Christmas 1970
Love,
Philip

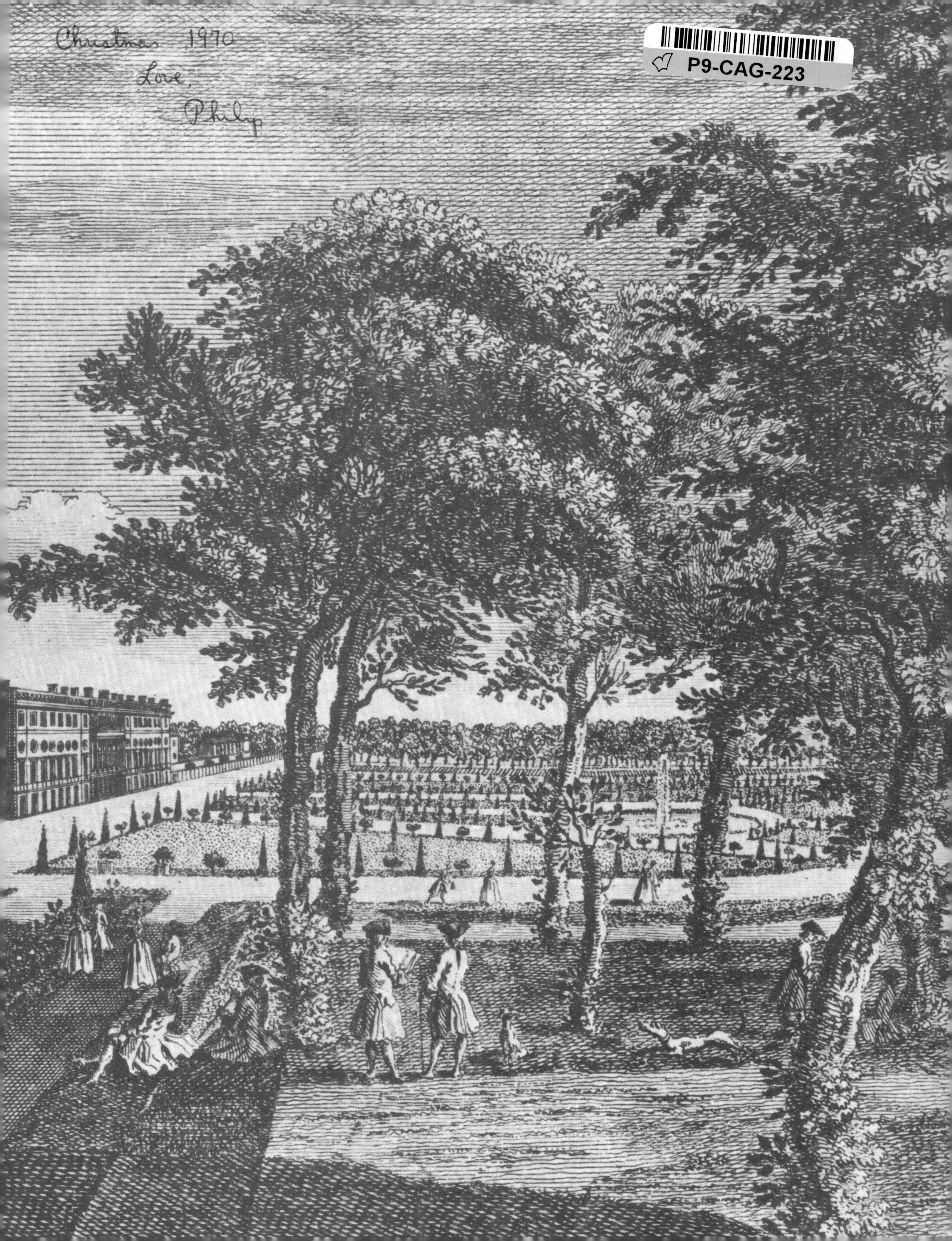

Mother,

A slight token in this season of joy and giving to express a feeling that oftens goes unspoken. I hope the book will bring you much pleasure.

A symbol of friendship, a symbol of love.

Your loving son,
Philip

Great Gardens of Britain

Great
of

Peter Coats

Gardens
Britain

Spring Books
London·New York·Sydney·Toronto

Originally published 1967 by
George Weidenfeld & Nicolson Limited
© 1967 Peter Coats
This edition published 1970 by
The Hamlyn Publishing Group Limited,
London · New York · Sydney · Toronto
Hamlyn House, Feltham, Middlesex, England

Printed gravure by D. H. Greaves Limited,
Scarborough, Yorks.

SBN 600 33844 4

Contents

Introduction

left Sir John Vanbrugh (1664–1726) playwright and architect, had a hand in the design of the first garden for Blenheim Palace
centre William Kent (1685–1748), according to Horace Walpole, 'leaped the fence, and saw that all Nature was a garden'
right Lancelot Brown (1716–83) was the greatest 'place-maker' or landscape gardener in England

opposite Spring brings the daffodils, while the branches of the trees are still bare: Hush Heath Manor in Kent

Are the gardens of Great Britain the best in the world? It is often said so, and yet the greatest enthusiast must admit that the English, Scottish and Northern Irish have nothing to compare with the great gardens of the continent. We look in vain for a Villandry in Surrey or a Versailles carved out of the Sussex Downs. There is, in Great Britain, no garden to compare with the celebrated pleasure grounds of Italy. There is no Gamberaia in Gloucestershire, and the hanging terraces and stairways of Collodi would be draughty indeed in the North Riding of Yorkshire. There are plantations of azaleas at Bodnant and Exbury, the brilliance of which 'makes the rash gazer wipe his eye' – but at Bodnant and Exbury their colour is not reflected, dramatically, in ink black water, as they are in the great gardens on the Ashley and the Cooper rivers in South Carolina, nor are they, bright congregation though they are, set in a nave of soaring swamp cypresses. Though conditions and scale are much the same as those to be found in Japan, there are no temple gardens of Bonsai, and certainly no Zen gardens of rock and raked sand, so subtly devised, and so significant to the tutored mind. There is no Ryoanji in Hampshire, no Kyoto in Kent.

In the field of garden sculpture, too, it must be conceded that the French and Italians are infinitely superior. The most xenophobic British garden lover must admit that his native sculptors are far inferior to those whose work is admired in gardens abroad.

No one could claim that Van Nost wielded as fine a chisel as Le Hongre. Peter Scheemakers was a fine artist but he is not to be compared with Tubi, and in any case both he and Van Nost were Dutch. The very English Cheere is no Coysevox. And the great sculptor, Grinling Gibbons, usually carved in a medium unsuitable for the open air. Perhaps with Henry Moore, whose work looked so impressive in the garden of Battersea Park, or Barbara Hepworth, whose anatomical abstractions complement the tulips in the garden of Churchill College, Cambridge, the situation may improve.

In garden architecture, however, the British may, with diffidence, claim to compete with foreign gardens. *Templa quam selecta* – how amiable, indeed, are the temples at Stowe and Rousham, set in their lovely man-made landscapes which brings us, at last, to a side of gardening at which the British can with confidence proclaim their excellence – the landscape garden.

For the landscape garden, it is often said, and often will be said again, is the great English contribution to the art of gardening, even to art itself. The park at Rousham, conjured by William Kent in the early eighteenth century, and, in my opinion, the two most beautiful of all, Stourhead and Blenheim, have no equal anywhere else in the world. No *jardin anglais*, no *Englischer Garten*, no *parco inglese* can compare with them. They stand alone - green misty perspectives, such as Claude painted, but his countrymen were quite incapable of planting; dreamy opalescent distances, sometimes peopled with deer, but more often, with cows, for this is England, not Arcadia. The landscape garden is surely the only art form to be perfected in Britain; it should be the British pride – a thing of beauty, and a joy for as long as they have acres left unbuilt on.

But these were gardens made centuries ago, parks conjured to surround the palaces of territorial princes. Such gardens are no longer planted today, though at Anglesey Abbey in Cambridgeshire, as will be seen later in these pages, a garden has been created of which the great Le Nôtre would certainly approve.

What is it then about the gardens of Britain which makes them the envy and model of the world? I think the answer can be summed up in two words – quality and diversity. First, quality. A garden-plan, after all, is made up of different component parts – lawns, hedges, trees, shrubs and, of course, flowers. All these depend for success on being cultivated in the right way, and the British can grow better than gardeners of any other country in the world. The vagaries of the climate may occasionally exasperate them and test them highly, but it happens to be the best climate in the world for gardening. The English lawn, one of the few things that the British are not tiresomely modest about, is without doubt the best in the world. And nowhere in Europe or America will you find finer trees, better grown. The giant redwood trees at Melbury or Longleat cannot compare with the 4,000-year-old *Sequoia sempervirens* of California, but there is in Britain a far greater variety of trees than in the whole of America. There are fine box hedges at Williamsburg, and excellent topiary—

The sea-horse fountain at Chatsworth in Derbyshire

The Emperor Fountain at Chatsworth was built in honour of a Tsar

opposite Summer sees the garden filled with flowers: roses and foxgloves at Cranborne Manor in Dorset

The elegant Pin-Mill building in a formal corner of the garden at Bodnant in Wales

an art which was born in Roman times and is still practised in Italy – but nowhere, save in Britain, will you find clipped hedges of the perfection and antiquity of those in the garden at Levens or Powis Castle.

Shrubs, too, those accommodating practical plants which in the last hundred years have come to play such an important role in gardens, for they need so little upkeep, 'We are but shrubs – no cedars, we', as Titus Andronicus modestly claimed. Surely it is not presumptuous to claim that the British grow the best and most varied shrubs in the world. And not only at Kew or in the celebrated public botanical gardens, but in private botanical gardens as well. (Dr Johnson could not understand the term botanical garden: 'is not every garden botanical?' he asked with his usual unanswerable logic.) And not only in the gardens which are famous for their collections of rare shrubs – several of which are illustrated later in this book – not only at Nymans, or at Wakehurst or at Exbury or Pylewell, but there are first-class

opposite Azaleas growing in the shade of silver-boled beeches at Bodnant

In the garden of Tresco Abbey in the Scilly Isles grow many topical plants: *above* Mexican dasylirion. *below* An impressive aloe

At Earlshall in Fife there is one of the finest gardens
in Scotland. Here a balustrade of stone separates a cobbled
courtyard from a lawn set with clipped yews

At Leonardslee in Sussex there is a garden which is
famous for its rare trees and shrubs grown in a
woodland setting. The scented Loderi strain of
rhododendron was first raised there in 1901 by the
present owner's grandfather, Sir Edmund Loder

above, below and *opposite* The art of topiary is shown in great variety in the garden of Levens Hall in Westmorland, one of the very few topiary gardens to eschew the change of fashion to a more natural style in the eighteenth century

collections of shrubs, and other plants, in numberless quite small gardens all over the country, though their owners, vicars, retired RAF officers, young married couples or country ladies in herbaceous hats, would be surprised to hear them referred to as such. Collections of shrubs and other plants, which are more varied than those found in any gardens of comparable size elsewhere.

Of hardy shrubs, only dogwood, that lovely flowering tree which makes the joy of American gardens and countryside in spring, behaves churlishly on the other side of the Atlantic.

But few gardens are anything without flowers, and surely the list of flowers that grow in Britain is longer than the list of flowers to be found elsewhere. The wayside cottage gardens, though not so many or as well tended as they were fifty years ago, are unique in the world. Cottages are rare in America, though the communal lawn and flowerbeds which are the beauty of the American suburb might well be duplicated in Britain. And the French are too thrifty to waste on flowers space which might grow vegetables.

Even in the field, literally, of wild flowers, British riches are limitless, though many of the flowers that they think of as natives were imported from distant lands. What, for example, could seem more English than the snowdrop? And yet Shakespeare,

Sheffield Park in Sussex, now the property of the National Trust, is set in a park laid out by Lancelot Brown about 1775, and later developed by Humphry Repton. This engraving is from a drawing by Repton

Autumn. It is in September and October that the garden at Sheffield Park takes on its full splendour, with the maples and nyssas reflecting their changing colours in the lake

who loved flowers and mentioned over a hundred different varieties in his works, has no word for the snowdrop, and indeed there is a theory that the snowdrop that everyone knows and loves – *Galanthus nivalis,* which seems as English as the may, was introduced to Great Britain as recently as 1854, little more than a century ago, when soldiers in the Crimea dug up bulbs round Balaclava and sent them home in letters to their sweethearts.

As can be imagined it was a difficult task to choose, out of the innumerable good gardens of England, Scotland and Northern Ireland, the gardens to illustrate and describe in this book. Still more so, as a few years ago, in my book *The Great Gardens of the Western World*, several of my favourite English gardens appeared. I decided, I think rightly, that it would be repetitive to have full-length chapters on these gardens in this new book. But no book on the gardens of Britain could claim to be complete without mention, however passing, of Hidcote, where that great American gardener Lawrence Johnston planted borders 'as no one had ever planted borders before' and created a beautiful garden, great in everything but size. Or of my favourite, Stourhead – one of the first of the great landscape gardens – or of the Savill gardens at Windsor, where that gardener of vision and zest, Sir Eric Savill, has been the moving spirit in a great enterprise, the creation of one of the finest 'wild' gardens in the world. Some other gardens in that book of mine were: Levens, for its unique topiary, Chatsworth for its fascinating history, Earlshall

in Scotland and the ever-to-be-lamented Victoria Sackville West's Sissinghurst – surely the loveliest English garden of all.

But what a rich store of gardens still remain. The final choice for this book was entirely mine and I do not expect everyone to agree with it. But, as I have claimed, the excellence of a garden can be summed up in the two words quality and diversity, so these were the qualifications which I most carefully sought. The British are rich, for instance, in rhododendron gardens. I have chosen to include the ones I think most representative. I would like to have shown pictures of the garden on the Island of Gigha, where Colonel James Horlick has conjured, in only a few years, a garden of rhododendrons and other acid-soil loving plants second to none.

Another naturally planted garden I would like to have included in my book is Muncaster, that splendid garden in Cumberland, where terraces of rhododendrons overlook the Esk valley. But in any books on gardens one has to limit the number shown of gardens which specialize in rhododendrons, as in pictures and in description they are bound to have a certain sameness.

And there are many other gardens I would have liked to have included: Nether Lypiatt in Gloucestershire, for its splendid borders enclosed in perfectly proportioned yew hedges; Minterne, for its superb blue *Rhododendron augustinii*, its maples and its banks of aconites; Melbury for its splendid trees. I would like to have shown pictures of the beautiful garden at St Nicholas in Yorkshire, where the Hon. Robert James first introduced me to some of the finer points of gardening, and Bramham Park in the same county, where, until disastrously damaged by a gale some years ago, the avenues recalled a planting by Le Nôtre. And there are many more.

But the gardens which were my final choice for this book are all, I think, fully representative of the diversity and quality of gardens in Great Britain.

For natural gardens, wild gardens, rhododendron gardens we have surely included the best: Nymans, Exbury, Leonardslee, Rowallane, and Pylewell.

For formal and historical gardens we have Haddon Hall, Kinross, Hever and Luton Hoo.

The great landscape gardens are well represented – Rousham, the only garden laid out by William Kent which has survived, Blenheim, with its river by courtesy of Capability Brown, and 'transcendant Stowe'. And fantasy could not be better represented than by Sezincote.

There are, too, several gardens illustrated in this book which are primarily plantmen's gardens, where the visitor finds collections of plants that are either unusual or difficult to grow elsewhere, gardens like Great Dixter, where Christopher Lloyd has assembled so many fascinating plants, or the gardens at Logan and at Mount Stewart, where the kindness of the climate permits tender, even exotic plants to grow as they would nowhere else.

Then there is the sort of garden which to me is perhaps the

The British have the best gardens in the world, though 'the vagaries of the climate may occasionally exasperate them and test them highly': camellias at Nymans in Sussex

above The Savill gardens in the park of Windsor Castle are the finest natural gardens laid out in England in the twentieth century. Rare rhododendrons, azaleas and many other shrubs find shelter among trees which once may have echoed to the ghostly horn of Herne the Hunter, *below*

INTRODUCTION

opposite The greatest, and one of the earliest, landscape gardens of England, Stourhead. A smaller replica of the Pantheon in Rome built by Henry Flitcroft about 1745

At Hidcote in Gloucestershire there is a garden considered by many to be as fine as any in England. Through a filigree of magnolia branches is seen a fountain casting up its sprays against a dark pediment of close-clipped yew

dearest of all – the garden which enjoys no particular benefits of climate, whose claim to fame does not lie in an eighteenth-century master's touch, whose charm is not necessarily set off by three-hundred-year-old topiary or a two-hundred-year-old folly. These are the gardens in which you will not find rarities like *Eritrichium nanum* or *Myosotidium nobile*, but these are the gardens which have been created, perhaps in quite a few years, by the taste, knowledge and, above all, love of their owners. These are the gardens which maintain the high reputation of the gardens of Great Britain today. Lyegrove in Gloucestershire, Great Dixter, again, Hush Heath in Kent, three of the most English gardens I know; and Haseley Court in Oxfordshire, where perfection of taste need be no further sought, Julians with its roses, and Kelvedon with its differently coloured enclosures. Kelvedon was the first garden that I ever had a professional hand in planning, and it is one which will always mean much to me.

While writing this book I have made many friends among gardeners of long ago, and some, I hope, among gardeners of today. In my desire to salute the shades of the past, I would like to adapt, if I might, the saying 'a green thought in a green shade' by substituting the word 'for' for 'in', and give an affectionate thought – not green, but coloured with every warm hue of gratitude – for the shades with whom I have made friends while gathering material for this book. It has been a treasure hunt, however, upon which some of the most fascinating facts I have unearthed were not always those I had set out to seek. And this brings me, unchronologically, to the shade of Horace Walpole, whose succinct descriptions of gardens and the way of life in the eighteenth century are such a rich legacy to all garden writers of today. And I have another debt to Horace Walpole to acknowledge – for it was he who coined the word 'serendipity'. It comes from a story he wrote about 'Three Princes of Serendip' who set out on a quest for their fortune and 'were always making discoveries, by accident and sagacity, of things they were not in search of'. Serendipity, therefore, has come to mean the faculty of making happy and unexpected discoveries by accident.

This exactly describes why writing this book has been so enjoyable. For instance, in my search for information about old Scottish sundials, I came across Dr Johnson's remark about botanical gardens, already quoted. In checking the dates of Sir Robert Atkyns I found that his home was called Swell Bowl. My search into the provenance of the Nassau Zuylestein family in the Complete Peerage led me to some interesting facts about the imprudent Countess of Strathmore, whose infatuation for a gambler led to the neglect of her garden, which she had formerly tended 'with her own hands'. In seeking how to spell brunswigia, I learned that the difficult to propagate variety josephinae got its name from poor Josephine, who was divorced for inability to give Napoleon an heir. And in my search for information about the great old lady of English gardening, the intimidating Gertrude Jekyll, I discovered that she was known to the young Lutyens family by the name of Aunt Bumps. Serendipity – 'happy

and unexpected discoveries', indeed.

There are some other garden figures from the earliest times I would like to salute and whose acquaintance I have made, or improved, while collecting material for this book, such as John Gerard, in whose classic *Herball* I have found some of the best of all plant descriptions, for it was he who suggested that to enumerate 'each pear apart, were to send an owle to Athens'. John Reed, that early northern gardener whose writings make as sound Scotch sense today as they did three hundred years ago – with his 'Shrubs ... well plyed and pruned' and 'Bordures, orderly intermixed'; and the fascinating, lovable Vanbrugh, whose wit and diversity of talents I never appreciated till I came to write about him in this book; Capability Brown, and his fears that the Thames would be jealous of his new river at Blenheim; Henry Wise, who thought that everything in a garden should be symmetrical; and Batty Langley, for whom there was nothing 'more ridiculous or forbidding than a garden which is regular'.

Most garden lovers or students of garden history would agree with me that Versailles is the greatest garden in the world – but I would like to salute the shade of William Robinson, who thought Versailles terrible. *Tous les goûts sont dans la nature.*

The Nut Walk at Sissinghurst leads down to the old moat and the statue of Dionysius. Beneath the trees grow massed azaleas

opposite The tower of Sissinghurst Castle in Kent, seen from a corner of the South Cottage garden. Created amid the ruins of a Tudor castle by those great gardeners Victoria Sackville-West and Harold Nicolson, it is 'surely the loveliest English garden'.

Among the shades there are some women too – the elegant Lady Amelia Hume, whose memory like a whiff of perfume from her own incense plant, humea, comes down the years to perpetuate her fame, and Gertrude Jekyll, Aunt Bumps, whose garden chair (it must have been a most uncomfortable one) inspired Sir Edwin Lutyens with his design for the Cenotaph, and whose exact sense of colour forbade the introduction of goldfish into a pool in a Gold Garden.

These are just a few, a very few, of the shades of yesterday, kept green by their writings or their contributions to botany, with whom for a few happy months I have been lucky enough to associate; but there are as many, not shades but bright lights of today, to whom a grateful word is due. I thank the owners of the gardens included in the book for letting me invade their domains, for answering my importunate questions, and for being so generally helpful. I thank the publishers of *Country Life*, the files of which marvellous publication, going back nearly seventy years, have proved a Klondike of valuable information. Looking through old copies of *Country Life* in search of a date or fact is a short-cut to Serendip. In my notes on Rousham I have expressed my admiration for the writings of Christopher Hussey and have compared them to those of Horace Walpole in their ability to introduce us so personally to gardens that we seem to be walking down their paths, considering their plan, smelling their roses. Likewise I am grateful, for his garden descriptions have taught me much, to Lanning Roper, that distinguished American connoisseur of gardens, who like Lawrence Johnston, the creator of Hidcote, left his native land to settle in England, proof, if any were needed, of the British gardens' siren charm.

I would like to thank, too, the photographers who have worked, in all weathers, to collect the material. Though the sun often looks as if it is shining in our pictures, it was not necessarily doing so when the photographs were being taken. That the camera is wholly truthful is a statement I have come to doubt.

My gratitude, too, is due to the various ladies who helped to type my manuscript, in particular to Felicity Calthrop and Margaret Coupland, who revealed happy talents in deciphering my writing and rare gifts for spelling botanical Latin.

In conclusion, gardening, according to a less well-known line of Bacon's very well-known essay, 'is the greatest refreshment for the spirit of man'. Our own gardens, like our own children, need no commendation. Other people's gardens are ever fascinating. To visit them, and many are open to visitors several days every year, is to gain inspiration and relaxation. Some were planted centuries ago by kings and great landowners, some in the last fifty or sixty years by quite ordinary people. But all have been loved and looked after. And gardens take a lot of looking after. Even with the best gardening climate in the world, gardens are not made overnight. There is no such thing as instant gardening – no such things as the gardens of Adonis 'that one day blossomed and fruitful were the next'.

PETER COATS
*A*1 *Albany, Piccadilly*

Camellia Reine Hortense

Rhododendron souliei

Rhododendron dennisonii

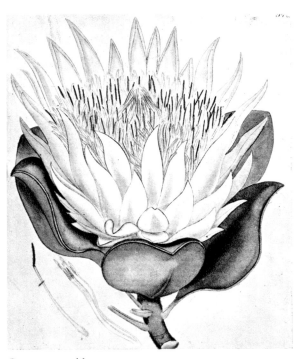

Protea cynaroides

Beschorneria yuccoides

Puya chilensis

Rhododendron decorum

Rosa centifolia

'. . . Not only in the gardens which are famous for their collections of rare shrubs . . . . there are first-class collections of shrubs and other plants, in numberless quite small gardens'. No other country can grow a greater variety than are cultivated between the Scilly Isles and the north of Scotland

Blenheim

A great garden for a great house

above Sarah, Duchess of Marlborough, wife of the great general for whom Queen Anne built Blenheim Palace. Her quarrels with the architect John Vanbrugh, especially over the bridge in the park, were famous at the time

Blenheim Palace – one of the most famous private houses in the world (though 150,000 members of the public visit it every year) – was the gift to John Churchill, Duke of Marlborough, of a grateful Queen Anne. It takes its name from a remote village, Blindheim, on the Danube, where in 1704 the Duke won a resounding victory over the armies of Louis XIV and his allies. Such a blow was it to the French King that for weeks he refused flatly to talk about it.

In the following year the Queen of England presented Marlborough with the ancient park and royal manor of Woodstock, and offered at the same time to build there, at her own expense, a new house worthy of England's hero. To build his new house the Duke chose the gay, witty, versifying, and playwriting, but inexperienced, architect Vanbrugh (1664–1726), at that time Controller of the Queen's Works.

Zestfully, Vanbrugh set about the designing, in concert with Nicholas Hawksmoor (1661–1736), of the new palace, or castle as it was then called, of Blenheim, using all the *fantaisie* and grandiose invention for which he will always be famous, and which he employed in the creation of such massive houses – 'hollowed quarries', as Voltaire called Blenheim – as Castle Howard and Seaton Delaval. Not for nothing did Dr Abel Evans devise for Vanbrugh when he died the heartless epitaph, 'Lie heavy on him, Earth, for he laid many heavy loads on thee'.

But what hand Vanbrugh had in the garden plans which went with his monumental building assignments is never clear. At Eastbury, which he built for Bubb Doddington, and in the garden at Lord Cobham's Stowe, he is said to have collaborated with Charles Bridgeman, though Vitruvius Britannicus gives the credit for the garden at Eastbury to Burlington. None of the gardens for which he was responsible survives intact, and nowhere is their disappearance more grievous than at Blenheim. On the gardens there, Vanbrugh worked in close co-operation with Henry Wise, Queen Anne's own gardener and a particularly delightful man. His affectionate biographer, Mr David

opposite To the west of the palace lies the water garden laid out by the ninth duke. Its architect was Achille Duchêne, successor at Blenheim to Vanbrugh, Henry Wise and Lancelot Brown

Green, describes Wise as a man with whom it was impossible to quarrel, and so their association was generally harmonious. The great parterre they devised for England's first soldier was laid out on military lines. Its ground plan, with its rigid lay-out and great bastions, recalls more a project for some fortification by Vauban than a pleasure ground. It was designed as a tribute to England's greatest soldier, who took it as a compliment, though not forgetting that the design, however appropriate, was primarily to be for a garden. But he had complete confidence in his garden designer, saying, 'for the gardening and plantations I am at ease, being very sure that Mr Wise will bee diligent'.

Diligent Wise was – and the great parterre at Blenheim was the admiration of all who saw it. What the fate of this magnificent creation was to be sixty years later, we shall see.

From the start the Duke took the greatest interest in his new garden, and though only fifty-five seemed sometimes to doubt whether he would live long enough to see it finished. Wise was well known for the successful removal of thirty-foot high lime trees to the park at Hampton Court. He must, the Duke desired, work the same wonders at Blenheim, and did so, when he planted, again on military lines, the two great avenues, The Great Avenue and The Mall, with well-grown elms.

As the palace grew, so did the garden. 'The garden wall was set agoing the same day with the house,' Vanbrugh reported to the Duke, campaigning in the Low Countries, 'and I hope will be done against your Grace's return . . .' The wall of the kitchen garden – which still exists – was built on Vanbrugh's usual gargantuan scale. Its bastions are a hundred feet wide and it is fourteen feet high. But it was the bridge, one of the sights of the park at Blenheim, which was a matter for wonder, derision, admiration, even rage, from its very conception. Some sort of bridge was certainly necessary – for the principal approach to the site chosen for the new palace lay across a steep-sided valley along which meandered the River Glyme, brimming over on either side to make a boggy area of pools and rushes, rich in snipe, but flooded in winter, and a wilderness of waterlogged reed beds in summer. A causeway existed but was not considered a worthy approach to what was to be 'England's biggest house for England's biggest man'.

John Vanbrugh envisaged the low-lying land traversed by a monumental bridge which would be the glory of the park at Blenheim. Such was his enthusiasm that he easily persuaded the newly-created Duke that only a bridge such as he had in mind would make a fitting approach. A more modest, and less expensive design – by Sir Christopher Wren, no less – was considered but cast aside, and Vanbrugh's conceit won the day. His successful comedy *The Provoked Wife* had been produced in 1697 and confirmed his reputation as a playwright. The Blenheim bridge nearly wrecked his reputation as an architect . . . and certainly provoked the wife of his distinguished client. 'I made Mr Vanbrugh my enemy', wrote the redoubtable Sarah, 'by the constant dispute I had with him to prevent his extravagance.'

opposite The elaborate fountain, epitome of the bravado of Edwardian taste, which makes the centrepoint of the garden laid out sixty years ago below the east front

Cedars of Lebanon (*Cedrus libani*) have been a feature of great English gardens since the reign of James I

Eighteenth-century sphinxes on the terrace below the water garden were given portrait heads of the beautiful American wife of the ninth Duke

Vanbrugh's Bridge, subject to so much criticism, and the lake created for it by Lancelot Brown. Before the water level was raised it contained thirty-three rooms

The grand cascade, devised by Lancelot Brown in 1764, at the junction of the river Glyme and his new lake

What annoyed her most was the fact that the architect had had the fanciful idea to incorporate dwelling houses, complete with windows and fireplaces, into the fabric of the bridge. These unusual abodes, which incidentally were never inhabited, aroused the Duchess's anger, and she sarcastically told someone that she had counted no less than thirty-three rooms actually inside the bridge.

Chief criticism of the bridge, of course, was the fact that the river it crossed was negligible, but letters of Sarah herself survive which state that 'Sir John had set his heart upon a lake', so fresh attempts were made to create an adequate flow of water by digging canals. But even by 1725 – when the canal system was finished – the bridge still seemed out of all proportion to the water it had to cross.

Vast though the arch seems, even today, with its base partly submerged by the lake, Vanbrugh would have liked to see it even vaster, and the idea for the arcaded gallery with which he wanted to crown it was only dropped after a more than usually acrimonious dispute with the Duchess. These disputes grew more and more frequent, and, as the Marlboroughs' favour at Court declined, the Queen's payments became more irregular. Finally, with its proud owners in virtual exile, work came to a standstill and was not resumed until 1716, after the accession of George I, when the palace was finally completed.

Sixty years after the original development of the park around the former Royal Manor of Woodstock – in 1764 – Lancelot Brown was asked by the fourth Duke, who embraced 'with too much enthusiasm the naturalism of the late eighteenth century', to develop the park in the fashionable style of the day. Brown's first care was to give Vanbrugh's enormous bridge something worth crossing. By constructing a series of dams he harnessed the waters of the Glyme and created an artificial lake which Sacheverell Sitwell has described as 'the one great argument for the landscape gardener. There is nothing finer in Europe'. The waters of the widened Glyme were made to flow more impressively through the undulations of the park, and so great was the transformation of the little river that Brown doubted whether the Thames would ever forgive him. By raising the water level, some of the thirty-three rooms which had aroused Duchess Sarah's ire were submerged, and the view of the park was immensely improved. However, benefits Brown bestowed with one hand he took away with the other.

Vanbrugh and Wise's great six-sided parterre below the south façade of the house, already ridiculed by Addison as pompous and contrived, was swept away and replaced with a plain area of turf, and the palace was bereft of a formal garden which for half a century had been one of the sights of England. If only Lancelot Brown had been less heavy-handed in his quest for the natural garden – if only he had recognized and left untouched the, by then, matured beauty of the formal gardens laid out a

The view to the west, over Duchêne's baroque patterned parterre with its fountains, pièces d'eau, obelisks, to Brown's lake and serried trees beyond

century before his time, how much worthier he would have been of our acclaim. But with him there was no compromise, the Romantic aspect was all, Nature, or his own idea of Nature, must be triumphant.

And the great parterre of Blenheim disappeared for ever, until in 1925 the ninth Duke set about recreating Wise's lay-out with the aid of the well-known French architect Achille Duchêne, who had restored so many of the gardens of the old *châteaux* of the Loire, their work was in every respect successful, and with the *broderies*, fountains and coloured gravel, or *brique pilée*, of the new formal garden, today lay a worthy carpet before Vanbrugh's great Baroque palace.

The present Duke, too, has sought further to embellish the gardens of his splendid inheritance by adding a spring garden which in its delightful simplicity is in startling contrast to Vanbrugh's grandiose architecture, Brown's vast perspective and Duchêne pastiche sophistication. This garden, small by comparison with the rest of the gardens at Blenheim, is the tenth Duke's special care, and exhibits his knowledge and taste in gardening as understood in the twentieth century. In it winding paths lead between high planted beds of shrubs and small trees which, though they are at their best in spring and early summer, present pleasing vistas of flower and leaf contrasts until the first frosts. Particularly fine are the species hydrangeas – the huge velvety-leaved *sargentii* and the neater *villosa*, the last a particular favourite of the Duke. These grow among hostas, many different potentillas, drifts of the Tibetan blue poppy which was until recently called *Meconopsis baileyi* but has now been renamed *M. betonicifolia*. Elsewhere in this private garden are rhododendrons and azaleas growing happily in specially prepared beds of the acid soil they need.

It is a very personal garden and it has been created from nothing, in its setting of ancient trees, in comparatively few years. The speed of growth and general luxuriance of the planting shows what care and thought have gone into the garden's planning.

For many years Blenheim – now recognized as one of the country's great monuments – has been open to visitors. The small sum they pay to see the palace and its magnificent gardens goes to the upkeep of the whole. Daniel Defoe wrote, in 1724, 'It requires the Royalty of a Sovereign Prince to support an equipage suitable to the greatness of this Palace.' 'Today', writes Mr David Green, to whose erudition and research the author is deeply indebted, in his admirable account of Blenheim Palace, 'it is less a question of equipage than of plain survival'.

Blenheim will certainly survive, thanks to the care and interest taken in it by the present Duke and his family. And did not Dr Mavor write in his *New Description of Blenheim* in 1806, 'Its acknowledged supremacy in natural charms and highly embellished landscape is attested by the annually increasing number of visitors. And who that has seen Blenheim once, does not wish to see it again?'

The park and gardens of Blenheim Palace, showing the relationship of the gardens to the park and lake

Drummond Castle

A garden landscaped on the grand scale

Drummond Castle was built in 1491, in the reign of King James IV of Scotland, by the first Lord Drummond whose descendant, the Earl of Ancaster, is the present owner. During the last war the elaborate gardens suffered greatly, of necessity, from neglect and over-growth and it is thanks to Lady Ancaster that they have been restored. It is her hard work, careful study and patience which have given back to the gardens the lustre which once made them celebrated throughout Scotland.

The gardens at Drummond are terraced, like many in Scotland, where there are many more terraced gardens surrounding old historic houses than there are in England. The reason is not hard to find. In the early seventeenth century, when the taste for decorative gardening was growing in Scotland as it was in England, the houses of the great landowners were still fortresses. The times were still too unsettled for country houses like Hatfield, Woollaton or Longleat, with their smiling façades and 'walls of glass', to be practical propositions. There were still feuds and forays and midnight attacks to contend with, and houses had to be easy to defend. It was far too soon for the chieftain to abandon the old castle on the hill and build himself a pleasant country house, in the English style, on the plain.

But nevertheless some faint breath of culture, of a gentler way of life, was wafting from France, especially following the arrival of Mary, Queen of Scots. The chiefs still clung to their strongholds, but they were conscious of the changing fashions of the Renaissance. Many of them had stayed at the French court, the Auld Alliance was still in force and ships plied back and forth between Leith, the port of Edinburgh, and France. Scottish castles were castles still, but gradually were to take on a continental air with more decorative spires, turrets, carved façades and high, crenellated gables. Soon the steep, easily defended slopes up to the castle walls were being carved into terraces, to provide gardening space for the castle's occupants, at least when times allowed. Sometimes the garden, and this is still a feature of many old Scottish houses, was situated some way away from

above The gardens of Drummond Castle 150 years ago, with box-edged borders, hollyhocks and peacocks. In those days gardens of such size might require sixty gardeners to keep them

opposite The terrace walls and central stone stairway of the garden are little changed since Victorian days. The gardens are remarkable for the way an elaborate layout has been adapted to modern conditions

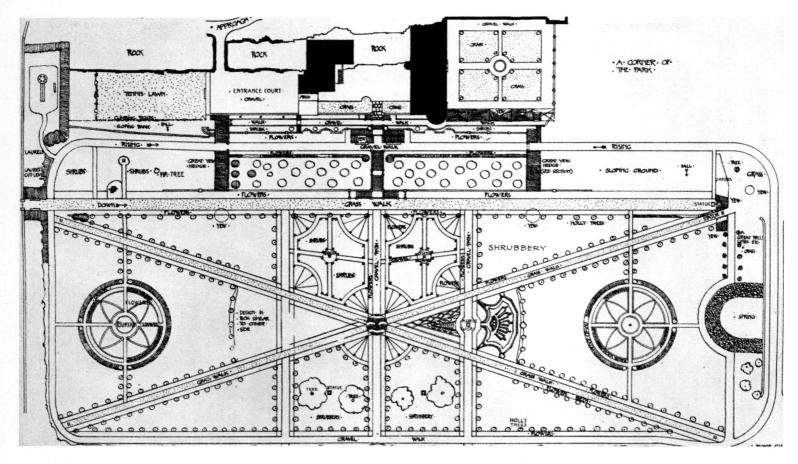

A plan of the gardens in 1900 from *The Formal Garden in England and Scotland* by Inigo Triggs, published in 1906 by B. T. Batsford Ltd

An old gateway of carved stone with swags of fruit and flowers in bold relief. Also shown is the white buddleia 'Peace'

the house – in a walled enclosure of its own, and with its storage sheds, potting houses and bothies attached. But terraced gardens, hugging the foundations of the frowning walls of castles, were more often the rule, and the architects of the day used all their ingenuity in constructing them.

The story of the gardens of Drummond Castle begins in 1630 or thereabouts, when the gardens were laid out, much on the plan that we admire today, by John Drummond, second Earl of Perth, 'a nobleman of learning, probity and integrity . . . benevolent to his friends, prudent and economical in the management of his affairs and just in all his dealings . . .'. It was he who terraced the steep incline up to the castle walls, and laid out the vast walled parterre which still lies below.

Early in the last century the parterre was italianized, and decorated with many fine statues which were brought from Rome. This work was done about the time of Queen Victoria's accession, and the designer was George Kennedy. The striking lay-out is in the form of a St Andrew's cross – the diagonally crossing bars being formed of gravel walks, intersected at right angles to the castle by a broad central path. The whole complicated pattern was, until the second world war, bedded out and planted with the greatest elaboration. Photographs of the garden taken sixty-five years ago display an almost bewildering kaleidascopic pattern of interlocking flower beds, diamond, oval and fan-shaped, some bordered with low hedges, some with paths of sparkling white gravel. There were scrolls and broderies of box everywhere. The beds were filled, it is safe to assume, with all the most loved flowers of the Victorian gardener – scarlet geraniums, blue and white petunias, powdery blue ageratum and gaudy

opposite Below the terrace lies the extraordinarily complex pattern of the formal garden. Colour is provided as much by evergreens and permanent planting as by the brightness of bedded-out flowers

marigolds. But even in those lavish days the vast area to be bedded out must have daunted the garden staff, for an unusual and generous interplanting of evergreen was added, rather in the modern style of herbaceous border planning, to give, one supposes, some colour and cheer in the winter. Today, many of the evergreens are still there to provide a rich pattern of different greens, golds and silvers. But Lady Ancaster has wisely reduced the bedding out, gravelling some areas and turfing others, but always retaining, as far as possible, the original plan.

The two diagonal bars of the St Andrew's cross are now bordered with silver-leaved, white flowered anaphalis, which is in bloom from June to October, while the adjacent paths are edged with lavender, Miss Jekyll's own Munstead variety, and with low box hedges. The few bedded-out flowers in this part of the garden are chosen to reach their peak of beauty in August and September, so as to be at their best when the house is occupied for the shooting season. But though the autumn is the period when the garden is at its brightest, the many evergreens with which it is planted make for some colour all year long. Among the evergreens which are outstanding at Drummond are the fastigiate yews, both green and gold, and hollies Golden and Silver Queen.

From the great central sundial, paths radiate to all four points of the compass. Two are of gravel, two of turf. We have described the wedge-shaped areas in between, and their very individual planting. A fine staircase of carved stone, gracefully balustraded and ornamented with some good garden statues, mounts from the great parterre to the castle walls, giving access to the terraces on the way.

It is on the walls of these that the more delicate plants of the garden at Drummond find shelter, such as good specimens of *Romneya coulteri*, the Californian poppy which we admire at Mereworth; a beautiful *Buddleia davidii*; White Profusion, a delight for butterflies; and the steely blue-leaved thistle *Eryngium oliverianum*.

Though, thanks to the original thoughtful planting, the gardens at Drummond are beautiful at any time, late summer sees them at their best. It is then that the borders are ablaze and that their bright colour is reflected in the flaming autumn leaves of the trees around. There is a splendid collection of colouring trees which are shown off to the greatest advantage against the eight-foot-high beech hedge which surrounds much of the garden, and it is in autumn that the maples, *Acers japonicum, dissectum, palmatum*, and *Osakazuki*, display their radiant tints.

The terraces of Drummond Castle which McCulloch, years ago, described as 'placed in the most advantageous position to enjoy the magnificent and varied expanse around' and looking 'over scenery scarcely equalled', provide one of the most beautiful vantage points in Scotland. The gardens are open to the public under Scotland's Gardens Scheme, and well repay a visit. Lord and Lady Ancaster are to be congratulated on the success of their devoted labour of rescue and re-creation.

opposite Purple lavender, silver-leaved, white-flowered anaphalis and the bright, but transient, colour of late-summer flowers make the beauty of the Drummond garden in August *right* The great sundial, dated 1630 and designed by the second Earl of Ancaster's architect, John Mylne

Oxfordshire
Stowe

A garden celebrated for its architecture

Richard Temple, first Viscount Cobham, who built Stowe and redesigned the garden in the new style of Bridgeman and Kent. Portrait by Jean Baptiste Van Loo

opposite 'The garden temples of Stowe . . . are some of the eighteenth century's most charming legacies'. John Vanbrugh's Rotunda has graced the park since 1719

That tireless country house visitor Celia Fiennes, who visited Stowe in 1694, described 'A vista through the whole house, so that on one side you view the gardens which are one below the another with low breast walls and taress walks . . . beyond it are orchards and woods, with rows of trees'. No more. Soon Miss Fiennes, unimpressed, was jogging off on her sidesaddle 'To Horrwood 7 mile, by severall other seates'. The Stowe she saw, with its simple gardens, was soon to disappear, as if by magic. Had Miss Fiennes visited it forty years later she would surely have shown more enthusiasm, for she would have liked the new fashion in gardening which was to sweep the country early in the next century. 'There is a new taste in gardening just arisen,' wrote Sir Thomas Robinson to Lord Carlisle in 1734, 'which has been practiced with so great success that a general alteration of some of the most considerable gardens in the Kingdom is begun . . .' But we have begun our notes on the garden at Stowe in the middle of the story.

Before 1590 Stowe was the property of the Bishopric of Oxford. Soon after that date, it was sold to John Temple. It was his grandson Sir Peter Temple who can be said to have been the first of the landscape-gardening Temples, and they were to be great landscape gardeners, as they were to be builders of temples. Was their curiously apposite motto *Templa quam delecta* (How Delightful Are Thy Temples) a conscious pun? Sir Peter enclosed a park of 200 acres, and his son Richard built the house that Celia Fiennes visited in 1694. It was his son, also called Richard, who succeeded in 1697, who during the next fifty years built much of the great house that we see today and laid out and embellished the park which was to become one of the great sights of England. 'Transcendant Stowe'. Richard Temple became a peer, Lord Cobham, Pope's 'And you, brave Cobham'. Brave he was, having made his name at the siege of Lille in 1708 and fighting with distinction at Ramillies under the Duke of Marlborough. By 1742 he had become a Field-Marshal. He was a devoted adherent of the new Hanoverian dynasty, who rewarded him and his family

42

The south front, 'as long as one side of a London square', once looked over a great formal garden two-thirds of a mile across

with their friendship for many years. Their friendship is commemorated in a dozen different ways in the gardens at Stowe, where there was a temple for Queen Charlotte, a statue of Prince George, and an arch for Princess Amelia.

Lord Cobham increased his already large fortune by marrying a great heiress, Anne Halsey. Designing and planting gardens in the new style of Bridgeman and Kent was his passion, and he spent lavishly on the development of the grounds of Stowe. Lord Cobham died in 1749 and having no son, his great property passed to his niece Hester Grenville, who soon was given, by the accommodating Hanovers, the title of Countess Temple. Her son succeeded her as Earl Temple in 1752, and her daughter, another Hester, married the elder Pitt – William, later Prime Minister, who once, as a young man, had held a cornetcy in Lord Cobham's troop of horse. He was a frequent visitor to Stowe, and even, it is said, advised on the lay-out of the gardens (he was fond of giving advice). He stayed often at Stowe, for the first time in 1735, when he played cricket there, in intervals of suggesting improvements to the grounds. Pitt was a great enthusiast in all he undertook, and always sure that he was right, whether it was gardens to be planned or politics. He possessed, he owned complacently, the 'Prophetic Eye of Taste', knew exactly how gardens should be arranged, and even, on occasion, would undertake to replant the flower beds of his friends, with or without their help, by torchlight.

above The Temple of Ancient Virtue was one of William Kent's contributions to the garden and is said to be his best. Its design was based on that of the Temple of Vesta at Tivoli, but with Ionic instead of Corinthian pillars. The temple was built about 1734

right A plan, dated 1763, of the gardens at Stowe, showing how William Kent de-formalized Charles Bridgeman's lay-out, softening the outline of the lake and opening up far-spreading vistas

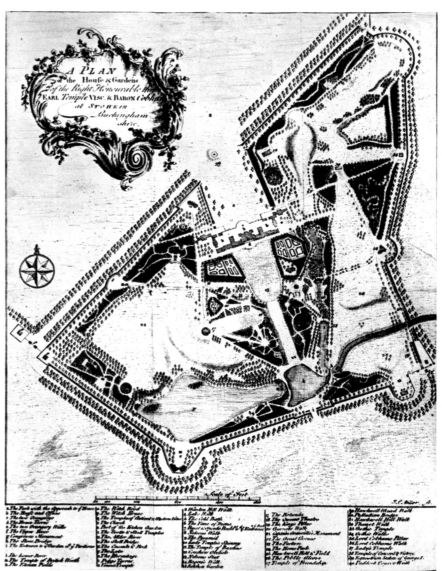

Lord Temple was like his great uncle, a very rich man – the richest, it was said, in England. Like his uncle he married a great heiress, much of whose money was lavished on the beautification and development of Stowe, especially in the closing years of his life when, exhausted by the manoeuvres of politics, he retired to Stowe, a tall, scraggy figure, 'Lord Gawky', hobbling round the gardens on two sticks, and planning more temples.

It was during the lives of Lord Cobham and Earl Temple that the park at Stowe took on the appearance it has today. Work of laying out and replanting the park began about 1713, when the village of Stowe, which was considered to be too near the house, was bodily removed to nearby Dadford. The garden work was under the direction of Bridgeman, creator, it is said, of the ha-ha, of whom Horace Walpole was to write,

After London and Wise, Bridgeman was the next fashionable designer of gardens, and was far more chaste; he banished verdant sculpture, and did not ever revert to the square precision of the foregoing age. He enlarged his plans, disdained to make every division tally to its opposite and though he still adhered much to straight walks with high clipt hedges, they were only his great lines; the rest he diversified by wilderness, and with loose groves of oak, though still within surrounding hedges.

The great panorama he created at Stowe lay below the south and west façade of the house, a façade as long as one side of a

The Oxford Bridge with its rusticated stonework and urn-capped balustrade has been attributed to Kent, though its architect is uncertain. Beyond is one of the Boycott pavilions, once lodge gates to the park at Stowe. They were built by James Gibbs (1682–1754) about 1728 and took their name from a village which afterwards disappeared to make way for the park

above In the northern part of the park is the Queen's Temple, by Gibbs, dedicated to Queen Charlotte. It was greatly improved by the portico added by Giovanni Borra about 1777. It is now used as a Music School

opposite Inspired by the Palladian Bridge at Wilton, built in 1737, the bridge at Stowe was built soon after. Of Lord Pembroke's bridge it is said 'It was a *jeu d'esprit* in the Palladian manner, then fashionable, and original to the extent that it is different from any known bridge by Palladio himself, and better'

London square. From the steps the garden lay like a vast five-sided carpet, two-thirds of a mile across, with parterres and avenues of poplars leading to an octagonal *pièce d'eau*, in the centre of which was a *guglia* – a spouting fountain in the form of a slender pyramid. There were more fountains on either side, and the whole elaborate garden *coup d'oeil* was enclosed on either side by clipped yew hedges set with statues. In a plan by Sarah Bridgeman, published in 1739, the vast design looks like a plan by Vauban for one of Louis XIV's forts – walls, moat, bastions and all. The rest of the garden was laid out in bosquets of trees, cut by paths, the main ones straight but the lesser, more secluded ones curling in the new style. At intersections, and acting as eye-catchers – his own word – were William Kent's masterly *fabriques*, his temple of Ancient Virtue and Vanbrugh's Rotunda. Kent's work at Stowe, midway between the rigid formality of Le Nôtre's Continental School and the contrived naturalness of Capability Brown, is of the greatest interest. At Stowe, as we see at Rousham, he aimed at the re-creation of the romantic landscapes of Salvator Rosa or rather Poussin. At Rousham his work, in all its ingenuity, remains. At Stowe it has only survived in part. But in the leafy plantations which lie near the Temple of Ancient Virtue, and the less successful, architecturally, Temple of British Worthies, his gift for siting, pictorially, his *fabriques* may still be acclaimed.

Vanbrugh, too, had a hand in the garden at Stowe, and designed the graceful ten-pillared Rotunda, afterwards altered by the Italian architect Borra, which, mellowed by the years, today still tops a grassy rise. How much the garden design owes to Vanbrugh, how much to Bridgeman, and how much to Kent is difficult to say. All three had a hand, certainly; and what Vanbrugh and Bridgeman began, Kent continued and, according to one's point of view, corrected.

Thus Stowe, the greatest garden of England in the eighteenth century, attracted all the most celebrated names in garden design. It is without surprise that we learn that Lancelot Brown, too, came there, at the very start of his great career. But he was young and comparatively inexperienced. Kent was still in command and though in his eleven years at Stowe he was quickly promoted to be head gardener, Brown had not yet the influence to affect, to any great extent, the lay-out of Lord Cobham's new garden.

But his nascent talents were recognized by his employer, who recommended him to the Duke of Grafton, for whom he designed a lake – and how many other lakes he was to plan in the future – which established his reputation as a 'place-maker', and led to fame. There is no record of Brown returning to Stowe to remake the gardens when he became England's leading gardener. But his influence was certainly felt there, and in the later years of the century what Kent had left of Bridgeman's crisp outline was blurred by the general change of taste. The pools took on yet more natural shapes, yew hedges finally disappeared or grew into lofty trees, statues were scrapped. It was at this time that many unwanted and no longer fashionable lead statues were shipped to America where they were melted down into bullets

KING WILLIAM III

WHO BY HIS VIRTUE, AND CONSTANCY
HAVING SAVED HIS COUNTRY FROM A FOREIGN MASTER
BY A BOLD AND GENEROUS ENTERPRIZE
PRESERV'D THE LIBERTY, AND RELIGION OF GREAT BRITAIN

opposite The Temple of British Worthies was designed by William Kent about 1735 and contains busts of Queen Elizabeth, Bacon, Shakespeare, Hampden, Locke, Newton, Milton and William III *above*

and used against the British Redcoats. But the temples, for which Stowe will ever be celebrated, survived.

Many eighteenth-century visitors thought that there were far too many of these. Horace Walpole condemned them scathingly. But as 'J' wrote of Stowe in *Country Life* many years ago:

If there are half a hundred monuments, there are four hundred acres to set them in. We can see just what Lord Cobham intended in his sprinkling of this monotonous surface with column and temple, so that the flattish green English landscape was refined and varied, until it seemed to him and his contemporaries classic ground.

The first Lord Temple died in 1779. On his death Stowe passed to his nephew who became Marquis of Buckingham in 1784; the family achieved a Dukedom in 1822, but died out sixty years later, and the ownership of Stowe passed in the female line to the Kinloss family. Soon after the first world war it was sold and became the home of one of England's finest public schools. The authorities of Stowe School preserve as far as possible the great park of Lord Cobham and Lord Temple as it was two hundred years ago. They have made one important change, in the immediate vicinity of the house. They have demolished the Temple of Bacchus, a deity to whom the high-living Lord Cobham was particularly devoted, and on its site built a new school chapel, designed by Sir Robert Lorimer, worthily enough.

As the Stowe schoolboys raise their voices to sing the eighty-third Psalm *Templa quam delecta*, how many think, one wonders, of the sybaritic, easy-going Temple, who made the opening line of the psalm his family's motto and created the superb house and park where 'Stoics' are lucky enough to spend four or five years of their early life. Though, when the school opened in 1923, Mr J. F. Roxburgh, the inspired headmaster, creator of the great public school that Stowe now is, said, 'Every boy who goes out from Stowe will know beauty when he sees it all the rest of his life'.

So much for the boys of Stowe, but what memories do day visitors to Stowe take away? A vivid impression, surely, of its unique garden architecture, of temples set in *bosquets* of trees, temples reflecting the careful precision of their architecture in water. A Temple of Concord and a Temple of Ancient Virtue. Stowe, of all places, is famous for its garden architecture, that manifestation of the delight in building which was so apparent in the eighteenth century, a time when the designing of 'follies' offered the perfect exercise in architectural skill and expertise. Purely and shamelessly decorative, they were not like the great Palladian houses of the period, meant to be lived in. They needed no bedrooms, no kitchen quarters, no mundane offices. Their architect was free to let his fancy take charge, his only trammel a respect for the tenets of scholarly building. The garden temples of Stowe and of the other great houses of the period, are some of the eighteenth century's most charming legacies. They have a charm both frivolous and erudite. Useless, yet fair to look upon; their 'simple doom', like Stephen Phillips' roses, 'merely to be beautiful'.

Sussex

Wakehurst Place

A garden taken under the aegis of Kew

The estate of Wakehurst Place is a very ancient one. Mention of it is made in a chronicle of the early fifteenth century, when one John Wakehurst 'of ancient lineage' had 'tenments with appurtenances at Wakehurst in the parish and lordship of Ardingly'. The house as it stands today, in all its time-mellowed maturity, was built in the last decade of the reign of Queen Elizabeth (1590) by Sir Edward Culpeper. Sir Edward chose the site for his new house with care, and took care to place it – an unusual thing at that time – on rising ground.

The Culpepers lived at Wakehurst for two hundred years, until Sir William – fourth and last baronet of his line – sold the great house and two thousand acres of the surrounding land to William III's Controller of the Treasurer's Accounts of the Navy, Dennis Lyddell. From the Lyddells, Wakehurst passed to the Peytons, to the Marchioness of Downshire and finally to the late Sir William Boord. It was Sir William and Lady Boord who restored the old house to its present grandeur, with the aid of the distinguished architect, Aston Webb, RA.

The gardens of Wakehurst, though almost perfectly sited by nature, owe much to Lady Boord, whom her friends remember as a passionate gardener, and a keen rock-gardener in particular. The rock-gardens at Wakehurst were her special interest, and indeed creation, for she herself designed and planted them, and at a time when English women usually took rather a remote interest in their gardens, and were rarely seen at work at their drawing boards, still less wielding a trowel. Though Lady Boord's favourite corners of the garden have been largely re-modelled since her day (one of the rock gardens by the late Walter Ingwersen), many of the conifers and shrubs she planted seventy years ago still grow there, giving a pleasing look of maturity and a richly upholstered appearance to her rockwork.

In 1903 Wakehurst Place changed hands, and was bought by Sir Gerald Loder, afterwards Lord Wakehurst, of the well-known Sussex family and brother of Sir Edmund Loder, of nearby Leonardslee. Sir Gerald Loder was as keen a gardener as his

opposite Black swans float on the lake, which is closely planted with the rare trees and shrubs for which the garden is famous

above Wakehurst in the eighteenth century. The façade has changed little over the years *below* Wakehurst today. The garden has been chosen, because of its variety of soil, as a 'satellite' of Kew

brother and his special interest was rhododendrons, and in particular any plant which came from New Zealand or Chile. For all these plants the climate and terrain at Wakehurst offered promising conditions. There was open woodland round a lake, streams running through sunlit coppices and belts of high forest trees for shelter. The rich, porous soil was ideal for lime-shy plants; and soon rare plants from all over the world were growing in it.

But before listing just a few of the notable shrubs and trees at Wakehurst it would be pointful to trace the garden's story up to the present day, because, to adapt Mary Queen of Scots' saying, in its end is its beginning.

All through the Wakehursts' time the garden grew in beauty, until it was recognized as one of the great gardens of Sussex and indeed of the whole country. In 1935 Lord Wakehurst died and soon afterwards the house and its magnificent estate was bought by Sir Henry and Lady Price. It was during their occupation

opposite The rock garden has gravel paths, and the stone-work is closely overgrown with cushions of alpines. The garden is enlivened by slender conifers and red-leaved Japanese maples

The garden with 'its variety of soils (clays, loams, sands) rich with humus, wet in parts, well drained in others' offers perfect growing conditions for unusual and tender plants

WAKEHURST PLACE

In 1903 Wakehurst Place was bought by Sir Gerald Loder, brother of Sir Edmund Loder, of nearby Leonardslee. The Loder family gave their name to the famous Loderi strain of rhododendron, a cross between *R. griffithianum* and *R. fortunei*

of Wakehurst that the author of the book first visited the garden, twenty years ago, and he has never forgotten the delight and interest with which its plantations and thoughtfully-planted parterres provided him.

In 1963 Lady Price was widowed. She continues to live at Wakehurst, though the garden, by way of the National Trust, was soon to come under no less august an aegis than that of the Royal Botanical Gardens of Kew.

For many years, it appears, Kew had been in search of a 'satellite' garden. Of the selection of Wakehurst, Mr Richard Shaw, now curator of Kew, but formerly assistant curator of the great Sussex garden, told the author:

Wakehurst Place was chosen most wisely by Sir George Taylor, who had received other tempting offers. But he bided his time until Wakehurst Place, with its completely different terrain (Kew was naturally featureless), its more humid climate, its clean and clear atmosphere, its variety of soils (clays, loams, sands) rich with humus, wet in parts, well-drained in others, with its natural features of rock outcrops, water, hills and dales, meadows and woodlands and the many microclimates they provide, became available, via the National Trust, on a 99 year lease.

Mr Shaw went on to say:

Because Wakehurst is so different from Kew there is every possibility that plants which are less successfully grown there (light, porous soil, atmosphere pollution – lessening, by the way – arid conditions) will thrive at Wakehurst. The same may be said of frost-tender plants. Wakehurst Place is not frost-free, but it is a more favoured locality than Kew as far as frost is concerned. Furthermore, there is the question of space. The collections at Kew have increased over the years and the existing plants which thrive are constantly expanding. The genus rhododendron is unhappy at Kew, and so are other ericaceous subjects.

The writer asked Mr Shaw, who has great knowledge of and affection for the collection of plants and trees at Wakehurst, which he considered some of the most interesting. First among those he chose for special mention was the beautiful late-flowering red *Rhododendron eriogynum*, a native of Yunnan which was discovered by Forrest in 1914. This lovely tender shrub he described as quite at home at Wakehurst. Two other notable plants were a rare Chinese conifer *Keteleeria davidiana*, very rare in cultivation in this country, but which actually 'cones' at Wakehurst, and the sub-tropical Japanese evergreen laurel *Litsea glauca*.

It has been noted that all Chilean plants were favourites of Gerald Loder when he first planted his garden. One at Wakehurst which is quite outstanding is the climbing *Berberidopsis corallina* which shows its red flowers in late summer, and its Chinese cousin *Idesia polycarpa*, which in England is very seldom grown, though it is comparatively hardy; it looks like a catalpa, and its chief beauty is its handsome fruit. And no list of the plants of the garden at Wakehurst would be complete without mention of the famous Wakehurst form of *Pieris formosa forrestii*, a plant noted in several gardens described in this book, and quite one of the best garden shrubs we have. It has tufts of brilliant red leaves in spring which are far more attractive than its flowers, like lilies of the valley and sweetly scented though these be.

Among the many New Zealand plants that Lord Wakehurst acclimatized successfully in Sussex and which still grow in his garden to prove his gardening taste and ability to give plants the conditions they need, are the conifer *Phyllocladus trichomanoides*, which in its original form in the Antipodes grows sixty feet high and used to provide the Maoris with a scarlet dye; many olearias, including the very rare *lacunosa*, discovered in the mountains of Rotoroa, several pittosporums, and the curious *Pseudopanax ferox*, discovered in the North Island of New Zealand by Captain Cook.

The writer paid the last of many visits to Wakehurst in June, and he was reintroduced to the garden by Mr Wallis, head gardener there for many years. It was a cloudless sunny day. The azaleas were at their peak, and the air in the woodland walks was heavy with their scent. Some of the earlier rhododendrons were casting their flowers, though others, rising from a carpet of fallen blossoms, seemed still to have as many blossoms on their branches as lay about on the grass beneath.

The rock-garden was bright with flower and the rocks, accented here and there with Lady Boord's conifers, were encrusted with saxifrages, hummocks of sempervivums and starry with rock roses. All round the lake grew shrubs and trees so rare that, even had they simple English names, it would seem presumptuous to refer to them in the vernacular: and what, after all, is the English for *hymenanthera*?

On the surface of the lake, and somewhat resentful of our cameras, floated two fine specimens of *Cygnus niger*. Shame that when flora smiled so sweetly, fauna should be unfriendly. But apart from the black swans, there was no discordant note in the idyllic theme, and Sir Edward Culpeper's fine old house mirrored its face contentedly in the waters of the lake. All around lay shady lawns and plantations: there was a hum of bees – and lawn mowers. Sun-burnt gardeners, both men and women, were at work on the borders and shrubberies. It was an inspiring scene. At a moment in our history when the future of a garden of the size of Wakehurst might necessarily seem to be in doubt, here was a large garden, a great garden, whose future, in the doughty care of Kew, is certainly assured.

It is hoped to open the garden of Wakehurst to the public as soon as the necessary arrangements are made. The project would be an interesting one to bygone owners of the great estate: to John Wakehurst 'of ancient lineage', to Sir Edward Culpeper – did he plant a herb garden at Wakehurst? – to the Lyddells and the Peytons, and to Lady Boord with her trowel and trug. More especially perhaps would the future of the garden have pleased the great gardener Sir Gerald Loder and his successor at Wakehurst, Sir Henry Price. And from the terrace of her home Lady Price will doubtless watch, with interest and approval, the garden take on such a new and promising lease of life.

In a wild garden there are infinite possibilities for the thoughtful gardener to achieve striking juxtapositions of different foliage: here the lacy fronds of ferns contrast with the bolder leaves of *Rheum palmatum*, the ornamental rhubarb

Hertfordshire

St Paul's Walden Bury

A splendidly planted eighteenth-century garden

The garden at St Paul's Walden Bury is a rare example of a garden laid out by an enthusiastic amateur, in or about 1735, which has survived more or less unchanged. That it was designed in the way it was, at that date, is of interest too, because in 1735 the new taste for a more natural style of planting was already well established, and gardens laid out on the formal lines of that at St Paul's Walden Bury were no longer fashionable. Perhaps the owner at that time was uninterested in the foibles of fashion (he was a serious business man) or perhaps he was too set in his ways to follow every new trend. We do not know – what we do know, however, is that the garden is a rare one of its type and that it is still there.

Mr Edward Gilbert bought the property in the early eighteenth century and it was during his time – a long time, for he lived to be well over eighty – that the garden as it exists today was created.

It seems that at the same time as much of the work on the garden was being undertaken considerable alteration was being made to the house itself, and the present smiling bow-windowed façade was added to the north front. It is from the door in the centre of this that the main lines of the garden radiate, on a plan which recalls, though it is on a much smaller scale, a garden by Le Nôtre, or perhaps more particularly the ground plan of the garden at Hampton Court. Though the garden at St Paul's Walden Bury was laid out in the years following 1735, the alterations to the house were still uncompleted as late as 1767, so it was late in the day to be planting *allées* and avenues, with statues as eye-catchers. At that time, all over England the fashion for such formality was already past, and avenues were being broken up, by Capability Brown and his school, all over the country, to be replaced with more natural plantings, and statues were being scrapped, to be broken into hard core or, if of lead, even sold abroad to be melted down into bullets.

However, perhaps Mr Gilbert was old-fashioned. He clearly preferred the old style. He was certainly a man of taste, for he redecorated the chancel of St Paul's Walden church in the

Mary Eleanour Bowes, wife of the ninth Earl of Strathmore, brought St Paul's Walden Bury (depicted in the background of her portrait) into the Lyon family *(Country Life* photograph)

opposite A lead sphinx, one of a pair which flank a grassy rise towards a Doric pillared temple

above As spring merges into summer and the sunlight falls through young
foliage, the green avenues of St Paul's Walden Bury are at their most
beautiful

opposite Lilium mimodelphum growing by the fish pond The architect of the
graceful temple, a later addition to the garden, was Sir William Chambers
(1726–96)

Baroque style, with a beautiful screen, an imaginative addition to the fourteenth-century church which aroused the ire of the Victorians. It is possible that he was influenced in his garden development by his son-in-law Mr George Bowes, a Conservative landowner and an enthusiastic amateur gardener, who had laid out a pleasure ground on the most impressive scale, again in the old style, in the north.

The child of the marriage of George Bowes and Mr Gilbert's daughter was called Mary Eleanour, and she was one of the great heiresses of her day, in due course becoming ninth Countess of Strathmore. We will hear more of her later. It was through this marriage that St Paul's Walden Bury came into the Bowes Lyon family, who own it today. A daughter of this distinguished family, descendant of Mr Gilbert and Mr Bowes, Lady Elizabeth Bowes Lyon, mother of the present Queen, spent much of her childhood at St Paul's Walden Bury, where the gardens full of leafy glades and walks cut through shady woodland must have offered the perfect playground for children.

The gardens, which are on heavy clay, are not vast, though very much in the grand manner. They lie mainly to the north of the house, and the main vertebrae of their plan are three avenues, radiating *en patte d'oie*, as we see at Hampton Court, from the lawn near the house. These avenues are cut through woodland which contains some old oaks and beeches which, from their size, may be assumed to have been there before new plans for the garden were laid.

Of the hedges which line the three avenues, Sir David Bowes Lyon once said, in a talk on the problems of gardening on heavy clay which he gave to the Royal Horticultural Society,

We have three long grass avenues which are bordered with beech hedges. They ought to be hornbeam, which does much better, and is the natural hedge plant on clay, but I preferred beech because it keeps its leaf well on into and sometimes even through the winter, while hornbeam sheds its leaves early . . . our hedges are different in all the four seasons.

And it is true that the visitor to St Paul's Walden would be hard put to it to say at which time of the year the hedges there, in their spectacular radiating plan, look the most effective: in their spring green or autumn russet.

The central *allée* runs due north in a line from the garden door (once the front door) of the house, a full 600 yards, to an imposing statue of Hercules with his lionskin and club, on a pedestal of stone which is decorated with neat panels of 'frostwork'.

The avenue to the north-east has for eye-catcher at its further end the spire of St Paul's Walden church. Cross paths cut these main *allées* – the first aligned on an elegant domed temple which came from the ruined Copped Hall, near Epping.

Near the temple rescued from the wreck of Copped Hall is an open space of sunlit lawn, surrounded by high trees. Here the *genius loci* is a lead statue of the Disc Thrower, which generations of Lyons have referred to as the Running Footman. The lawn, of which the elegant Baroque outline had become almost entirely

Father Time, with his sundial and hour-glass

In the shelter afforded by the ruined orangery grow many delicate plants. Its walls are wreathed with *Rosa hemisphaerica* and different clematis

The garden at St. Paul's Walden Bury is known for its statuary, including this lead figure of a discus thrower which once marked a place of romantic assignation

overgrown, was rehabilitated in 1938 by Sir David and Lady Bowes Lyon with the advice of the well-known architect Mr Geoffrey Jellicoe, whose sure touch we admire elsewhere in this book, at Pusey and at Haseley Court.

This enclosed lawn, with its lead figures and brooding temple, seems to be the very heart of the garden at St Paul's Walden Bury. The sunlit lawn and darkling shade of the trees recall Horace Walpole's words about William Kent introducing 'perspective in landscape making, and breaking . . . with groups of trees, too uniform or too extensive a lawn, opposing woods . . . to the glare of the champaign'.

All the garden statues and temples at St Paul's Walden Bury, many added by Sir David and Lady Bowes Lyon, are remarkable for their quality and for the perfection of their placing. They are always in proportion to their surroundings, and are features of the garden which earn the admiration of every visitor.

The pair of stone figures of wrestlers on the north lawn are probably by Van Nost, whose work we see also at Powis, and the delightful figure of Charity by Sir Henry Cheere (1703–81) was set in place on the south side of the house by the ninth Countess of Strathmore, whose story we are about to tell, in memory of her mother, the excellent and kind-hearted Mrs George Bowes, Mr Gilbert's daughter. The lead Discobolus we have already mentioned, and he plays a romantic part in the story of the garden at St Paul's Walden Bury and in particular of Lady Strathmore. This lady, daughter of so excellent a mother, had a stormy private life. Though a keen botanist, whose flower albums, some illustrated by herself, some by the foremost flower artists of the day, are preserved in the house, and though she was the friend of such serious horticulturists as Sir Joseph Banks, she was regrettably flighty. After the death of her husband she made a highly unsuitable second marriage – with the notorious gambler, Andrew Stoney. During their courtship they used to meet in the garden of St Paul's Walden Bury. Jesse Foot, in a life of the Countess, quotes Andrew Stoney writing to her in 1776: 'You may think me whimsical, but on Thursday next at one o'clock I shall be in the garden at St Paul's Walden. There is a leaden statue, and near that spot (for it lives in my remembrance), I shall wait.'

The marriage which followed a series of such assignations was a disaster, and Stoney spent as much of Lady Strathmore's money as he could. The gardens of St Paul's Walden Bury fell into neglect. In 1783 Lady Strathmore appeared 'altered and dejected' and a visitor wrote of the

once beautiful pleasure ground, where, in spite of the ruinous state of it, much was left for admiration; because the taste which gave it creation was not yet totally obliterated. The Countess pointed out to us the concern she had formerly taken in the shrubs, the flower-beds, the alcoves, the lawns and the walks, even the assistance her own hand had lent to individual articles.

This setback in the story of the garden at St Paul's Walden Bury was repaired in time. All through the Victorian period the garden was carefully kept by its various occupants, successive

members of the Bowes Lyon family. But it can only be said to have really flowered again when it became the home of a younger son of the Strathmore family, the Hon. David Bowes Lyon and his wife, in 1931. David Bowes Lyon, afterwards Sir David and President of the Royal Horticultural Society, was one of the most distinguished gardeners of his time, and he and his wife were active in every aspect of the garden work at St Paul's. Lending assistance to 'various articles' with their own hands was very much the order of their gardening day.

In 1961 Sir David died, and the world of gardening in England lost a much loved figure. At the time it was written,

He was passionately interested in every aspect of horticulture . . . and at one time intended to make horticulture his career. He found relaxation from his busy life in the City in his work for the Royal Horticultural Society . . . and in his own beautiful garden.

As a gardener, Sir David was full of resource. Undaunted by the unpropitious soil of the garden, he succeeded in growing there many of the plants one would least expect to find thriving on heavy clay. Some of these he would mention with special pride, such as the great *Magnolia soulangeana*, surely one of the best loved magnolias in our garden, with its white petals stained on the outside with purple, and its kindred variety *Magnolia soulangeana*

Stone figures of wrestlers, said to be by Van Nost, on the north lawn

A lead swan spouts water in the centre of a green leaf-shaded pool

A five-pillared temple, with a dome of open ironwork, stands near a fine magnolia in the rose garden

brozzonii. Other favourite plants, all of which grow to perfection at St Paul's Walden Bury, are species peonies, such as the creamy wittmanniana and obovata, and the tall, strong-growing yellow lutea ludlowi, and the specially beautiful *Paeonia mlokosewitchii*. The Milkman's peony (or to be accurate the Milkman's son's peony) is certainly one of the best of all yellow peonies, and extremely good-looking from the moment in early spring when its pinkish-mauve shoots first appear, through its all too short flowering period until autumn, when its pods burst to reveal scarlet seeds within.

What other trees and plants thrive especially in this well-laid-out, well-planted garden? The spreading, ground-covering *Juniperus pfitzeriana*, several fine weeping willows, *Salix babylonica*, their branches unhung with harps, many eremurus, iris and a collection of agapanthus which came from the Hampshire garden of that great expert of the genus, the Hon. Lewis Palmer. Lilacs do well, like the deep purple Massena, the popular Souvenir de Louis Spath and the double white Madame Lemoine. The white, fading-to-rose flowered *Cornus kousa chinensis* has been found to be unexpectedly successful on the local clay. A magnificent wistaria, also no clay lover, has topped a full thirty feet in twenty years. Many lilies do well, *L. aurantiacum* in particular, a selected canary yellow form of *L. szovitsianum*, unusual in that it has no spots, and the strong growing Maxwill hybrids.

Much of his success at St Paul's Walden Bury, in growing plants which are known not to like a heavy soil, Sir David attributed to a method he practised for many years, of burning clay. This he called his 'scorched earth' policy and however drastic it sounds, it was most effective. The heavy local clay was packed round a well established bonfire and left for days to burn slowly. Any opening that appeared was stopped and the burning programme continued. The resulting substance was friable and easy to handle, and most plants loved it.

The author would like to cite another example of Sir David Bowes Lyon's resourcefulness. The heavy clay soil of the garden at St Paul's Walden Bury presents no difficulty in the culture of roses, both the hybrid teas and shrub roses. But about the culture of these Sir David expressed a most original opinion, 'I have one basic rule,' he said, 'about growing roses. I grow them as tall as I can. Most roses can be made to grow upward. It is largely a question of how you use the knife. I only slightly shorten good growth . . . in this way you get roses at eye level or even to look down at you, and that to my mind is more satisfactory than to have to look down on them.'

On his last visit to St Paul's Walden Bury the writer remembers that there were roses everywhere – roses on walls, roses grown as shrubs or as flowering hedges – or roses in friendly neighbourhood with other plants. And he recalls especially the honeysuckle growing on the trees of the lime avenues, tempering formality with an almost cottagey appeal, the broad swathes of pink fraxinella, the old-fashioned, charming Burning Bush, growing by a high shrub rose Fantin Latour, which was almost the same

shade; and the low-growing feathery flowered verbascums, growing next the pink shrub *Rosa californica* near the tennis court.

There has been a garden at St Paul's Walden Bury for two
hundred years, but it is fairer today than it has ever been. The
spell it casts on the visitor is the result of its very personal quality,
and the garden has only achieved that personality through the
affection and hard work, over the years, of its devoted owners.

Beech hedges, which keep their russet leaves well into winter, were chosen,
rather than hornbeam, to outline the radiating avenues which are a feature
of the garden at St Paul's Walden Bury

Berkshire

Pusey House

A garden of rare beauty surrounding a lake

John Wood (1704–54), architect of Pusey House near Faringdon, was the creator of Georgian Bath, and there is something about the façade of Pusey House, though it lies in a typically country setting, which breathes an urban air. The grey stone house, framed in trees, looks southward over its lily strewn lake towards the distant White Horse Hill of Uffington.

The garden is largely the creation of the present owners, Mr and Mrs Michael Hornby, who bought the place in 1935. But before visiting the garden, a moment might be spared to trace the history of Pusey House and the estate which goes back over a thousand years – to the misty times of King Canute. It was at a time when England was being invaded by the Saxons and the king's army and the invaders encountered each other where Pusey House now stands. One of Canute's officers, William Pewse, was able to enter the Saxon camp disguised as a shepherd, and managed to overhear plans for a plot to ambush Canute on the following day. By this daring exploit he saved the king's life and was rewarded with a generous gift of land and a 'Horn of Tenure'. Tenure of land by Cornage or, as it is also known, Horn Service, laid the duty on the recipient of warning the king by horn of the approach of the enemy. It was an ancient English custom, and the Horn of Pusey, almost miraculously, still exists. It is now in the Victoria and Albert museum. In the fifteenth century it was mounted with a silver band which was engraved with a Gothic inscription which runs, 'I King Knowde [Canute] give William Pewse this horn to hold by the land'. The horn remained in the Pusey family till 1935 when it was bought by William Randolph Hearst, the American newspaper magnate, and then bought back by Mrs Bouverie-Pusey and given to the Victoria and Albert Museum where it still attests the antiquity of the Pusey name. It was a name to become more famous centuries later, in the annals of the Church, when the gentle Edward Pusey the theologian (1800–82), wrote in collaboration with John Keble and John Henry Newman – afterwards Cardinal Newman – his *Tracts for the Times*, and became founder of the Oxford

above The theologian Edward Pusey, one of the founders of the Oxford Movement. His family lived at Pusey in the nineteenth century

opposite Framed by trees, the grey stone façade of the house, built by John Wood of Bath, looks over a flower-bordered terrace towards the lake

67

PUSEY HOUSE

Movement. The other Pusey House, the Theological Centre in Oxford, is named after him.

When Mr and Mrs Hornby bought Pusey, thirty years ago, the lawn swept right up to the house, very much in the style approved by Lancelot Brown in the eighteenth century, and one of their first cares was to set the house on a terrace, below which the lawn fell gradually to the edge of the lake. To create this terrace they commissioned the distinguished architect Mr G. A. Jellicoe, already well-known for his garden work. The addition he made to Wood's façade was wholly sympathetic: a terrace, raised six feet above the former garden level, providing a wide paved area which might have seemed daunting if it had been left an unbroken stretch of stone. But he allowed it to be softened with planting, not only of the low, usually prostrate, paving plants, but also by larger, bolder clumps of such shrubs as lavender, and *Phlomis fruticosa*, the felty leaved, golden-flowered Jerusalem sage. Today, after thirty years, mellowed and flower-starred, the terrace at Pusey spreads a welcoming carpet of mellow grey stone for the garden visitor to step down to as he emerges from the garden door. In the stonework grow silver cushions of dianthus, tufts of the unusual sysirinchium, the Satin Flower, a yellow-flowered cousin of the iris, blue flax and a sulphur yellow spurge, one of the euphorbias, that plant family that is so popular today with informed gardeners, which Mr and Mrs Hornby collected in the Auvergne, and have had running about the stonework of their garden ever since. On either side of the door, in pots, are standards of sweet-leaved verbena, and against the wall, growing in old lead vases, showing up brilliantly against the stonework of the house, roses Crimson Conquest and Mary Wallace, which seem to defy all the established rules by growing and flowering well in a root-space of barely 2′ × 6″. The terrace at Pusey has been described in some detail as it seems to the writer to be a perfect example of its kind. Its formality is tempered by thoughtful planting, and the view it overlooks is delightful, with the lake in the foreground and a distant prospect of fields framed in high trees beyond.

Leaving the terrace, the garden visitor to Pusey has a choice of routes, left, to the borders of old roses and across the bridge to the well-planted shrub-borders; or right, past the new swimming pool, along the herbaceous border, to the walled garden, known as Lady Emily's garden. We will turn left, cross the bridge, admire the shrubs and waterside planting on the other side, cross the main vista from the house by way of Mr and Mrs Hornby's new and most ambitious plantings, skirt the west end of the lake and return to the house by way of the walled garden.

Below the terrace, in a border of floribunda roses and lavender, interspersed in July with clumps of lilies, and against Mr Jellicoe's wall, we admire some well-grown specimens of that seldom met with shrub *Piptanthus nepalensis* – a member of the laburnum family with the laburnum's rabbitty-yellow flowers, but larger, and attractive three-fingered leaves. Soon one comes to a border of old roses, such as Mme Pierre Oger, Louise Odier,

The chinoiserie bridge, with its crisp white woodwork and pointed finials 'elegantly spans the lake only a foot or two above the water'

Mme Calvat and that exquisite rose Paul Neyron, with one splendidly flowering group of the hybrid musk Penelope, almost smothering a graceful Victorian shepherdess statue in terra cotta. Half right, and the lawn is crossed, and the bridge, another particularly attractive feature of the garden at Pusey, is at hand. The date of the Pusey bridge is uncertain, but it cannot well be much later than the house – 1745 has been suggested.

It is typically oriental, but in the European manner, with decorative railing and finials. It elegantly spans the lake only a foot or two above the water, and the image of its crisp white woodwork, mirrored in the water, recalls the lines: 'The silver lake, from its meandering tides, reflects each object which adorns its sides'.

On the further bank, one's way lies to the left, past a waterside planting of primulas, several gold-flowered clumps of *Lysimachia punctata*, and bold groups of hostas. These, like euphorbias, enjoy greater popularity today than ever before. There seems to be something about their blue-green glaucous leaves which modern garden-makers find especially satisfying. Their foliage is striking from early spring till late summer, whether it is *H. glauca* which is planted or *H. marginata*, with its white-edged leaves, or the golden variegata. Though the flowers of hostas, or Plantain Lilies, are comparatively uninteresting, their splendid leaves rightly win them a place in every connoisseur's garden. Nearby, at Pusey, grows another popular plant of today, a plant which is a great favourite of flower arrangers – *Alchemilla mollis*. The flowers of Ladies' Mantle are a pale but vivid green and its leaves are dressed with silky hairs which take raindrops, and hold them like jewels, long after the shower is past.

Leaving the lakeside behind we enter an area planted with flowering shrubs and rare trees. Fine specimens are on every hand, and to mention just a few, there is a vast *Rhus cotinoides*, a giant *Hydrangea villosa*, fine *Cytisus battandieri*, *Cornus nuttalli*, stranvaesia, and more piptanthus. A most effective planting here is of *Rhus cotinus* – the purple-leaved variety, against a backing of the silver-leaved Willow Pear, *Pyrus salicifolia*, one of the best of all grey-leaved trees, with groups of *Deutzia rosea* at the sides. It is juxtapositions such as these, which only thought and knowledge could have brought about, which make Pusey and Mr and Mrs Hornby's achievement there so remarkable. In this part of the garden, too, there are several remarkable trees – good specimens of liquidambar, the autumn colouring *Cercidiphyllum japonicum*, *Acer griseum* and the lovely, and too seldom planted, yellow-flowered cherry *Prunus yukon*.

Soon we pass, on our left, the tiny church of All Saints, built in 1743 by the then squire of Pusey at his own expense. The architect of this graceful little building was probably John Wood, creator of Pusey House itself. The church contains an impressive monument to its builder John Allen Pusey by Peter Scheemakers whose work we salute elsewhere in this book. Leaving the church the visitor to Pusey passes more interesting trees and emerges on to a wide swathe of lawn, with a fine view to his right towards

above Lady Emily's Garden, with its paved paths and closely planted borders of roses, peonies, artemisias and dianthus. Beyond its creeper-hung walls is a temple of grey stone with an oddly Oriental air

the house. In the new beds running on either side of this new lawn, Mr and Mrs Hornby have lately planted many interesting shrubs which have quickly settled down in their new quarters, making a wide tapestry of leaf and flower. Here grow so many shrubs, roses and trees that to enumerate more than just a few would make tedious reading. Outstanding are the philadelphus – *P. aureus* of the golden leaves, purple-eyed Belle Etoile, pure white Virginal and well-named Manteau d'Hermine, and there are several unusual and sometimes rather tender shrubs which deserve mention – *Indigofera gerardiana*, the pink Indigo plant, *Rubus tridel*, the little grown *Lespedeza thunbergii*, called after a long ago Spanish governor of Florida. In these new borders at Pusey some of the trees are of great distinction. There are good maples, *Acer drummondii, laxiflorum* and *capillipes*, and a thriving specimen of the Honey Locust, *Gleditschia triacanthos* which turns a bright yellow in autumn, and got its name from an eighteenth-century director of Berlin's botanical gardens.

To return to the house, the visitor must now bear left and make his way under some magnificent trees where in spring the ground is thick with daffodils and periwinkles. Another bridge, of plainer design, crosses the lake, and on the other side the visitor soon comes on a temple of grey stone with an oddly oriental dome.

Nearby lies Lady Emily's garden – called after Lady Emily Herbert, a daughter of the second Earl of Caernarvon, who married Philip Bouverie-Pusey in 1822. It is a small secluded garden, planted in the main with roses, silver *Artemisia palmeri*, and here and there the white woolly-leaved *Verbascum bombyciferum*. The walls around are wreathed in more roses, Albertine, Alberic Barbier, Lady Waterlow and New Dawn, with, here and there, white clematis and the huge velvety leaves of *Hydrangea sargentiana*. As the visitor leaves this garden, reluctantly, for it casts a kind of spell, he admires on the right a bold group of achillea – Golden Plate – lifting their flat yellow faces to the sun. Passing through the gate once more, he finds himself back on the herbaceous border path, which runs eastward back towards the house. The herbaceous border at Pusey is one of the best the writer knows, and comprises in its full 150 yards all the herbaceous plants which one could expect to see in a well-planted garden of the 1960s. Blue would seem to be the predominant colour, blue sparked with silver, and softened by different mauves. So it was, at any rate, last July, with delphiniums, *Salvia superba*, Canterbury Bells, and silver artemisias blending harmoniously into an azure haze. If blue was the predominant note of the long herbaceous border at Pusey, white seemed to be the theme of another, newly made border nearby – a border planted with magnificent white delphiniums, white peonies, white Iceberg roses, white-leaved Scotch thistles *Onopordon arabicum*, and, growing behind, the silver architectural leaf sprays of the Cardoon artichoke. What a subtle charm a white border has – 'Blanche comme un dimanche'.

One more corner of the garden remains to be visited before

opposite Busts on columns stand in niches of rusticated stone in the curving walls of the south façade. Below is a border of plants, including acanthus, chosen for their rich and contrasting foliage

the terrace is regained. A few years ago Mr and Mrs Hornby installed a swimming pool in one of the several stone-wall enclosures which their garden contains. It surely is one of the most successful of its kind, and the pavilion which overlooks it a peculiarly graceful example of garden building. Its architect was Mr Godfrey Allen, who modelled its Gothic arches on the nearby stable clock. Outside it is painted white, inside terra cotta, and at the corners of the pool it overlooks, stand tubs of agapanthus, the blue African lilies, which flower in late summer when the pool is in constant use. These seem to be the perfect tub-plants, for they will live happily in the same container for years on end, flowering season after season and with the greatest generosity.

One more gate, and we are back on the terrace, and once more the view it 'discovers' confronts us. Of all the delightful features of the garden at Pusey, and there are many, it is the terrace which we are most likely to remember, for on a June evening, when the pinks are in flower and scenting the air around, and the swallows are dipping over the lake, it has a serenity and a peacefulness that are all its own.

A gate of airy wrought iron gives on to the white border. To either side of the grass path grow iris, nepeta and silver-leaved *Stachys lanata*

Rowallane

A garden where some famous plants were first raised

Primulas delight in the moist peaty soil of the garden at Rowallane. *P. japonica rosea* has flowers of rich pink, arranged in tiers

The name Rowallane is a word known to thousands of gardeners in Europe and America – for it has been given to several magnificent plants which have spread the fame of the Northern Ireland garden far and wide. There is a Rowallane primula, a Rowallane viburnum and, perhaps best known of all, the Rowallane hybrid hypericum, a St John's Wort, which is doubtless the best of all the St John's Worts in cultivation, with its enormous golden yellow flowers which are sometimes three inches across.

The garden at Rowallane is just a hundred years old and, until it was taken over by the National Trust for Northern Ireland in 1954, had only known two owners. Briefly its history is as follows. In the sixties of the last century it was a small agricultural estate, twelve miles south of Belfast, near Saintfield in County Down. It was then bought by the Reverend John Moore who, soon after taking possession, set about improving both the house and garden. In 1864, he built a series of high walls to enclose more of the garden and in 1867 he added a large range of outbuildings. Receipts exist which show that at that time he bought large numbers of trees – 2,000 oak, 2,000 beech, 2,000 larch and 1,000 spruce. These trees have now grown to full maturity, and form useful windbreaks which protect the many tender shrubs and trees with which the garden has subsequently been planted. The Reverend John also dotted his new pleasure grounds with cairns of stone similar to those which Queen Victoria had made fashionable at Balmoral. He died childless in 1903, the year after the great queen, and left his demesne – delightful Irish word – to his nephew Hugh Armytage-Moore, at that time a land agent at Castlewellan, twenty miles distant.

At Castlewellan there still exists an interesting collection of shrubs and trees, and it is possible that this collection fired the imagination and interest of Hugh Armytage-Moore, for he soon became horticulturally ambitious for his new garden. To start with, he planted nothing very sensational – herbaceous plants and ponticums mostly – but soon he was taking in more and more farmland, enclosing it and planting rarer things. The

Under a canopy of spring leaves lies the spreading garden planted in the last hundred years by the Reverend John Moore and his nephew. To the right, a fine group of *rodgersia*, named after US Admiral John Rodgers, 1812–82

In the reconstructed rock garden, with its built-up beds of specially prepared, sharply drained soil, it is possible to grow such demanding plants as the silver-leaved New Zealand celmisias

opposite Hosta undulata medeo variegata thrives in damp shade. Its leaves are attractively curled, and splashed with soft green and white

natural grey Whinstone of the district was, and still is an attractive feature of the gardens, and, making the most of it, he planned a rock garden which records show was one of the garden sights of Ulster in 1912. The name Rowallane itself derives from a Celtic word which means outcrop of rock.

Francis Bacon, in a much quoted passage, once wrote, 'God almighty first planted a garden, and indeed it is the purest of human pleasures'. Hugh Armytage-Moore certainly found it so, for in 1917 he gave up his practice as a land agent, and henceforward, till he died in 1955, he dedicated his life to his garden.

Rare plants and seeds poured into Rowallane. There were spoils from such world-famous gardens as Glasnevin in Dublin, Kew, and the Botanical Gardens at Edinburgh. The reputation of the garden grew, and today is visited by ever-increasing numbers of garden enthusiasts from all over the world. Since its takeover by the National Trust of Northern Ireland, Rowallane has been most fortunate to have on its board of directors Mrs Terence O'Neill, wife of the Prime Minister of Northern Ireland and a keen and most knowledgeable gardener. Mrs O'Neill comes of a gardening family, for she is the sister of Mr William Whitaker and was born and brought up at Pylewell Park, in Hampshire, of which there are pictures of the garden elsewhere in this book. Of the garden at Rowallane and the best season to visit it Mrs O'Neill has written:

Locally, Rowallane has the reputation of being a 'spring' garden, and it is true that it is at its most spectacular in spring, with species and hybrid rhododendrons and azaleas in flower and daffodils naturalized in the grass; but it looks splendid at nearly all times. There are no conventional herbaceous borders but several borders with herbaceous plants, which is something different. Hostas, rodgersias, perennial and monocarpic meconopsis and candelabra primulas all thrive, and

above Among the attractions of the garden at Rowallane are the natural outcrops of rock *below* A wide gravel path bordered by cushiony alpines and groups of tulips. In the foreground grows *Rodgersia pinnata*, with striking leaves and crimson flowers

there are mixed borders of shrubs and sub shrubs, with New Zealand and South American plants in sheltered places. Other later flowers include hydrangea, agapanthus, nerines, and colchicum, and there is always good autumn colour and fruit.

Some of the interesting plants at Rowallane include, in the walled garden, the twining *Schizandra rubrifolia*, of the magnolia-cae, from China, the coral fruited *Berberidopsis corallina*, and *Myrtus luma* with its bright yellow bark, both from Chile. There are many magnolias, including a magnificent specimen of *Magnolia veitchii* thirty feet high, many hoherias, especially the late summer flowering *Hoheria lyallii* and *sexstyla*. In a protected corner, though it is perfectly hardy, grows a splendid *Viburnum tomentosum* var. Rowallane, parent plant of thousands of Rowallane viburnums all over the world. In sheltered beds grow euphorbias, hostas, and thousands of primulas, their colouring reflecting the orange tones of the bugle flowers of the rhododendron Lady Chamberlain, a beautiful, delicate plant, first raised in Mr Edmund de Rothschild's garden at Exbury.

In her notes of Rowallane Mrs O'Neill goes on:

Leaving the walled garden, the visitor gains the top of the spring garden, and in early April can survey several groups of rhododendrons already starting into bloom. *Magnolia campbellii* towers above arboreum rhododendrons, while *Nothofagus obliqua* and *N. antarctica* form landmarks. A path from the Trio Hill leads to the Bishop's rock. The magnificent panorama of the County Down countryside lies ahead, while to the left rhododendrons nestle happily in the natural rock.

The path leads to a small pool surrounded with primulas and meconopsis, followed later by hydrangeas and astilbes. From here a gate leads into the original, but now newly planted, rock garden, and it should be mentioned that generous gifts from Scottish gardens have enabled this rock-garden to be re-established after twenty years abandonment.

The author still remembers his first visit – many years ago – to Rowallane. He had driven over one hot afternoon after luncheon from nearby Mount Stewart with Lady Londonderry. The party, not all of whom were garden enthusiasts, were soon daunted by the size of the garden they had been brought to visit, and one by one fell by the wayside, preferring to rest in the shade of the blossom laden trees or on one of the Reverend John Moore's strategically placed stone seats. Only Lady Londonderry and Mr and Mrs Armytage-Moore, an erect, indefatigable Queen Marylike figure in a pale blue toque and veil, carrying a parasol, completed the tour. The affectionate, almost paternal way in which Mr Armytage-Moore had talked of his much loved trees and shrubs, which he had watched growing for fifty years, was most endearing. 'The purest of human pleasures' indeed.

In conclusion, to quote Mrs O'Neill once more:

I would like to pay tribute to Hugh Armytage-Moore for planting with such skill and discernment. He used so wide a diversity of plants, that he created a garden of exceptional beauty and interest: one of the finest, perhaps, in the British Isles.

opposite In April and May many of the Asiatic magnolias, such as *M. wilsoni* and *M. watsoni*, come into flower in the garden at Rowallane

Kinross

A splendid seventeenth-century garden

In the land-locked Scottish country of Kinross, in the centre of the flat countryside bordered to the north by the Ochill Hills, lies Loch Leven, made famous by Mary Queen of Scots. Directly to the west of the island castle in which she was imprisoned stands Kinross House, the masterpiece of its first owner and architect Sir William Bruce. Sir William, as an architect, is known for his reconstruction, for King Charles II, of the Palace of Holyrood House, in Edinburgh, and for the architecture of several of Scotland's finest houses. As a politician he is remembered as an adroit place seeker, a clever manipulator whose career was greatly advanced by the role he played as go-between, between the exiled Charles II and General Monk, afterwards Earl of Albemarle. Following the Restoration he enjoyed a series of important and lucrative posts, culminating in his installation, ten years after the Restoration, as 'Contriver and Overseer of all the Works at the Palace of Holyrood House'. Contriver, Sir William certainly was.

More political places fell into his hands, making him a rich man, a rich man with a hobby which was architecture, an art in which he had talent enough to earn him the name of Kit Wren of the North. Another Sir Christopher he perhaps was not, if one is to judge him by his work, begun in 1667, at Holyrood, and later work at Hopetown, West Lothian, and at Mertoun. But Kinross is, in its peculiarly Scottish way, severe yet grand, a masterpiece. The stone of which it is constructed is cut with lapidary care . . . a glowing sandstone, which seems to change colour with the weather, tawny in sunshine and a soft pigeon colour in the rain. And the house is superbly sited, with a magnificent avenue of beeches, oak and lime as an approach, and panoramic views over Loch Leven, with its storied castle, and the purple hills beyond.

At the accession of James II, Sir William's career reached its apex. He was appointed a member of the Scottish Privy Council, and work was begun in 1686 on a new house grand enough for someone who was now a very great personage in Scotland.

Sir William Bruce (died 1710), politician and architect of Kinross House. He has been called 'the Kit Wren of the North'

opposite To the west of Kinross House lies a formal rose garden with gravelled paths, clipped yew trees and statues

A contemporary plan (*c.* 1686) of Kinross House and its garden; the walls, fountain and general lay-out remain much as they were when Sir William Bruce designed them

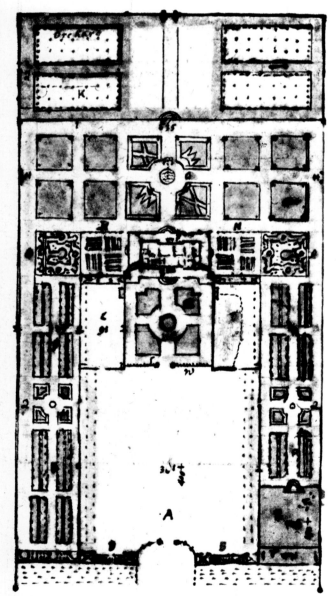

opposite The Fish Gate, with a view of one of the herbaceous borders for which Kinross is celebrated. The gate is probably the work of a Dutch sculptor. On both sides grow *Cotoneaster horizontalis*

From then, however, for various reasons, political and religious, Sir William's fortunes declined. Though his great house stood four-square to the chilling breezes which blew in on Kinross from nearby Fife, its upper floors were not finished, at least not as splendidly as those at ground level. The architect of Kinross died in the year 1710 and after that the house passed through the female line, going downhill all the time. It was saved from complete dereliction by being bought in 1777 by George Graham, who had made a fortune in India. From him the property passed to his descendants who, however, did not live in the house, which stood ghostly and untenanted from 1822 until 1902, when the late Sir Basil Montgomery restored the house, and re-created the policies. The present owner is Sir David Montgomery and the house is lucky to have as occupant Sir David's mother, whose chief care is the beautiful gardens.

The main axis of the garden at Kinross runs from the central window of the west façade to Loch Leven castle. Of Sir William's original garden little remains, except his great stone walls, the attractive twin pavilions with their elaborate swagged medallions carved with the entwined initials of the first owner of Kinross and his wife, some handsome urns and the delightful 'Fish Gate', with its gate of airy ironwork and snaky cornucopia meeting below a carved basket of fish. All these attractive conceits at Kinross are the work of the Dutch sculptors who are known to have worked there in 1686, and the receipt for whose work exists among the family papers. That is all of Sir William's garden that survives, though it is known that elaborate work was carried out at Kinross, some even before the house itself was started. The eight acres between house and loch were levelled, and records exist that Sir William's son John sent home from France a collection of plants, including horse chestnuts, Croix de Jerusalem, jonquils and anemones – with an apology for not having been able to discover their Latin names – 'which must be sowed up and down your parterre'.

This parterre was re-created by Sir Basil Montgomery in 1903, when he entirely re-designed the garden, within the framework of Sir William's decorative walls. It now takes the form of a fine formal garden, enclosed in yew hedges and centring on a circular fountain and a lily pond. This still occupies the same position as marked on the original seventeenth-century plan. To either side

Scale and space contribute much to the grandeur of the garden at Kinross. Here a couchant lion presides over a wide lawn

A figure of Atlas with his heavy load stands in the centre of the walled rose-garden

Topiary, as well as statues, can give contrast and character to a garden, as with this spiral of yew set in the centre of a bed of floribunda roses

lie broad stretches of lawn and between garden and loch runs Sir William's wall, pierced by the Fish Gate and broken by bold buttresses of yew. Along this wall runs a herbaceous border which has most imaginatively been divided into sections with different colour schemes, the blue and yellow section being particularly effective.

To achieve the overall effect of different azures that Mrs Montgomery aimed at in her blue border, she planted, always in bold patches, galega, a Goats Rue with ferny pea-green foliage and sprays of pale blue flowers which look rather like wistaria; the always-successful *Salvia virgata nemerosa* – now known more popularly as *Salvia superba* – of which the rich purple flowers in July are followed by russet red heads which have a decorative value of their own.

More blue or mauve flowers in the blue border at Kinross are tall monkshoods, *Aconitum wilsonii*, willow gentians, *Gentiana asclepiadea*, the blue-flowered *Campanula latifolia*, King George asters, and bold plantings of iris which add to the colour of the border in June, to be followed by phlox, which always seem to do better in Scotland than anywhere else – and the brilliant, eye-catching blue of *Salvia patens*, difficult to place sometimes owing to its strong colour, but being surrounded by other blues and mauves it blends well in Mrs Montgomery's border.

For the yellow border a host of plants have been marshalled of which the flowers, or leaves, show tints of gold. Among these are some good helenium, such as *H. autumnale* and *patulum*, two of the best of the sneezeworts, plants that flower at a time when their bright faces are particularly welcome. In a damp patch *Senecio tangutica* has been planted, a bold-leaved groundsel with ragged but handsome flowers, and inula, Flea-bane or elecampane. Two more good yellow-flowered plants in the border are solidago Golden Gates, a more distinguished Golden Rod than many of the family, and the old favourite yellow Oxe Eye Daisy, *bupthalmum*, which has flowered in British gardens since 1722. In the front row of the border the note of yellow is maintained and Mrs Montgomery has planted there bold cushions of golden thyme which have grown into handsome mats of pungent foliage, so tight knit as to discourage the most enterprising weed.

It is difficult to say when the gardens at Kinross are at their best. Perhaps in August, when the roses and clematis are out, filling the beds with colour and festooning Sir William's walls. As we see at Haddon, Mrs Montgomery, too, uses floribunda roses *en masse* to create her bold colour effects, and these are especially brilliant in the fountain garden, which was re-planted with floribunda roses soon after the war. They are confined to two colours only, red and pink, which make a most effective

left A pavilion with a swagged pediment of carved stone bearing the initials of Sir William Bruce, architect of Kinross

opposite Gravelled paths, buttresses of yew and three-hundred-year-old walls make a classic setting for flower-filled borders

The formal gardens were re-created by Sir Basil Montgomery in 1903 within the original framework. The house is severe yet grand and built of a tawny glowing sandstone

show. Six of the beds are set with the dark red Kirsten Poulsen. The other six are planted with the pink floribunda rose Tivoli, and Karen's sister, our old friend Else Poulsen, one of the first of all floribunda roses, and one that has been embellishing our gardens ever since its introduction fifty years ago. Unfortunately, poor Else is subject to mildew and discerning gardeners now prefer the excellent new Silberlachs; which is the rose that Mrs Montgomery is intending to plant at Kinross in Else Poulsen's place.

It is said that early morning or a summer's evening are the best times to visit any garden. In the opinion of the author the gardens of Kinross are at their very best just before sunset. It is then, with the warm façade of Sir William Bruce's great house glowing, its window glass alight and the shadows lengthening in the evening light, that the full beauty of the gardens can be appreciated.

left A lead child and swan in the centre of the lily pond around which (*opposite*) is laid out the great formal parterre of the garden at Kinross. Beyond is Loch Leven, with its island and Loch Leven Castle, where Mary Queen of Scots was imprisoned in 1567

Yorkshire

Newby Hall

A beautiful garden surrounding a great house

On a hot afternoon in 1792, Mr William Weddell, art connoisseur, dilettante and the owner of Newby Hall near Ripon, was taking a stroll in Surrey Street in London and passed a bathing establishment. Unable to resist the temptation of a cool plunge, he entered, and the *Gentleman's Magazine* of the day records the sad and immediate consequences: 'Regretted by all who knew him and in the sixty-eighth year of his age, William Weddell, Esq., MP for Malton . . . walked into the bath up to his middle, . . . was seized by an internal chill, and before he could retire, expired. His name written in his hat discovered who he was to the bath keeper, who immediately went round to his house, where some friends with his lady were awaiting his return to dinner; but on receiving the melancholy intelligence, Lord Down and Mr Frederick Montagu hastened to the bath and found it but too true. Mr W. was distinguished by his taste in virtu. . .'

From the susceptible Mr Weddell the estate of Newby passed to a fairly remote relation, the third Lord Grantham, who in course of time became Earl de Grey, and was an ancester of the present owner, Major Edward Compton.

The garden, as re-created by Major Compton, is one of the most important gardens in the north, the northernmost English garden, in fact, shown in this book, so at this juncture it might be to the point to make some comment on the gardening climate it enjoys. Unlike two of the Scottish gardens illustrated, Logan and Lochinch, Newby is not near the sea, and so cannot look for the relief from frost which the proximity of the Gulf Stream affords. Yorkshire winters are hard and long, and yet they offer some advantages. Being more consistently severe than in the south, they do not encourage plants to make their spring growth too early. The plants in Yorkshire gardens are better able to withstand late frosts. On the other hand the sun does not shine for so long and as warmly in Yorkshire as it does in the south. But Yorkshire has not got a bad climate for gardening, and a great expert on bulbous plants – the late Lt-Colonel Charles H. Grey, Hon. Director of Harlow Car (the Northern Horticultural

'Distinguished by his taste in virtu', William Weddell formed the collection at Newby in the late eighteenth century. A bust by Joseph Nollekens (1737–1823)

opposite The rose garden has neatly paved paths 'cushioned here and there with rounded, low-growing shrubs to give warmth and character in winter'. Here Major Compton grows many of the old shrub roses

NEWBY HALL

Society's Gardens at Harrogate), who moved to Yorkshire from Kent once said that everything he grew in the south 'did' as well, if not better, in Yorkshire.

What certainly helps the owner of Newby Hall to grow the wide variety of plants for which the garden has become well known is the variation in the soil, which differs from light sandy soil in places to heavy clay, with good alluvial deposits near the river Ure, which flows past the bottom of the garden. In the garden's full twenty-five acres, parts are almost lime-free and here Major Compton grows the usual acid-loving plants, especially his favourites, which are those which flower on the naked stem, like some magnolias, hamamelis and azaleas and species rhododendrons. Further from the river, and on heavier soil, he grows philadelphus, lilacs, and many roses.

When Major Compton inherited Newby Hall in 1925, much had to be done. This is how he describes the garden scene at Newby at that time and how, over the years, he changed it.

A number of paths wandered pointlessly through rough grass. There was a period piece rock garden designed by Miss Ellen Wilmott (of garden fame) and a Victorian parterre on both south and west fronts. I was determined in those early days to make a garden worthy of the beautiful house and I soon realized that to enable me to do so I would have to have shelter as the whole twenty-five acres were very windswept. I planned the garden on a central axis, which seemed the obvious thing to do. This axis sloped from the house down to the river some 350 yards away, and to form the axis itself I extended the existing short double borders so that they ran the whole length from the upper terraces down to the river, and backed them with walls of yew. The rest of the garden I built round this axis and the few existing trees, so that by degrees the individual gardens planned themselves, so to speak. In this I was much influenced by Mr Johnny Johnston's garden at Hidcote of which I was a great admirer. The Victorian parterres were replaced by plain lawns and flagstone walks, and Miss Wilmott's large rock garden was joined up to the rest of the garden by suitable paths. . . . Further features were added and the original shelter belts either thinned or had vistas cut through them. I think at the back of my mind I wanted each self-contained garden, so to speak, to represent a certain picture at a certain time of the year; for instance, one enclosure is called the 'Autumn Garden', another the 'Species Rose Garden', and others . . . 'Sunk Garden', 'Blue and Yellow Garden' and so on.

The target to be aimed at seemed to me to be (a) privacy and shelter and (b) sound architectural construction, both of these, to my mind, being of greater importance than mere colour itself. In many ways one can better appreciate a garden by viewing it in winter rather than in summer. Background again is so important. Take, for example, roses. So much of their beauty, to my mind, lies in their foliage, so admirably designed to set off the flowers. This foliage beauty is so often lost by surrounding the roses with grass and greenery. At Newby we tried the experiment of a sunk garden with flagstones and a surround of copper beech – to my mind a perfect foil for the delicate foliage and lovely flowers of the rose.

The gardens of Newby Hall cover the long slope which runs from the southern façade of the house down to the river Ure. Their plan is a simple one, bearing in mind the two axes: the

The urbane façade of Newby Hall, rumoured to have been architected by Sir Christopher Wren, rising above the elaborate pattern of its garden

Weather-worn statues, brought from Italy, stand on pedestals lapped in *Cotoneaster horizontalis*. Behind grow Irish yews and red-leaved *Prunus pissardii*

wide grass path edged with herbaceous borders which runs north and south, and the equally wide gravelled path, known as the statue walk, which runs east and west. This walk consists of an *enfilade* of weather-worn Venetian stone figures rising on pedestals from a planting of *Cotoneaster horizontalis*, beloved of bees in early summer. These statues of gods and goddesses, with whom the rigours of the Yorkshire winter has not dealt kindly, make strange blurred silhouettes, recalling nostalgically the Brenta, as one walks past them, now against the sky, now against the red foliage of *Prunus pissardii*, now against Irish yew. The other gardens at Newby lie in the angles formed by these two main paths, and, in the modern way, each has its own character and its own colour scheme.

The author remembers with particular affection the sunk paved parterre enclosed in a yew hedge and shadowed by a fine cedar tree which bears the name of Major Compton's late wife – Sylvia's garden. Here grow all the favourite flowers of the first Mrs Compton and the long stone paths are bordered with low plantings of dianthus, aubretia, thyme and such cushiony-mat forming subjects. The only height is supplied by modest flowers like lavender and nepeta and silver-leaved senecio and santolina. Just above this haze of grey and blue and mauve, when the author visited Newby, floated here and there the white trumpets of Regale lilies. Sylvia Compton was a beautiful woman and a good gardener, and her own garden at Newby is kept just as she planted it, a delightful memorial.

Not far from Sylvia's garden, below the statue walk, lies the rose garden, with neatly paved paths, cushioned here and there with rounded, low-growing shrubs to give warmth and character in winter and with beds of the 'old' or shrub roses, their flowers carried high, against Major Compton's copper beech hedge, a most effective background. In June the scent and colour in this rose garden casts a potent spell and not only does the visitor revel in the look and fragrance of the roses, but can also make their acquaintance. No garden is better labelled than Newby, and this quality is particularly valuable in the rose garden, where their names can add so much to the charm of the plants. Who could resist a rose called *Cuisse de Nymphe Emue*, and would it, by any other name, smell quite so sweet?

But it is the two herbaceous borders at Newby which frame the sloping path from the south terrace down to the river which must command the admiration of all. Planted as boldly as the borders at Hascombe Court, they would seem to be the very models of what herbaceous borders ought to be. They contain all the favourite flowers for borders, yet every group seems to breathe an air of health and quality which makes them each an individual pleasure to look at. And the Newby borders contain some unusual plants not met with in many gardens, and always remarked on by every visitor. Plants such as *Delphinium casmerianum atropurpureum*, the enormous-leafed, cloudy-flowered *Crambe cordifolia*, and those two excellent silver-leaved artemisias, *ludoviciana* and Silver Queen, but even more remarkable is the curious false hellebore,

Veratrum nigrum, a most difficult plant to find in catalogues. This has leaves like a deeply ribbed hosta and flowers in spires of chocolate black, or green, if the even rarer *V. album* is chosen.

Near it, and for contrast, is planted the pure white floribunda rose Iceberg, the cool tones of the roses acting as most effective foils to the dark flower spikes of the veratrum, and to give contrasting heights, and to create more interest, Major Compton includes, in the modern way, groups of shrubs. But these are most carefully chosen, for he feels that some shrubs are too heavy to grow among the more delicate type of perennial flowers. So the plants which have won a place in the Newby borders are mostly small-leafed, a few old roses, the oddly coloured *R. versicolor*, and the red-leafed *rubrifolia*, rosemary, Hypericum 'Hidcote', *Genista virgata*, a weigela with purple leaves, philadelphus, and potentillas, and species peonies, especially *P. delavayi, lobata*, and the exquisite *mlokosewitschi* with its tourmaline anthers and flowers like sophisticated buttercups.

The writer visited Newby in the early days of his garden experience, and he was introduced there to plants which have remained firm friends, and which he has grown himself ever since. *Euphorbia wulfenii*, for instance, a spurge which is perhaps the finest and most impressive of its race, and which is often mentioned in descriptions of other gardens in this book. Another is *Pyrus salicifolia* – the Willow Leaved Pear, a tree of modest size with pendant silver leaves and a habit of rare beauty. The only attractive pampas grass, in the opinion of the writer, *Cortaderia bertinii* was a find at Newby – a grass of unsurpassed neatness of habit, which only grows five feet high, never breaking off and looking untidy like most pampas grasses. *Photinia fruticosa* was another, as well as several excellent chaenomeles (the 'japonica' of long ago) such as the pink *moerlesii* and pure white *nivalis*. One last plant which grows at Newby, and which the writer has planted in many gardens ever since he first saw it there, is *Rheum atropurpureum*, a splendidly impressive plant for a damp place, a giant rhubarb with wide webbed leaves of rich claret and high pinnacles of creamy, woolly flowers. 'Meeting' plants in other people's gardens, making friends with them, so that from then on you either grow them yourself or recognize them as friends when you see them elsewhere, is surely one of the great pleasures of gardening. Not comparable to the joy of planting or creating a garden such as Major Compton has created, but still a lasting joy.

The writer asked the owner of Newby what particular satisfaction he got out of gardening. His answer sums up very well what many gardeners must feel about their favourite hobby:

... the same sort of pleasure that an artist would get out of painting a picture ... selecting the most harmonious colours ... appreciation of the interplay of light and shade, the 3-D effect of tall plants and short plants and spaces between, and the sheer and simple beauty of shadows on a long summer evening, and above all the fact that by walking round one's garden one can almost forget the miserable world outside in which we now live.

Beyond the balustrated terrace with its lily-strewn pond, a long vista leads the eye down to the river Ure

White delphiniums growing among evergreens illuminate the corner in which they are planted

Cambridgeshire
Anglesey Abbey
A garden laid out in the eighteenth-century manner

To have created in less than forty years a garden of which the avenues would have pleased Le Nôtre, the statuary and urns not been out of place at Versailles, the herbaceous border been a credit to William Robinson, and the trees impressed a Forestry Commissioner, is no mean achievement. But this is what the late Lord Fairhaven, since 1926, conjured at Anglesey Abbey in Cambridgeshire. But before describing the garden let us salute in passing the Abbey itself, for it is a historical building of great interest and architectural charm, and it has overlooked the wide fenland countryside between Cambridge and Swaffham Prior for over eight hundred years.

Originally Anglesey Abbey was an Augustinian Priory, dating from the twelfth century. Towards the end of the reign of Queen Elizabeth it was secularized and became a manor house, though much of the old monastery remained. When the old fabric was destroyed, parts of it were incorporated into the new building, especially the vaulted dining room of clunch with Purbeck marble pillars, which dates from 1236. Several buttresses are of the same period, and a stone, built into a much later doorway, shows the arms of Elizabeth of Clare – who gave her name to Clare College at nearby Cambridge. The property was owned by various families, but was really saved in 1861 by the Reverend John Hailstone, who preserved and cared for it. In 1926 it was bought by Lord Fairhaven, the more recent history of the Abbey and its fortunate acquisition by the present owner being outlined in measured Latin phrases, written by the late Earl of Birkenhead, and carved on another stone set in the hall by the new front door.

> Hanc Aedem In Pios Vsvs Fvndatam
> Primo Regnante Henrico
> Disrvpit Princeps Ejvsdem Nominis Octavvs
> Recreavit secvlaremqve Fecit
> Thomas Parker Anno MDCIX
> Hailstonivs Vir Reverendissimvs

opposite The south front of Anglesey Abbey. In the foreground, Pan in a sheepskin blows a welcome

Gardening in the grand manner: a classical statue and close shorn hedges contrast with towering trees beyond

Restavravit Cvravitqve Anno MDCCCLXI
Officivm Tam Pivm Vltimi Confecervnt
Hvddleston Et Henricvs Brovghton
Fraterna Sollicitvdine Anno MCMXXVI
O Si Haec Domvs
Tantas Passa Vices
Jamdvdvm Qviescat
Birkenhead Scripsit

Lord Fairhaven modernized the house and added considerably to it, and within a few years he had completely transformed and greatly enlarged the gardens.

The first view of the gardens at Anglesey Abbey is obtained through the garden door in the centre of the southern façade – little altered since 1620. A wide vista greets the visitor as he steps on to the spreading lawn outside – a perspective of shorn turf, fringed with elm, chestnuts, a magnificent copper beech with wine-dark leaves, and Lord Fairhaven's favourite tree at Anglesey, a towering silver lime. The two last trees, both over a hundred years old, grow to the left of the Abbey, with, below them, a perfectly proportioned yew hedge, which was one of the new owner's first additions. This has been allowed to meld, tactfully, with a line of tall Irish yews, making a particularly pleasing contrast in texture, and giving an effective look of maturity, though the yews are less than forty years old.

Beyond lies a smiling landscape of lawn and trees, and in observing its treatment the thoughtful visitor has further occasion to acclaim Lord Fairhaven's planting acumen. Elsewhere, as we shall see, the gardens at Anglesey Abbey are noteworthy for the almost audacious way new avenues, groves and glades of new trees have been planted. But where maturer plantations already existed, Lord Fairhaven had the good sense not to add new planting of trees which by their smaller size would of necessity diminish the whole. The trees around the Abbey itself, besides fulfilling the important function of providing shelter – ever necessary for houses, like Anglesey Abbey, built in the quite flat and windswept country of the fens – have wisely been left unencumbered with latter plantings, and indeed have been in places thinned to allow each specimen greater room for development.

The plan of Lord Fairhaven's new landscape garden, with its avenues and vistas, is a complex one and depends for its great success on the owner's knowledge and love of trees, their character, their temperament, and most important of all their different rates of growth. The green friezes they form against the enormous cloud-swept skies of East Anglia are compellingly effective and their proportions most impressive. The Main Avenue is over half a mile long, and composed of four rows of alternate planes and chestnuts. Another, called the Warrior's Walk, is over 350 yards long – a magnificent double row of Norway spruce and larch. Parallel to it is the Emperor's Walk, formed of Norway spruce alone and of equal length. Lesser avenues radiate from these three great *allées*, and at their intersections or to act as

left The open temple was assembled in 1953 to mark the coronation of Elizabeth II. In the centre stands a version of Bernini's David carved by G. Fossi. The base bears Lord Fairhaven's cipher *opposite* At the entrance to the temple there is a lead figure of a crouching lioness by Jan Van Nost (1668–1729). The Corinthian pillars capitals came from Chesterfield House

A Caryatid in Coade stone. The formula for this frost-resistant material, which was much used about 1800 for garden statuary, is unfortunately now lost

A sundial, dated 1785, by B. Cox in an angle of the Abbey's rose-clad walls

eye-catchers at their further ends are the statues, urns, sphinxes, obelisks, and temples which, after the tree plantings, are the most memorable features of the gardens at Anglesey. The placing of these is nothing short of masterly. In one part – near the rose garden – a long yew hedge is enlivened by having set before it four magnificent urns of marble. Two are signed by Peter Scheemakers, Nollekens' master, and the crisp carving of one shows Iphigenia's sacrifice, and the other a Bacchanalia. The two others are by Laurent Delvaux (1696–1778), who was Scheemakers' partner. Records exist that these urns formed lots 267, 371 and 392 at the great Wanstead sale early in the last century, and that they fetched £21, £80 and £78 respectively. Today these urns and the way their marble and perfect proportions shine out against the dark evergreen recall a corner of the French gardens of Courances or Vaux le Vicomte.

Elsewhere in the gardens at Anglesey there are other examples of the happy juxtaposition of stone and verdure, such as at the end of a broad avenue of planes, where two lead sphinxes on high pedestals share their secrets with the skies. In another part, near a wide circle of copper beech hedge, tenanted by four gracefully draped statues of women in lead, which were once at Stowe on the Temple of Concord and Victory, Lord Fairhaven has placed a temple to shelter a very fine vase of porphyry. This magnificent piece measures six feet across, and must be one of the largest single pieces of porphyry outside the Vatican.

But perhaps the most impressive example in Lord Fairhaven's landscape garden of the happy coming together of stone and foliage, is the pair of enormous urns which stand in the triple rings of trees at either end of a single avenue of planes and chestnuts; these had to be at least fifteen feet high to look adequate, and as one can imagine were not easy to find.

Though emphasis at Anglesey is certainly on trees and statuary rather than flowers, flowers are in no way lacking. Under the honey-coloured walls of the Abbey there is an attractive rose garden, symmetrically planted, with each bed planted with a single variety of rose. There is also a hedge-enclosed garden which is planted out most spectacularly twice a year – in the spring with blue and white hyacinths and in the autumn with Elsdon dahlias, in a bright scheme of red, orange and yellow.

The herbaceous border at Anglesey Abbey was devised and planned by a master of that particular art – Captain Vernon Daniell, one of the earliest gardening friends of the writer. As might be expected, it is laid out on the grandest scale, and backed with a splendid hedge of beech more than nine feet in height. The border is semi-circular in form and is planted not only with all the favourite herbaceous flowers, including delphiniums sometimes taller than the hedge which shelters them, but also with some more unusual flowers. Especially the writer recalls some fine groups of *Dictamnus fraxinella* – the Burning Bush – usually so slow growing, which at Anglesey has quickly made bold clumps that are most striking in early summer, with their spidery white or purple flowers. Another plant which

makes a fine, if short-lived, show is the flowering Sea Kale, *Crambe cordifolia*, which shows its cloudy heads of white flowers over large, architecturally sculptured leaves in June. As the herbaceous border we describe is at Anglesey, it naturally has its own *genius loci*, in the shape of a statue of Time, said to be by Michael Rysbrack (1639–1770). And when the heyday of the herbaceous flowers is past – does Time discourage delay? – a nearby dahlia border takes over and, until the first frosts, make a swathe – at least when the author visited Anglesey – of different coloured flowers of a brightness to make 'the rash gazer wipe his eye'. Once the brilliance of the dahlia garden has faded, the only colour left is the russet of the beech hedges – the blue of the vast East Anglian sky, never so blue as when autumn turns to winter – and the fading green of the turf. Yet such is the grandeur of the scale of the gardens at Anglesey, that they are impressive at any time of the year. They are a living memorial to the vision, taste, knowledge and optimistic patience of their creator.

A happy combination of sculpture across the centuries: an eighteenth-century lead vase, from Drakelow Hall, on a second-century Roman altar

'One of the largest single pieces of porphyry outside the Vatican' is sheltered by a temple of Doric pillars, with a scaled roof of green copper

Haddington

Tyninghame

A distinctive garden on the Firth of Forth

above Tyninghame in early Victorian days, as altered by William Burn in 1828 *below* An original wing

opposite White roses frame a pensive Venetian statue in the new garden laid out by Lady Haddington in the early 1950s

There are some gardens – even when they belong to houses famous for their history or their architecture, which seem to be the immediate child of their present occupants, the creation of their imagination and fancy, an extension and expression of their personality. Such a garden, at least in the opinion of the author of this book, is the garden at Tyninghame. It is a very beautiful garden. The Countess of Haddington, a very modest woman, would be quick to say that there was a garden at Tyninghame long before she came there fourteen years ago. True enough. But it is since Lady Haddington has occupied herself with it that the garden has taken on its extraordinary character. It is a very personal garden, and to have imbued an old-established garden with so much of her own light-hearted fancy is an achievement on Lady Haddington's part, of no mean order.

The garden at Tyninghame is large and lies around a house which, in spite of its Pompeian-red walls and Hans Anderson turrets, no one could describe as architecturally beautiful. But, while retaining its Victorian plan, the garden displays, at every turn, taste, imagination and deftness of touch. Pompousness has been made pretty without loss of dignity, and one part of the rather daunting façade, in the Scottish Romantic style, has been elegantly clothed with creepers and masked with a honeysuckle-covered trellis. The severe gravel walks have been enlivened with crisp white *caissons de Versailles* containing pyramidal bay-trees. Six columnar cherries – *Ama-no-gawa* – give point to a Victorian stone seat as they stand behind it, erect as footmen. The proportions of the Victorian parterre have not been changed, but the flower-beds have been set with the best varieties of the best plants of today. And yet, in the embellishment, there is no fuss, no silliness. All has been achieved by a thoughtful artistry which warms the heart of the most *blasé* garden connoisseur.

Below the east façade of the house lies an elaborate parterre, which also retains its early nineteenth-century plan with its conically clipped yews and symmetrical beds. Here some suitably rugged terracing of old Edinburgh paving stones under the house

above Running at right angles to the main garden path is a two-hundred-year-old apple tunnel

opposite A gate, with key-stone carved with the date 1666, leads from the main garden

An enclosed parterre of box-bordered flower-bed lies in the shelter of tall trees and columnar evergreens

walls is the only modern addition to the parterre.

Centrepoint of this garden is a towering sundial, of a typically Scottish seventeenth-century design, like the one we admire at Drummond. The Tyninghame one is a copy of one at Newbattle, in Midlothian, and has an elaborate set of dials, raised on an octagonal base and decorated with grotesque animals.

Beyond this parterre – to the east – lies a part of the garden, once known as the Wilderness, which comprises the original eighteenth-century bowling-green.

But between this and the east parterre is a corner of the garden, little larger than a tennis court, which was laid out in 1953, from an eighteenth-century plan in an old French garden book. Here the planting is entirely the choice of Lady Haddington and an excellent example of her taste and gardening knowledge. Informally planned, in a series of beds set in turf, each bed is brimful of all the garden-owner's favourite plants. In Lady Haddington's own words it is 'stuffed with all the old roses . . . Tuscany, gallicas, Bourbons, damascs, and in addition a few modern shrub roses like the Victorian looking "Lavender Lassie" of the same colouring and form as the old roses, to extend the flowering season.' As well as many plants of silver foliage, like the seldom-grown eureops, a frosty-leaved small shrub from the Drakensburg, artemisias, senecios, santolinas, lavenders, salvias with furry opalescent leaves, variegated hostas and the rare peony *mlokose-witchii*. Several different euphorbias, the strange, slightly sinister spurges so popular with the garden *cognoscenti* of today, are in great evidence. Old roses and plants with good leaves – two typical modern trends which are well exemplified at Tyninghame.

The delighted visitor leaves this part of the garden with regret, and with the feeling that he is leaving a very carefully selected company of friends, of favourite plants chosen for some very special quality that has endeared them to the garden's creator. His way lies through an iron gate, set between piers of brick, capped on either side by stone figures of children from the Veneto, quite reconciled, judging by their smiles, to their translation from the banks of the Brenta to the shores of the Forth.

The path from here leads under splendid old trees, and is bordered on one side with deep plantings of rhododendrons and azaleas, and on the other open to the park, studded with more fine trees and watered by the river Tyne. The path, a quarter of a mile in length, leads to the old walled garden, which is more than two hundred years old. This is laid out in the old-fashioned Scottish style, with broad grass paths, clipped hedges, box-edged borders of mixed flowers, with here and there some good eighteenth-century lead statues. A graceful fountain, with water falling from four horses' heads, is the central point of this part of the garden, and is enclosed in a circle of closely trimmed yew hedges.

But it is further on, through a gate with the date 1666 on its mossgrown keystone, that a surprise awaits the visitor: an apple tunnel, running at right angles to the main garden path, and a full hundred yards long. The pleached walk leads under blossom-filtered sunlight in spring and cool green shade in summer.

Autumn hangs the apple hoops with fruit, in the manner of a Mantegna fresco, until the fruit is gathered and winter strips the leaves, leaving only a filigree of branches against the sky. It is the finest apple tunnel that the author of this book has ever seen, and well over eighty years old. At one of its ends the vista is closed by a slender statue in marble of Flora, and at the other Ganymede, cupbearer to the gods, patiently year in, year out, offering refreshment from his marble cup.

From the apple tunnel the visitor to the garden at Tyninghame retraces his footsteps, through the walled garden and back to the pleasure-grounds which lie round the house itself. On the south side, below the terrace, lies a parterre of lawn with raised flower-beds contained in grey stone walls and low buttresses. These rather ponderous early Victorian conceits (they date from William Burn's alterations to the garden in 1828) have been enlivened by a typical example of Lady Haddington's fancy, and are now crowned with pyramids of wood, over which are trained yellow roses and clematis, and under-planted with purple sage and dark red *Rhus cotinus* – all plants chosen to blend with the pink red walls of the house. Treated in this way, Mr Burn's raised beds make garden features that are practical and decorative.

Passing the rose pyramids on his right, the visitor mounts some steps, and is about to re-enter the house when a completely different sort of garden catches his eye. This is a corner which is Lord Haddington's especial care, a heath garden as well planted as any in Scotland.

Heath gardens have not only great appeal, but sterling quali-ties too. For if thoughtfully planted, they can provide flower and colour almost all the year round. They look particularly well in Scotland, and the view of Tyninghame's pepper pot turrets seen over the rose, grey and sea-green colouring of Lord Haddington's heath garden is a telling one.

Before leaving the gardens of Tyninghame, it must be recorded that they are set in parkland with avenues of trees that are second to none in Scotland. These were planted by the sixth Earl of Haddington over two hundred and fifty years ago in the year of the Union, aided and abetted by his enthusiastic young wife, his cousin Helen Hope. Always very much in evidence at Tyninghame are the shining waters of the Firth of Forth which lie, like a silver sword, to the east. Half an hour's walk on springing turf and under a canopy of trees brings one to the shore; here, golden sands stretch to right and left of the tumbled rocks of Whitberry Point. The trees grow down to the water's edge, conjuring an almost Mediterranean feeling. To the north-west, across the Firth, lies the misty shore of Fife. Nearer in the land-and-sea-scape, is the primeval shape of the Bass Rock, wreathed per-petually with its cloud of gannets, and white-caps breaking at its base. The sea brings to Tyninghame the blessings of gentle winters, the centuries have conjured the park and dressed it with splendid trees. But it is the present holders of the ancient name of Haddington who have cast their own spell on the place – the magic which invests now the gardens and policies of Tyninghame.

Fastigiate cherry trees, *Prunus ama-no-gawa* 'erect as footmen', stand behind a semi-circular Victorian seat of carved stone

The centrepiece of the large, walled garden at Tyninghame is this fountain in a flower-bordered pool

Haddon Hall

A historic garden planted with modern roses

Built on a steep hillside, with long views over the peaked hills and rolling fields of Derbyshire, stands Haddon Hall, perhaps the most romantic of all the great houses of England. Legend clings like ivy to its ancient walls. Often-told tales of Dorothy Vernon and her lover linger, and have been made the subject of a highly coloured historical novel by Charles Major and an early film of Mary Pickford, for which, in the 1920s, a Hollywood version of Haddon Hall was built in California. The gate through which Dorothy eloped and the packbridge over the infant river Wye, here little more than a stream, which she crossed to meet her lover Sir John Manners are still shown, all part and parcel of the Haddon story. How much is truth and how much is legend it is difficult to say. Dorothy Vernon, heiress of Haddon, certainly married Sir John Manners, and their descendant, the present Duke of Rutland, still owns Haddon. But did they elope, as Charles Major graphically recounts?

Certainly, after her marriage, the story of Dorothy's connection with her famous and supposedly much loved home became more *terre à terre*. After the death of her husband's elder brother she was translated to the greater grandeur of Belvoir Castle and seems seldom to have visited Haddon again, and to have let it stand empty. But it was never allowed to fall into disrepair, and the fifteenth-century house is so massively constructed that the walls of the Great Hall, built in 1452, before the Wars of the Roses, are as sound as they were in the reign of Henry VI. The long gallery was added in the reign of Queen Elizabeth and its panelling displays the arms of both the Vernon and the Manners families, put up by Dorothy Vernon's father, soon after her marriage, runaway or not, to Sir John, which, alas for the romantic, does not suggest any violent disapproval of the match.

It is from the three great bow windows of the long gallery that the best view is obtained of the garden at Haddon, but before passing through the anteroom and out on to the sunlit, rose-scented terraces, let us briefly note the history of the house since Dorothy's day. For years it stood empty, though it was always

Mary Pickford in an early film version of *Dorothy Vernon of Haddon Hall*

opposite The bow windows of the long gallery at Haddon Hall look over an old garden planted with the best modern varieties of roses well cared for. Its walls were so strongly built that the panelling, carvings and much of the ancient fittings of the house are perfectly preserved. One of the most celebrated amongst the historic houses of the country, Haddon was always a place of pilgrimage, though Celia Fiennes, who has left such a fascinating record of country house and garden visiting in the late seventeenth and early eighteenth century, was not impressed by the grounds.

Thence to Haddon Hall – The Earle of Rutland's house near Bankwell. It is a good old house built of stone on a hill, and behind it is a fine grove of high trees, and good gardens but nothing very curious as the mode now is . . .

The new fashion in gardening had obviously not reached Haddon by 1700. But all admired the ancient building of the Hall and its splendid site.

The gardens of Haddon Hall are little changed in form since the Vernons' day. They form a series of terraces, built sturdily of the local stone, which clamber up and down the hillside on which the Hall is built, hugging the steep inclines and offering shelter to the many flowering plants, especially roses, which in summer clothe them. They are linked by a flight of seventy-six steps, of stone but without mortar. The uppermost terrace, until the gardens were completely cleared and replanted by the ninth Duke of Rutland, was heavily shaded by tall trees which crowned, somewhat top-heavily, the whole complex of the garden, and shaded what was known as Dorothy Vernon's walk. These were felled and their place was taken by a lawn, neat paths, and flower-filled beds, in which the planting is kept low, not only because owing to the terraces' elevation tall flowers might suffer from being exposed to wind and dashed about, but also so as not to obscure the magnificent views over the fields and hills of the surrounding countryside. Of the Renaissance of the garden at Haddon Hall, Kathleen Duchess of Rutland has said: 'I can not describe what a joy it was . . . to make these old terraces come to life again with roses, honeysuckle, rock roses and lavender . . .'

More clearing took place on the second terrace, where a row of yew trees, once possibly neatly trimmed in Tudor style into pyramids or peacocks, had over the centuries grown wild, and completely shaded the terrace, making it dark and gloomy. So these, too, were felled and replaced with a wide lawn and neat cones of new yew. This lawn, when the author visited Haddon, was being used as a bowling green instead of the original one which crowned the hill on the site of which the gardens lie. Celia Fiennes does not mention the bowling green at Haddon, though had she done so, she could well have described it as she did the one at Somerhill in Kent: 'an advanced piece of ground above all the rest, which discovers the country a great circuit around'. For the outlook from the old bowling green at Haddon is very fine, and raised so high above Peverells Tower and the clustered rooves of the Hall as almost to look down the chimneys.

From the second to the third terrace runs the flight of stairs balustraded in stone and quite smothered with roses in June and

A flight of stone steps, with ball-capped balustrade, rises from the rose garden to a terrace

The garden was largely re-created, in its ancient
framework of walls and terraces, in 1912

The plan of the terraced garden at Haddon Hall
from Inigo Triggs' *The Formal Garden in England and
Scotland*

The packbridge over which Dorothy Vernon is said have eloped with her lover, Sir John Manners

July. These steps are the central feature of the garden, linking the upper and the lower parts. They are at least three hundred years old, as are the limestone terraces which form the strait jacket of the garden which its hillside site imposes. But if the garden's plan is an ancient one, the plants which fill it today are modern, especially the roses for which the garden is justly celebrated in summer. These were planted by Kathleen, Duchess of Rutland, when she recreated the garden in 1912, and have recently been most successfully added to by her son and her daughter-in-law, Lord and Lady John Manners, who chose the best and most modern roses available.

Most spectacular of these are certainly the floribundas, which were flowering magnificently in the garden at Haddon when the author visited it in June. Floribunda roses, one might mention in passing, were first raised in Denmark where the great rosarian Poulsen introduced the first two floribundas in 1924. These were first known as hybrid polyanthas, and the first two varieties to be widely planted were Else and Kirsten Poulsen. They were the outstandingly successful results of a breed between hybrid tea and polyantha roses. Since those early introductions, floribunda roses have been astonishingly developed, and are now the masterpiece of recent garden achievement. Few other plants give so generously in flower, and ask so little in the way of maintenance. They are the ideal plants for the labour-short gardens of today. True, the early floribundas had little scent, but the more recent varieties are deliciously fragrant – roses like Papa Meilland which has petals of dusty crimson velvet, shining leaves and a flowering season from June till the first frosts. It is with new roses like these that the old garden at Haddon is planted. A few the author particularly remembers are the Poulsen-raised Chinatown, with scented yellow petals edged with cherry, the light pink Poulsens, the scarlet Frensham and, one of the most charming roses of modern gardens, the pink Dearest, raised by that well-known hybridizer in Northern Ireland, Alex Dickson.

Of course, floribundas are not the only roses in the garden at Haddon. The terrace walls are festooned with climbing roses, like the wine-red Clos Vougeot, the pearly pink New Dawn, and the coral budded Albertine. There are beds of hybrid tea roses to lay their perfume on the air – no question of lack of scent about them, for their fragrance on a warm June evening seems to tint the very air with colour.

In an old catalogue, dated 1900, the author found a rose listed called Dorothy Vernon, which he understands is now long since out of commerce. It was described as being 'gallant pink in hue, of lovely form and with foliage that is practically evergreen' – evergreen, like the romantic legends which still haunt Haddon Hall. It is a pity there is no Dorothy Vernon rose there to add its sweetness to her garden, of which that acclaimed garden connoisseur Mr A. G. L. Hellyer has written, 'such is Haddon Hall, a place of dreams and a garden of exquisite beauty. It would be a dull visitor indeed whose imagination was not stirred by it, or who did not think his journey well repaid'.

opposite Bold plants of tree peony, effective even when not in flower because of their handsome foliage, stand on both sides of a door in a rose-clad wall

Hever Castle

A historic garden with classic statuary

William Waldorf Astor's elaborate gates, leading to the Italian gardens at Hever, were set up soon after 1903

opposite In the series of small Tudor gardens which lie below the east façade of Hever Castle are planted many of the flowers of Anne Boleyn's time. In the centre, an astrolabe

Four hundred years ago the beam of history was fixed on Hever Castle in Kent. It was to illumine the place with a hectic glory for several years, a light which faded to a baleful glow and finally totally and disastrously darkened and disappeared. The sunlit peace which envelops Hever Castle and its gardens today is in startling contrast.

In 1530 Henry VIII was courting the daughter of the house – Anne Boleyn. All England knew of his constant visits to Hever, with an escort of glittering cavalry, his approach heralded 'by the winding of a horn on a nearby hill'. The courtship was indeed historic, for though Anne's marriage was to be a disaster for herself and her too ambitious family, it was to contribute directly to the religious reformation and the foundation of the Church of England. And its offspring was to be England's greatest ruler.

Until the Boleyns bought Hever its history was obscure. Records exist which prove that it was owned by the Norman William De Hever who was Sheriff under Edward 1. From William it passed to the Cobhams and Sir John De Cobham was granted a licence to crenellate in 1380. Names with a Shakespearean ring follow in the chronicle of Hever: Scrope, the Earl of Wiltshire, Baron Saye and Sele, even Sir John Fastolf – said to be the original of Falstaff himself. The list of very English names lengthens. In 1423 Hever was the property of Sir Roger Fiennes and it would be interesting to know if Celia Fiennes, that ardent country house and garden visitor of the eighteenth century, was his descendant.

Sir Geoffrey Boleyn – once Lord Mayor of London and also owner of beautiful Blickling in Norfolk, his home county, bought Hever in 1459. The newly-rich Boleyns were socially ambitious and by a succession of brilliant marriages, with the daughter and heiress of Lord Hastings, with a daughter of Lord Ormonde, with a daughter of the Duke of Norfolk, they reached the very highest rungs of the social ladder. Then Anne aspired to the hand of the King himself, and calamity followed.

After Anne's execution on a trumped-up charge of adultery, but really for her failure to provide an heir, her father continued to live obscurely at Hever and on his death Henry took possession of the castle and its lands, tossing it casually to Anne of Cleves, another discarded wife, but one who had been clever enough to keep her head. After her death in 1557 Hever's fortunes steeply declined. By the end of the nineteenth century the castle was occupied by simple farmers whose ducks and geese swam in the old moat, whose kitchens were the once proud banqueting hall, whose bacons and hams hung seasoning from the ancient beams and whose corn and potatoes lay stacked in chambers that were haunted by so many memories.

Then, in 1903, came Hever's renaissance, when Mr William Waldorf Astor, of the famous American family, and a devoted lover of England and its gardens, saw the little moated castle, fell in love with it, and set about its restoration.

Though an essay on the garden at Hever would not be complete without a brief résumé of the castle's historical background, there is no space to describe in detail Mr Astor's astonishing recreation of the house itself. But the farm outbuildings disappeared and in their place rose, as if overnight, a Tudor 'village' which, while not competing architecturally with the Tudor castle, provided guest rooms, kitchens, and all the essential accommodation which Mr Astor, with his lavish American ideas, needed for the elaborate *train de vie* of entertaining in Edwardian England.

In the garden, the developments were as spectacular. Roads and nearby river were realigned – and moved further away from the castle. The little meandering river Eden was transformed into a lake. These alterations were all too necessary. The castle lay in a hollow, only 120 feet above sea level, and in winter the land around was often flooded. So the river was dammed and made into a lake not only for ornamental reasons, but also with lock gates for the purpose of controlling the water level and preventing flooding. To the south of the castle the level of the ground had to be raised as well, and a series of connecting moats and channels cut to carry away flood water in winter. These immense works were duly carried out, and the lake, when completed, covered more than thirty-five acres, and was in places ten feet deep.

Work then started on the pleasure grounds and soil was moved by the ton, with the aid of steam dredgers and an elaborate network of railways. Rocks were introduced on a scale unseen in England since Joseph Paxton moved the great rocks at Chatsworth for the sixth Duke of Devonshire, and caused his admiring patron to exclaim that the spirit of some Druid inspired Mr Paxton in 'these bulky removals'. Full-grown trees were transplanted from Ashdown Forest and it became a familiar sight on the twelve miles of country road which lay between Ashdown and Hever for early motorists to meet teams of ten men and four horses transporting lofty Scots pines to their new home on the banks of Mr Astor's new lake. Moving mature trees has long been a side of landscape gardening at which Americans have excelled but the planting of the woods round Hever must be an

opposite The statuary in the garden at Hever Castle is particularly impressive
right Water lilies on the moat, with the bridge leading to the main entrance of the castle

A pair of marble *putti* shaded from the sun by the flowers and leaf of honeysuckle

Valerian, vines and sprays of wistaria frame some of Mr Astor's collection of classic sculpture

early example of American enterprise in this field in England.

Thus a new landscape was created round Hever Castle. Nearer the house itself a series of small gardens were laid out, each enclosed in hedges of yew or box. These were kept in scale with the castle, whose great charm has always been its comparatively small size. In these gardens were planted all the flowers which might have grown there in the days of Anne Boleyn. Roses, lavender, herbs. There was, and still is, a maze for which the hedges needed a thousand yew trees; there was a bowling green and topiary chessmen which recall those we see at Haseley Court. In one of these enclosures has recently been dug a swimming pool, well concealed from the house by a six-foot hedge. At each of its four corners stand Italian terra-cotta pots planted not only with the usual geraniums but with heliotrope and the tender purple-flowered *Statice latifolia*, one of the best of all plants for tubs but one that is found in very few gardens.

Further from the castle, more ambitious garden features were brought into being. Rhododendrons were planted by the hundred to skirt winding paths, cascades were conjured; the balustraded 'Golden Stairs' were built on the main axis from the main gate of the castle, to close the view to the south from the inner courtyard and over the drawbridge.

For of course there is a drawbridge at Hever, which leads from the main entrance over the moat, another great beauty of the castle and its surroundings; and the moat at Hever, from June onwards, is afloat with water lilies, with countless flowers of white tinged with gold, lemon and deepest crimson.

But it was to the East that the most spectacular part of the new pleasure grounds lay. This is the Italian garden – with its pergolas, colonnades, fountains and astonishing collection of Roman classical statuary and sculpture which Mr Astor amassed during a period of time spent in Rome as American Minister. Great care was taken to situate this remarkable collection so that it could not be seen from the Tudor castle. Thus, leaving the medieval gardens, crossing the outer moat and following a wide path with lawn on either side, the visitor to Hever for the first time is astonished by the spectacle which greets him. The main collection of sculpture is placed under a long wall of old stone, an eighth of a mile long and richly clothed in roses, magnolias and wistaria, and with overflowing borders at its base. The assembly consists of Corinthian capitals, sarcophagi, a richly carved Flavian architrave soffit, all in marble; some, since most are Roman, are in fragments or at least hard hit by time. There are headless Aphrodites, armless Apollos, and a Hercules unmanned.

Marble, it has been said, and rightly, is not often suitable for English gardens. It needs brilliant sunshine, a clean bright light and pellucid skies to set off its lustre. Often in the soft light and misty air of England, Italian marble looks cold and forbidding. Also, unlike English stones, and Portland stone in particular, marble does not weather well, though it is the finest of all mediums for carving, but the subtleties of detail which marble makes possible to the sculptor are not displayed to best advantage by our

pearly light. Why, then, does the statuary at Hever look so well? In the opinion of the author of this book it is because it is constantly set off by foliage.

The juxtaposition of stone and leaf is a recognized way of achieving beautiful garden effects. Wistaria on a grey stone wall, moss on well-weathered steps, the cobwebby houseleek on a Cotswold roof; there are endless examples.

At Hever the telling effect of leaf against stone and stone against leaf are everywhere, and most happily manifest. What might otherwise have been a rather daunting enfilade of chilly antiquities has been made into a garden walk – a border, almost, in which stone and planting are most felicitously wed. Valerian tumbles over marble lions, vine leaves, real and of stone, crown a laughing Bacchus; the glaucous leaves of iris burst from the base of a carved sarcophagus.

The Italian garden at Hever is unique, and an excellent example of imaginative gardening. One suggestion might, most tentatively, be made: for a more classical choice of plants to be grown among these relics of Imperial Rome. The august permanence of marble surely calls for perennial planting. Vines and figs there are, but could not acanthus (the very own plant of architecture), for instance, find a place among the herms, and more rosemary be planted, which the asthmatic Pliny grew in his garden in Herculaneum, two thousand years ago?

In the south-eastern rotunda, with its walls clad in *Schizophragma hydrangeoides*, stands a Greco-Roman statue of a youth, in grey veined marble

Roses in bloom at Hever

Sussex
Nymans
A garden famous for its rare shrubs and trees

One of the author's many visits to Nymans was in April. A period of warm sunny days had raised his hopes as to what flowers he would find in a garden so well known for its beauty in early spring. And flowers in plenty he found. But it was snowing, and all the pink camellias, for which Nymans is famous, were capped with white, and their branches laden. The effect was strange but weirdly beautiful. A *Rhododendron macabeanum* of which Lady Rosse was particularly proud, as it had never flowered so well, was indeed in full splendour of blossom, but its giant leaves were top-coated with white, and it was in a tribute to the pure cream colour of its flowers that they did not seem dull in competition with the pristine snow; and round another corner, an Italian gate, with its coat of arms and supporters of naked cherubs, was etched in black and white, and the flowers of the *Clematis armandii* which festooned it showed up but wanly. Nearby the rosy petals of *Magnolia campbellii* stained the snow, and the blue flowers of *Rhododendron augustinii* were blanketed.

Particularly telling in the unseasonable picture was the scene presented by the topiary enclosure adjoining the courtyard. Here the spears of *Iris reticulata* showed black, and the dark pinnacles of the yew hedge were sharply outlined, as were the box-edged rose beds. The hush that always seems to fall when a garden is cloaked with snow was broken only when a cedar's branches shed their load, burying more deeply the daffodils beneath.

But that day was quite exceptional – a week before and the upper branches of the *Magnolia campbellii* had been glorious with blossoms, and a week after the blue flowered *R. augustinii* had cast its snowy coverlet, and shone forth once more in all its azure prettiness. The garden at Nymans was basking once more in the spring sunshine, the snow forgotten. And when the garden at Nymans smiles, it is a dazzling smile indeed.

The story of the garden begins eighty years ago when the property was bought by Mr Ludwig Messel. At that time Nymans lay deep in the country – miles from the nearest railway station, in a part of Sussex which was difficult of access in those

The gateway leading from the walled to the wild garden 'grown over, as it surely never was in its native Italy, with starry white *Clematis armandii*'

opposite Yew pillars with elaborately clipped finials surround a carved stone fountain at the junction of four paths in the walled garden at Nymans

NYMANS

motor-carless days. Even today, with the main London road and its incessant traffic running within a few hundred yards of the house, there is a feeling of tranquillity to be found at Nymans which makes it seem a place apart.

Mr Messel was an inspired gardener, and had many friends in the gardening fraternity of seventy years ago. William Robinson, author of the best of all gardening books, *The English Flower Garden*, the famous Gertrude Jekyll, Sir Edmund Loder of Leonardslee, who gave his name to the deliciously scented strain of loderi rhododendrons, were all friends. They came to Nymans regularly in those early days, and their advice and enthusiasm were surely a great inspiration to the new owner of Nymans, Ludwig Messel. He had, of course, the almost ideal terrain for a garden, with the mature trees of St Leonards Forest to give shelter and character, a rich sandy loam to plant in, and sharp drainage. The ground offered the perfect condition for rhododendrons, magnolias and camellias, and though over the years the garden at Nymans was to become a treasure store of rare and difficult plants, rhododendrons, magnolias and camellias remain its chief attraction still. And eucryphias – for the name of Nymans has been immortalized in a magnificent flowering tree which was first raised there in 1915 – *Eucryphia nymansay*.

In her careful notes (prepared for the Royal Horticultural Society's *Journal*) on the garden that she knows so well, Mr Messel's grand-daughter, the Countess of Rosse, suggests that the garden should be thought of as being in different sections, which we will visit in turn, starting with the forecourt. It must here be recorded with regret that the house at Nymans, a large comfortable building in an unusually successful Edwardian Tudor style, was largely destroyed by fire some years ago. But sad though that was, there were compensations. Few gardens in England can have such a romantic background as is offered by the ruined house walls of Nymans, and the author clearly remembers his first visit to Nymans, many years ago, when the grey calcined walls and glassless mullions were curtained on the outside with camellias, and there were creamy Banksian roses, growing up to what had once been the eaves, and red roses cascading down. The scene recalled that eminent gardener and poet, Victoria Sackville-West's lines in *The Garden*:

> Of such extravagance as pours the rose
> In windblown fountains down the broken walls
> In gouts of blood, in dripping flower falls.

In her notes, Lady Rosse next guides the visitors' steps to the heather garden, which, it is believed, is the first ever to be planted in England, an example that other gardeners were quick to emulate. There are now heather gardens all over this country, and a particularly impressive one in the gardens at Abbotswood described in some detail elsewhere in this book. When the author of this book first visited Nymans he particularly remembers great clumps of *Erica tetralix* in bloom, with its rose-coloured flowers filling the air around with honey scent, to the delight of the bees for miles around.

A gateway to the courtyard, with clipped laurel and rosemary

The courtyard of Nymans (*The National Trust*)

Camellias mark the beauty of the garden from earliest spring. The stone-roofed dovecote is swagged with clematis

But it is the walled garden, says Lady Rosse, which is the very heart of Nymans, 'intimate secluded . . . it is perhaps the most romantic part of all'. The author remembers it in May, when the herbaceous border, planted on the advice of the great William Robinson, was not yet out, though it showed great promise with its many clumps of different greens. But what other treasures were there! – pink magnolias like *M. sargentiana* and *campbelli*, already noted, the sweetly scented *Styrax japonica*, and *stewartia*, which is a feature too, of the arboretum at Westonbirt, and was named after John Stuart, Earl of Bute, whose garden, landscaped by Lancelot Brown, at Luton Hoo, we describe elsewhere. The pink-flowered dogwood, which seldom succeeds in England, grows well in the walled garden at Nymans, as well as the delicate *Rhyncospermum jasminoides*, and first and foremost, side by side, proud Philemon and Baucis – the two original parents of the Nymansay eucryphia – *E. cordifolia* and *E. glutinosa*, from which every *E. nymansay* in cultivation are descended.

Rhododendron sinogrande has magnificent leaves, dark green above, with under-surfaces of silvery grey. The flowers vary from creamy white to soft yellow

Perhaps this is the place to describe this famous child of the Nymans garden. First its name. It derives from the Greek *eu*, well, *kryphios*, cover, which makes allusion to the curious hooded formation of the plants' flower-sepals. All eucryphia flowers are white, four-petalled and have bosses of golden anthers of great beauty – *E. cordifolia* is evergreen, *E. glutinosa* deciduous and the only hardy species. The great garden value of *E. nymansay* is its toleration, unlike most eucryphias, of a lime soil, its glossy evergreen leaves, its delicately moulded flowers, its hardiness and its slender upright habit of growth.

One more plant – out of many that grow in the walled garden at Nymans – deserves acclaim: the Handkerchief, or more euphoniously named, Dove Tree, *Davidia involucrata*, the odd leaf formations of which look, according to the eye of the observer, like white doves or handkerchiefs.

We leave the walled garden at Nymans by way of the stone gateway, grown over, as it surely never was in its native Italy, with starry white *Clematis armandii*. Beyond lies a wood where the magnificent *Rhododendron sino grande* grows, with its noble leaves, green and wrinkled on top, gold or silver felted beneath, and *Lilium giganteum*.

Two more sections of the garden remain to be visited but there is no space here to give them each more than a quick glance. The top garden, where are the greenhouses built by Mr Ludwig Messel for the great work of propagating which went on in his day at Nymans; and a secret enclosed rose garden planned round an old well, where the air is scented in June with the breath of many of the so-called old-fashioned roses, some of which came from the well-known gardener Miss Ellen Wilmott at Great Warley in Essex. Further on, an old quarry has been utilized for plants with such bold foliage as yuccas, palms and the large-leaved gunnera. It is such imaginative touches as this which make a visit to Nymans such a rewarding experience. The garden appeals not only to the dedicated plantsman, but also to the gardener who just likes to relax and enjoy the beautiful garden pictures that only a real artist in planting can paint. Such pictures, at Nymans, are to be seen on every hand, in the garden itself and in the woods around, which seem to be an extension of it. Nowhere is the art of wild gardening so well understood.

What special memory of the garden does the visitor to Nymans for the first time take away? The eucryphias certainly, for it is no small thing to have given to gardens everywhere a flowering tree of the greatest beauty. But more especially, in the opinion of one visitor at least, it is the way that the garden, though of absorbing interest to the plant connoisseur, has found place too for all the quite simple, long loved flowers of England. Rarities which can only be named in Latin, but Lady's Smocks too. Rhododendron species from the uplands of Burma, but foxgloves, bergamot and bluebells as well.

opposite
'In wind blown fountains down
The broken walls
In gouts of blood, in dripping
Flower falls'

Luton Hoo

A famous rose garden in a Capability Brown park

On 2 December 1891, Luton Hoo, a large, comfortable house in Bedfordshire, was the scene of a distinguished romance. There was a house-party and one evening, while the other young guests were dancing in the ballroom, a pale young man with a seductive moustache proposed to a quiet, serious-looking girl with golden hair. The scene was their hostess', Madame de Falbe's, boudoir. 'Of course I said yes,' wrote Princess Mary, later, in her diary. The young man was the future King of England, and extremely charming: but Princess Mary's first romance was short-lived, and Prince Eddy, Duke of Clarence, died the following year; though at the time of the scene at Luton Hoo just described, all was happiness and expectation.

The next day, in the cold, wintry sunshine, the young couple were photographed in the garden overlooking Capability Brown's park. It was one of the first of the future Queen Mary's many visits to Luton Hoo, the last being in 1950, when, as an old lady, she inspected the famous collection of Fabergé objects which the house now holds, walked round the celebrated rose garden, and – who knows? – perhaps thought of that scene in the boudoir so many years before.

But the story of Luton Hoo begins many, many years before Queen Mary's proposal, and many years before the days of Capability Brown. There has been a manor house on the site since the thirteenth century, when the land belonged to the de Hoo family. Hoo itself is a Saxon word which means the spur of a hill, and is often met with in East Anglia. One of the de Hoos, in the third century of their ownership, was created, in 1448, Lord Hoo and Hastings, and his daughter and co-heiress married Sir Geoffrey Boleyn, grandfather of Anne Boleyn. This marriage we have mentioned in our chapter on Hever. The Boleyns were part-owners of Luton Hoo till 1523, when the place was acquired by Sir Robert Napier, in whose family the house remained till 1762 when it was sold to the unpopular Prime Minister of George III, John Stuart, Earl of Bute, shortly before his resignation.

The third Earl of Bute (1713–92, Prime Minister 1762) employed Lancelot Brown to remodel the park at Luton Hoo

opposite The rose-garden with its spectacular fountain and classical temple is one of the finest in England

The roses grow in immaculately clipped box-edged beds. Beyond the domed temple is a spreading cedar

Lord Bute was more popular with the gardening fraternity than with his fellow politicians and with the country generally, an unpopularity engendered by his reactionary political views and the equivocal position he filled in the Household of the Princess of Wales. But he was a great botanist and lavish patron of horticulture, and he can be credited with having used his influence with Augusta of Saxe-Gotha to have encouraged the foundation of Kew Gardens. Such was his fame in the world of horticulture that, as we have elsewhere noted, the Swede Linnaeus named stewartia, a beautiful plant of the aceae family (which includes camellias) after him. The celebrated Swede, to whom we owe the nomenclature of our plants, obviously had difficulty in spelling Lord Bute's family name, which is actually Stuart, but the wrong spelling persists, in spite of having been officially corrected by L'Heritier in 1781. Lord Bute, in retirement, was to write a nine-volume opus on the Flora of Britain, and he called in Lancelot Brown, then at the height of his fame, to do some important 'place-making' at Luton Hoo. This was to prove one of Brown's most important commissions and Miss Dorothy Stroud, the able biographer of Brown as well as of Repton, has discovered that Brown's work there, already begun in 1763, lasted over ten years, and brought him in £10,420 2s. 9d., though he was paid three times as much for work over a similar period of time at Blenheim. Miss Stroud also quotes the impressions of a visitor, the agriculturist Arthur Young, of the Park at Luton Hoo in 1770.

After praising the scene in general, Young particularly enthused over the lake with its 'sloop with sails and flying colours . . .' and in recent years craft of a different kind are still to be seen on the lakes at Luton, when the Sea Scouts use them for sailing, and the scene which Arthur Young saw two hundred years ago is re-created.

The house, half-built when Arthur Young saw it, was a graceful edifice whose architect was Robert Adam. When Dr Johnson visited Luton Hoo eleven years later, it was finished, and Johnson was, for him, full of praise. 'This is one of the places,' he conceded, 'I do not regret having come to see.'

Brown's changes to the Park were sensational. Already 300 acres in extent, a further 900 acres were enclosed. The river Lea was dammed in two places and, as at Blenheim, two lakes were conjured out of nothing. It is one of Brown's finest surviving landscape gardens.

After a disastrous fire in 1843 most of Lord Bute's house was destroyed, and the property was sold to a rich Liverpool solicitor, Mr John Shaw Leigh, who rebuilt the house, and from him it passed, in due course, to his daughter-in-law, Madame de Falbe, Princess Mary's hostess in 1891. Sir Julius Wernher, father of the present owner, Sir Harold Wernher, bought Luton Hoo in 1903; the house became the home of his famous collection of art. The gardens were laid out by Romaine Walker in the fashionable style of the day. Brown's park had originally swept right up under the windows of the house, but this was not to the Edwardian

Curving steps lead down from the upper terrace to the rose garden. At the corner of the border grow the evergreen leaves of *Saxifrage megasea*

taste, so a terrace was added, above a balustraded lower terrace edged with borders of flowers. Measured steps, in particularly graceful circular form, led down to the rose garden which is now one of the great rose gardens of England. But before visiting it in detail, the author must mention in passing that though, in his opinion, the rose garden is the greatest point of interest of the garden at Luton Hoo, there are mixed borders which in late summer are sensational, and a rock garden excellently conceived, well-constructed, and full of interesting plants.

But to return to the rose garden. Lady Zia Wernher is well known for her love of roses, and in 1959 that great rosarian Mr Bertram Park, crossing that wonderful rose Peace with the brilliant Independence, named the resulting seedling after her: Lady Zia; which the expert Mr Edwin Murrell has described as having 'a beautiful bloom of real substance, rich rosy flame with outer

Sir Julius Wernher, father of the present owner, Sir Harold, bought Luton Hoo in 1903. Soon after the garden was remodelled

A carved lion surveys the park designed by 'Capability' Brown, and studded with splendid cedars

recurving petals of a brighter and deeper fire. The flowers are always upright and the colour gets stronger and more glowing as they age.' High praise.

And though the author remembers with delight a bed at Luton Hoo planted entirely with this beautiful rose, it is not his intention to list all the roses growing in Lady Zia's rose garden as in a catalogue, visiting it bed by bed, and pillar by pillar. Suffice it to say that it is mainly planted with hybrid tea roses, and relies on that variety of rose for its beauty – as opposed to so many gardens these days which count on the newer floribunda for their chief display.

Perhaps it would be of interest at this point to trace briefly the history of the hybrid tea rose, which we still consider the perfect decorative rose although, in recent years, it has found a rival in the floribunda. We also often think of the hybrid tea rose as having been the leading light of gardens for many years. This, of course, is wrong. The floribunda was introduced in 1924, but the hybrid tea, to many of us the doyen of the rose garden, only made its appearance forty-five years earlier. It was in 1884 that the search was rewarded – the search for a decorative bedding-out rose which flowered not only in June and July, but well into the autumn.

The successful hybridist was Henry Bennett of Stapleford, who for ten years had been experimenting in crossing perpetual roses with tea roses in an attempt to produce a decorative rose, which was strong-growing and healthy, and which flowered in the autumn as well as in summer. His early attempts were not entirely successful, the trouble being that the tea roses were too delicate and the perpetuals were shy flowering, and prone to mildew. The resulting crosses often inherited the bad qualities of both parents. Of these, George Paul, a great rosarian (Paul's Scarlet – Paul's Lemon Pillar) wrote in 1952,

The first hybrid teas had too much perpetual blood in their character, and they carried with it the fault of being subject to mildew in the Autumn.

But when, with Lady Alice Fitzwilliam and La France . . . Tea predominated, then the value of the hybrid teas became apparent. The tendency to mildew disappeared, and the free habit of flowering and the autumnal character became apparent. A hardiness equal to that of the hybrid perpetuals was a distinctive feature of this new family.

The beautiful pink La France was the first hybrid tea rose to gain widespread popularity, and it is still to be found growing in English rose gardens. Since the year of its introduction – eighty years ago – dedicated rose-growers have raised thousands of other hybrid tea roses. Many of the most beautiful grow in the garden at Luton Hoo where they reward with months of flower the attention and care lavished on them by Lady Zia Wernher. Lady Zia, as we have recorded, has had a rose named after her – an accolade for anyone who loves roses, and a well-deserved one. For as a great gardener, the genial Dean Reynolds Hole wrote many years ago, 'He who would have roses in his garden must have roses in his heart'.

opposite Lady Zia Wernher's rose garden. Lady Zia has had a beautiful new rose named after her, a cross between 'Peace' and 'Independence'

Gloucestershire

Sezincote

An unusual garden in the Indian manner

Sezincote, built by Sir Charles Cockerell in the early years of the nineteenth century from designs by Thomas Daniell. A wood engraving by E. J. Tavener

opposite
Lush planting below an Indian-style bridge embellished with stone fretwork and couchant sacred bulls. In the centre a carved snake-entwined tree fountain rises from a planting of sulphur yellow *Primula florindae*

Of Sezincote it was once written, 'Discredited the domes arise out of beech and copper beech trees amid the scorn of those who own Tudor Manors in the neighbourhood'.

Years ago, the writer of this book read John Betjeman's lines in the *Architectural Review,* and the name of Sezincote was to haunt him ever after. But it was not until 1966 that he finally found himself visiting the place which had captured his imagination so long before. All through the thirties a visit to Sezincote, for one reason or another, eluded him. Then the war came and he was soon serving overseas, and though offered ample opportunities of admiring authentic Hindu architecture on the banks of the Jumna, he had to wait years before seeing Sir Charles Cockerell's astonishing pastiche in the Cotswolds.

The story of Sezincote begins in the late eighteenth century, when Colonel John Cockerell bought the estate, died soon after, and left it to his brother Sir Charles, who had spent many years in India, and had amassed a fortune there. It was Sir Charles who decided to decorate the exterior of the house, which was built on a conventional Georgian plan, in the architectural style of the country in which the proverbial Pagoda Tree had yielded him so generous a crop. Thomas Daniell prepared the drawings. The distinguished Humphry Repton approved them. Indeed they almost certainly gave Repton his inspiration for his first designs for the Pavilion at Brighton, which in turn inspired Nash.

Daniell's drawings of Indian architecture had lately been published, and had been enthusiastically received. Architects, it was felt, had too long found their inspiration in the buildings of Greece or Rome – or, if they were more fanciful, of China. Repton himself foretold that a change of taste was at hand 'in consequence of our having lately become acquainted with the scenery and building of the Inner Provinces of India'.

It was in the latest new style that Sezincote was furbished, and soon its Mogul dome rose among the trees – to surprise the rooks, and cause outbursts of indignation, though occasionally of enthusiasm, ever after.

130

above The formal garden, where 'conventional planting would have looked quite out of place'. The canal and rows of cypresses are recent and completely successful additions

right The new kiosk by the tennis court, designed by Mr Cyril Kleinwort on lines which Thomas Daniell would have approved

opposite The southwest wing of Sezincote has been recently restored, with its minaret, pinnacles and exotic fenestration

Campanulas, ferns and to the left, a gigantic *Gunnera manicata* grow round the lake at Sezincote

Though Sezincote certainly gave Repton his ideas for the Brighton Pavilion, the earlier essay in the Hindu style is infinitely more pleasing than the Prince Regent's gimcrack though endearing edifice. First, its situation, in rolling tree-clad countryside, instead of huddled among houses; and second, the material of which it is built, a glowing Cotswold stone, carved with lapidary skill by real craftsmen, instead of coarsely rendered stucco. But before the house, with its dome, its shadowy overhanging cornice, many minaret-like chimneys, and fretted window recesses was complete, Repton and Thomas Daniell had started work on the garden. Many of the flowering trees and tall cedars of their original planting are still there, to shade the garden with their far-flung branches.

The pleasure ground they devised lies to the east of the house and has for centre feature a deep gully – which one is tempted, to be in keeping, to call a nullah. Down this runs a stream which in due course becomes the Evenlode and joins its waters to the upper Thames above Oxford. The visitor arriving at Sezincote crosses this ravine by way of an Indian bridge supported on octagonal columns modelled on those of the caves of Elephanta. On either hand are balustrades of neat lattice work in Coade stone decorated with *couchant* sacred bulls. The sides of the ravine are closely set with planting carefully chosen by Daniell to reproduce an oriental and lush effect. Of this Christopher Hussey has written, 'From top to bottom the composition of this valley is most effective: magnificent and varied trees exaggerate its depth: water, mossgrown stonework, bamboos and ferns suggest a tropical luxuriance . . .'

Since Daniell's day, of course, many more moisture-loving plants which give this rich effect have been introduced to English gardens. *Gunnera manicata* from Brazil, first grown in England in 1849, now spreads its giant leaves at Sezincote, echoed by the bold, though finer leaves of rodgersia, unknown in England before 1880. In Daniell's day the imposing Skunk Cabbage of America, *Lysichitum americanum*, was a stranger to England, as was *Saxifraga peltata*, which now makes such an impressive clump in the shadow of Daniell's Indian bridge. Much of the planting in this most effective part of the garden at Sezincote was undertaken by Mrs Arthur Dugdale and her mother-in-law, who owned the property until 1944.

Above the bridge, at the head of the stream, there is the temple pool, which lies in front of a little shrine containing the Coade stone figure of Souriya, the Goddess of Pity. Behind are shadowy caves, overgrown with moss and ferns. Thickets of bamboos, of course, are on every side, and a solitary palm tree heightens the oriental atmosphere, as does the snake-entwined tree fountain below the bridge. It is Vishnuland indeed.

But though the nullah – if one may call it so – is perhaps the most telling part of the garden at Sezincote, there are many other points of interest. The trees, for instance, are magnificent, especially a rare weeping cut-leaf hornbeam, *Carpinus betulus pendula*, and several fine cedars. Nearer the house, with its egregious

The Temple Pool, designed by Thomas Daniell. The little building houses the Hindu goddess Souriya, the Goddess of Pity, carved in Coade stone

architecture, conventional planting and bedding out would have looked out of place – so Mr and Mrs Cyril Kleinwort, the present owners, have exercised restraint in dressing their garden. Lawns, some simple fountains, stone boxes of geraniums make up all the decoration. Recently a most successful stone-bordered canal has been laid in the west garden to align with the centre window of the bow-windowed façade. On either side of this canal, and most happy additions, are rows of slender cypresses, inspired, one feels, by Lord Curzon's planting by the Taj Mahal at Agra.

One more addition to the garden had been made recently by Mr and Mrs Kleinwort – a most elegant little kiosk near the tennis court, also in the Indian style. This is of a neat precision of design which would surely have pleased the perfectionist, Thomas Daniell himself. The architect of this most practical conceit, this most sensible folly, was Mr Kleinwort himself.

The gardens of Sezincote are unlike anything else in England, or indeed in the world. They certainly have no counterpart in India. Cool-climate plants, which would not survive a season in Rajputana, are used to create an Indian atmosphere which is disarmingly authentic.

The gardens are open every year in aid of the admirable National Gardens Scheme. For the lover of the original, the tasteful and the odd, a visit would seem an absolute necessity. For the gardens are most beautifully kept, and now that they are in the sensitive hands of the present owners, they are being every year improved.

Lotus-like leaves of *Saxifraga peltata* give a jungle-like effect to the planting by the Indian bridge at Sezincote

Powis Castle

A rare eighteenth-century terraced garden

Powis Castle in Montgomeryshire, with its park of ancient oaks, lies in what was once a Welsh principality which included six counties. When Henry II was King of England, one of his few allies over the Welsh border who was to be trusted was the Prince of Powis, whose fortress was the Red Castle. In the fighting, which was continuous at that time along the Welsh Marches, the Prince fought faithfully on the side of the English, and was three times reinstated in his territory due to his powerful protector. In 1283 the ruling Prince was Gruffyd Ap Gwenwynwyn. He was the last of the independent princes of Powis, for in that year he relinquished his title and accepted from Edward I, whose son was the first Prince of Wales, the English Barony of de la Pole. The de la Poles reigned at Powis until the reign of Edward VI, when the line died out and the castle was bought soon after by a member of the Pembroke family, Sir Edward Herbert, whose son became the first Lord Powis. The Herberts held Powis till their Jacobite sympathies brought them to exile with James II, Lady Powis having been one of the few witnesses of the birth of the Prince of Wales, the Warming Pan baby, whose mysteriously sudden arrival toppled James II's throne. Powis stood empty until William III gave it to one of his Dutch relations, William Van Nassau-Zuylestein, whom he made Earl of Rochford, and it was this Dutch occupant of Powis – and probably his son, Lord Enfield – who designed the series of magnificent balustraded and be-statued garden terraces for which Powis is celebrated.

By 1722 the exiled Powis's were allowed back, the Rochfords moved out, and the work on the terraces was completed, at crippling cost to the estate. Twenty years later the Powis peerage died out, and the estate passed to a remote Herbert cousin, descendant of Lord Herbert of Cherbury, the brother of the poet George Herbert, who wrote the poem which contains the verse:

> Sweet rose, whose hue angry and brave
> Bids the rash gazer wipe his eye,
> Thy root is ever in its grave
>   And thou must die.

On the aviary terrace at Powis there is an imposing lead peacock which Lord Clive may have brought from India

opposite The rare trees and shrubs which grow on the hanging terraces are protected by thirty-feet-high yew hedges to the north-east

Powis Castle and its terraced garden in 1742. The infant yews to be seen on the topmost terrace are now fully grown

Fame, in lead and a very ecstasy of enthusiasm, blows her trumpet in the forecourt

In the opinion of the author of the book, among the most beautiful lines to a rose ever written.

To die, too, appeared to be the regular fate of the Powis name, for in 1801 the title again became extinct. But it was revived for the third time in favour of Edward Clive, son of Clive of India, who had married a Herbert daughter. The present Earl of Powis, who lives at Powis Castle today, is a descendant.

We have traced the story of the owners of Powis Castle through the centuries in some detail, not only because there is much of English history in the tale, but also because each successive ownership played an important part in the creation and development of the garden. It was the old Welsh princes of Powis who determined the site when they built the original stronghold, though when they did so they certainly did not have gardening in mind, and chose the high bluff looking north-easterly towards the Breidden Hills purely for its impregnable position.

The castle, three hundred years later, stood empty, when the Powis family faithfully followed the Jacobite king into exile, and the gardens were neglected. Then the Dutch Nassau-Zuylestein – translated by his powerful uncle, William III, into an English Earl – inspired perhaps by the rocky terrain of Montgomery, so different from that of his native Holland – built the hanging terraces which are still such a spectacular feature of the garden.

Later, the wing of history brushed Powis again when its heiress, Henrietta Herbert, married the Victor of Plassey's son, and further additions were made to the already celebrated gardens. It was Henrietta's grandson, the third Earl, who planted many of the rare trees and shrubs collected from the four corners of the world, which make the garden so interesting botanically as well as historically. During his lifetime he is said to have planted over a million trees on his Welsh estate.

The garden faces south-east, and though it is 450 feet above sea level, can boast many delicate plants which, without the benefit of the Gulf Stream, could hardly be expected to thrive. This is due to two things – perfect drainage, not only of moisture, but also, and almost more important, of frost. It is well known that cold frosty air, weighing more than warm air, will flow down hill like water, collecting in hollows and valleys which can then become harmful frost pockets. This accounts for the sometimes surprising fact that exposed gardens on hilltops are less liable to frost ravages than gardens in sheltered hollows. It is a theory that is well proven, and Powis is an excellent example. It is miles from the sea, and yet shrubs and trees will grow happily there, which would surely not survive in similar latitudes in England.

On his last visit to Powis the writer was deeply impressed by the taste and originality shown in the planting of the terraces, and of the garden generally. For instance, as he entered by a gate in the lower garden he was greeted by Victorian basket-form pots, set high on either hand, and planted with white fuchsias and lofty dracaenas. These pots, with their thoughtfully chosen bouquets of plants, were to be the recurring theme, it seemed, of the garden planting. They seemed to be everywhere, some filled with more white fuchsias, some with pink, and some with crimson geraniums with crinkled leaves which breathed the very air of the Mediterranean. The knowledge and imagination of Mr Graham, now head gardener at Powis, but long at Mount Stewart in Northern Ireland, another garden illustrated in this book, were apparent on every side.

Brimming beds of flowers such as heliotrope, silver cineraria and lilies contrasted pleasantly with quieter areas of mown grass and box trees. One bed was entirely given over to musk roses, in every variety, with all their lovely girl-names, Penelope, Felicia, Cornelia, clearly labelled, a rare touch in gardens, and a very useful one in gardens open to the public. It is only a pity that visitors should so often reward the garden owner's thought by removing the labels as souvenirs.

As has been said, fuchsias were everywhere in evidence. Not only tender ones in pots but the hardy *riccartonii* and the beautiful *F. magellanica versicolor*, of which there was a large bed on one of the terraces at Powis, its smoky pink foliage blending with the stone-work which is one of the beauties of this great Welsh garden.

On the aviary terrace the author particularly remembers one of his favourite of all roses, *Rosa rubrifolia*, a delight not so much for its flowers but for its glowing ruby-coloured leaves, and the tender *Clerodendron bungei*. Clerodendrons, Victoria Sackville-West once described as 'stocky little trees, not often seen in our gardens . . . worth growing for the berries which surround the flower. Turquoise blue and scarlet . . . they are shiny, brilliantly coloured and look as though they have been varnished.' Near the south-west end of the aviary terrace at Powis there is a large peacock in lead, which stood in the great Lord Clive's day in his garden at Claremont. Did he, one wonders, bring it from India, and did it once spread its tail in the garden of Suraj ud Dowlah?

Casting their lofty shadows are magnificent Irish yews, which give great character to the hanging gardens at Powis, their vast, dark green bulks making an effective contrast to the limestone walls and the festooning plants which cover them. More huge yews, close clipped into a hedge over thirty feet high, protect

Below the red sandstone side of the castle is an architecturally treated wall capped with yews and underplanted with hydrangeas

The terrace walls at Powis face due south and offer ideal growing conditions for delicate and unusual plants

opposite The lead statues on the terraces are the *genii loci* of the garden. They are the work of Jan Van Nost and were brought by the Dutch Earl of Rochford in the seventeenth century

the terraces to the north-east. At every hand, there are seats, painted an unobtrusive grey, which invite the visitor to rest and enjoy the superb prospect which, as Celia Fiennes would say, the terraces 'discover'. An orangery is the central feature of the third, or main terrace. On this terrace, and growing against its wall, more rare plants are to be seen, many from the Southern Hemisphere, not hardy in many gardens but which the climate and the particular position of Powis, appear to favour. Among these are *Pittosporum tenuifolium* and *Hoheria lyalli* from New Zealand, *Drimys winteri*, the magnolia-like Winter's Bark from South America, the blue Passion Flower, *Passiflora coerulea*, the orange trumpeted *Campsis radicans*, and the Chilean *Abutilon vitifolium*.

The long herbaceous border planted below the third terrace is, in the author's opinion, one of the best herbaceous borders in existence – a rival to those at Hampton Court or Hascombe. It is set with great clumps of plants which make their bravest show in July and August. Many interesting plants find a place in it, but here for once they seem to have been chosen not for their rarity but rather for their good-natured generosity of flower. There are bold groups of *Artemisia lactiflora*, with flowers in a curious shade of cream – an unusual colour for a herbaceous plant – *Salvia superba*, low and close flowering and covered with flowers of rich purple in late summer, and to the front, *Lobelia cardinalis* which flaunts the most brilliant scarlet that one can imagine. The gardens at Powis are usually open every summer from May until the end of September, but perhaps they are at their peak of beauty when the herbaceous border is in full flower. The brilliant colour, set off by the pink limestone terrace walls and in contrast with the Irish yews, makes a memorable visual orchestration.

The Powis terraces are balustraded and embellished with urns and lead figures of shepherdesses and shepherds which are the work of Jan Van Nost who was in business at Hyde Park Corner in London at the time of William III. They were placed in the garden by the Dutch Earl of Rochford two hundred and fifty years ago, and have been there ever since.

It has been suggested that the garden at Powis is one of the few great gardens to escape the hand of Lancelot Brown, though it is difficult to imagine how even he could have done away with the hanging terraces, which, though artificial, were purely dictated by the precipitous site. It is difficult to conceive any alternative treatment.

Below the terraces lies a grassy slope, a wide bank planted with more flowering trees and shrubs which take the eye with blossom and lay their differing sweetness on the air. Trees like the exquisite *Magnolia wilsonii* from Szechuan, two magnificent *Cornus chinensis* with white flowers that are dappled red as they mature, hibiscus, *Feijoa sellowiana* – several from the uplands of Brazil – and the white Banksian rose *R. banksiae florepleno*, a rose which will only give of its best if very discreetly pruned. Here too grows the heavily armed *Rosa omeiensis pteracantha* from west China, of which the blood-red thorns are the chief beauty, and some

brilliant autumn-coloured *Cercidiphyllum japonicum* like those we admire at Nymans in Sussex.

By a path to the pool, in this garden of rarities, the knowing visitor is not surprised to find a *Ginkgo biloba*, the Maidenhair tree. This tree is one of the curiosities of horticulture, described in the Royal Horticultural Society Dictionary as 'a fine deciduous tree, unknown in a wild state, perhaps the most ancient of existing flowering plants, the remaining representative of an otherwise extinct race'. Had the ginkgo, especially revered in China, not been lovingly preserved in temple gardens through the centuries it would certainly have been lost to us. Once reintroduced into Western horticulture, however, as it was a hundred years ago, the ginkgo quite literally took on a new lease of life, and has since been widely propagated. It is tougher than is generally supposed. Some of the finest the author has ever seen grew in the heart of New York – on 57th Street.

The pool is fringed with all the jungly tropical-looking plants which love to grow with their feet in water. Lush and luxuriant subjects, like hostas, *Gunnera manicata*, rodgersia, the large-leaved *Lysichitum americanum* and a fine group of *Osmunda regalis*. Beyond the pool and against the skyline, the tallest tree in Britain holds high its head – a Douglas fir, which, when last measured in 1956, was 181 feet 2 inches high.

What other plants linger in the memory as the visitor leaves Powis? – the coral form of *Geranium kewensis* planted with the silver *Helichrysum petiolatum*, the unusual Australian plant, *Helichrysum rosemarinifolium* in a sheltered corner, lilies by the score, the heraldic red of *Lychnis chalcedonica*, an unusual white form of Lychnis Flos-Jovis, campion of the gods, *Clematis tangutica* starring the walls with gold, and an American honeysuckle in the lower garden clothing a line of pillars with flower and scent.

The history of the castle, the grandeur of its terraces, the taste and variety shown in their planting make a visit to Powis unforgettable. Few houses have been in continual occupation for seven hundred years, and though it is not the place here to describe the contents of Powis Castle in detail, in passing one must mention that the collection comprises pictures by Tintoretto, Gainsborough and Bellotto. There is also a room full of Indian relics of the great Lord Clive, and fine tapestries in Sir Edward Herbert's Long Gallery, where the original plasterwork of 1592 survives and is almost unique. All these treasures are there in the castle for the visitor to see. But outside, with their views of the Breidden Hills and the Long Mountain, are the three great terraces to beckon the garden-lover out of doors. In their shelter grow the plant-treasures for which, in the last of its seven centuries, Powis Castle has gained added fame.

The garden has been brought to its present perfection by generations of faithful Herberts. Their motto is *Ung Je Serviray* (One will I serve). True to their King and to their ancient home, there have been Herberts at Powis for centuries. The future of their garden, under the auspices of the National Trust, is as secure today as ever in its history. It is a very great garden indeed.

The apricot flowered *Geranium kewensis* is grown with silver helichrysum in a Victorian basket-design pot of terra-cotta

opposite A dracaena makes a panache of leaves above falling fuchsias

overleaf The terraces of Powis 'discover' as fine a view as any garden in Europe. Beyond the ground of the castle, with their treasure store of plants and sculpture, lie the Long Mountain and the Breidden Hills

Cranborne Manor

A garden fit for the loveliest manor house in England

John Tradescant, gardener to King James I, made a plan for the gardens of Cranborne Manor

opposite From the terrace, with its rose-grown balustrade, a broad grass path, bordered by low growing dianthus and miniature apple trees, leads to an ironwork gate set between ball-capped piers

Cranborne Manor is in Dorset, about ten miles north of Wimborne, in the Thomas Hardy country. Indeed, it is said that the local market town of Cranborne is the original of Chaseborough in *Tess of the D'Urbervilles*.

Cranborne Manor, originally a hunting lodge of King John, is one of the most beautiful houses in England, with a patina that only four hundred years of continual occupation, and unwavering affection, can bestow. It belongs to the Marquis of Salisbury, and is at present the home of his son and daughter-in-law, Lord and Lady Cranborne. Some sort of dwelling house certainly existed on the site for many years before the Manor as we see it today was reconstructed and embellished by Robert Cecil, James I's great Lord Treasurer, who was created Lord Cranborne in 1604, and Earl of Salisbury shortly afterwards. But it was Robert Cecil, the first of a long line of Cecils to live in and love Cranborne Manor, who gave it the fair face it still wears; and it was certainly he who built the two porches to north and south of the house which give the house such character. Indeed, so important a part do these porches play in many views of the garden that they almost come under the heading of garden architecture. They were built in 1600 and Inigo Jones has been suggested as their architect, and it is possible, for he is known to have worked at Wilton, and he almost certainly designed Cranborne's west wing. Of the two, the north porch perhaps is the most fascinating. It is strongly Renaissance in feeling with its Italianate pillars, alcoves and elaboration of strapwork. Above each pillar is a gaping mask – perhaps more grotesque than beautiful – which adds an endearing light-hearted touch to architectural nicety.

They are thought to refer to a period in Cranborne's history when courts of justice were held at the Manor. And there still exists a dungeon there, now used as a larder, into which convicted prisoners were once thrown, victims of the savage poaching laws which existed in the fourteenth and fifteenth centuries, a time when killing a stag unlawfully was a crime punishable by death.

In spring the grass under Cranborne's spreading trees is starred with thousands of daffodils

The lodges, with their peaked roofs and neat Jacobean brickwork, are set off by clematis and wistaria

The verderers and game wardens employed by the Lord of the Manor were empowered to mete out harsh punishment on poor forest dwellers who tried to defend their crop from the ravages of deer or wild boar. The Lord of the Manor, John Aubrey (1626–97), the old English antiquary and folk-lorist, holds that Cranborne Chase was once the property of Roger, Earl of Mortimer, and he thinks that the ancient oaks that surround Cranborne could a tale unfold if they 'were vocall as Dodona's'. (In classical times the oaks of Zeus at Dodona conversed and made predictions by rustling their leaves.) 'Some of the old dotards could give us an account of the amours and secret whispers between the great Earle and Queen Isabella.' The Chase was famous for its deer and according to Aubrey, 'the Deer of the forest of Graveley were the largest fallow deer in England, but some doe affirm the deer of Cranborne Chase larger . . . A glover of Tys Bury will give sixpense more for the buckskin of Cranborne Chase . . . and he says he can afford it.' But woe betide any poor forest dweller who tried to earn that extra sixpence without a permit from the all-powerful verderer, and was caught. A period in the dungeon would have been the best he could hope for. More likely he would be strung up on one of Aubrey's old oaks, giving them something else to talk about than 'amours and secret whispers'.

But when the object of one's visit to Cranborne is to see the garden, such grim days seem very far away indeed. It is a most unusual garden in that it retains much of the original plan. This is known to have been made by John Tradescant, and it is on record that he often visited Cranborne, ordered many plants for the garden and travelled down to Dorset with them.

If the two porches of Cranborne Manor are shared as features by both house and garden, the terrace can surely be claimed as an intrinsic part of the garden. It is one of the finest terraces of its date in England, recalling in its noble simplicity that at Haddon, shown elsewhere in this book.

From its balustrade, a fine view is obtained of the gardens. This contains two features which date from the days of Robert Cecil and John Tradescant: the bowling green and the Mount. Bowling alleys were very popular in gardens of the Jacobean period. Elsewhere it has been recorded how the French, in an early period of Anglomania, adopted this popular feature of English gardens, gallicizing the bowling-green into *boulengrin*, a curious word which is still in use in France to describe a long, usually (but not always) unbroken stretch of turf, with raised sides. But the bowling alley at Cranborne is typically English, a stretch of perfect turf, long and narrow, for the brooding yew hedges which enclose it on either side have encroached, and today the bowling alley has now more the appearance of a secluded walk.

Very few gardens still retain their original Mounts and Lady Cranborne, a student of garden history, and the story of her own garden in particular, has written: 'All Elizabethan gardens with any pretension of grandeur or fashion, had a Mount, and a paper

on gardens of this time tells us that "They are made to be clambered up to view a fair prospect".' The Mount at Cranborne is a good-sized one, and though the yew hedge which surrounds it, and the nearby beech trees, have been growing for hundreds of years, they do not obscure the view, and the fair prospect can still be enjoyed. The Mount itself has been made into an unusual rose garden, and it is here that Lady Cranborne grows many of her favourite old roses.

The writer asked her which of these ever-fascinating flowers she liked best, but Lady Cranborne found it difficult to say.

. . . You see one and think nothing could be lovelier . . . perhaps President de Sèze, then Madame Hardy, or Pale Pink Moss will catch your eye, and then it is equalled or surpassed in beauty. Proliferé de Redouté is a favourite, and Variegata di Bologna (though a martyr

above A fine collection of old roses growing in the shelter of high yew hedges *right* The silver foliage of lavender contrasts with the dark green of box

The north porch 'is strongly Renaissance in feeling with its Italianate pillars, alcoves and elaboration of strapwork'

opposite Roses festoon the grey stone walls of the north porch, said to have been designed by Inigo Jones

to black spot), but perhaps the great white roses I like best of all. They look as though they are indigenous here, and although there are none in the garden planted earlier than 1928, Tradescant lists them, and no doubt he brought some to Cranborne. There is a beautiful climber called Lamarque, and one Adelaide Orleans, and of course Gloire de Dijon is irresistible.

I am especially fond of the species roses; they flourish in our miserable chalk soil, which is endearing, and throw up great arching branches fifteen to twenty feet high. *Forrestii* is a beauty, and so are *hibernica*, *cantabrigensis* and *andersonii*.

Lady Cranborne's favourite part of the garden is

... the sweet garden, which is largely a herb garden, and full of flowers and savours and clothed even in winter because of the numbers of ever-green or ever-grey herbs; it is delicious to work in, as the various scents cling to one throughout the day. The north court I love. We have planted the terrace with all white flowers and the rest of the court garden is planted in white, cream and apricot colours. But I find that a part of the garden which has previously seemed dull and uninteresting can suddenly become a favourite spot, if one should think of a new plan or planting for it.

The warm grey walls of the garden and courtyard of the Manor are clothed with many roses and climbers. Among the roses are the heraldic-looking red Ramona – several noisettes and the beautiful double white banksian. Clematis, both species and hybrids enjoy the chalky soil and honeysuckle – especially the yellow-flowered americana, as do actinidia with its motley leaves, jasmines to scent the air, blue Morning Glories and the uncommon white form of *Cobaea scandens*, fastest grower of all, which shoots up the walls like rockets.

Cranborne seems to be the most English of all the gardens in this book. King Charles, King James, and almost certainly Queen Elizabeth walked there. In the Inventories there is an entry about preparations made for royal visits, such as that of King James in 1621: 'Paid for Weedeing the courts and gardens against His Lordship's Comminge to Cranborne'.

It is a garden which has been devotedly tended for many years, but never with such care as in the last fifty. It owes much to Lord and Lady Salisbury, both keen and knowledgeable gardeners, who left, when they moved to Hatfield, important legacies to the garden at Cranborne in the unique collection of species roses, the delightful pleached lime avenue, and the many rare trees. But though plants from the four quarters of the world flourish at Cranborne, once planted in the shelter of the walls of the ancient home of the Cecils they seem to lose any tinge of exoticism, and become wholly English. It is easy to forget that the Great White Rose, which figured in Tradescant's list and has grown at Cranborne ever since, originated in Bulgaria. And honeysuckle from America, and lilies from the uplands of China, now grow so contentedly in their new and gentle environment that it seems that, wherever they came from, their true home was always Cranborne.

Gloucestershire
Westonbirt Arboretum
A superb garden of trees

As with the other Gloucestershire gardens illustrated in this book – Lyegrove and Abbotswood – early mention of Westonbirt and the family that originally lived there is made in *The Ancient & Present State of Gloucestershire*, published by Sir Robert Atkyns, of Swell Bowl, in 1712. In the seventeenth century it appears that the manor belonged to a Mr John Crew. It was John Crew's daughter and heiress Sarah, who married in 1665 Richard Holford, Barrister-at-Law of Lincolns Inn. The young couple set up house at Westonbirt and the place's long and happy connection with the Holford family had begun.

The story of the arboretum – the garden of trees – which today makes the fame of Westonbirt, begins 160 years later when Robert Stayner Holford, at the age of thirty-one, succeeded his father. He was to remain in possession of his great estate for more than fifty years, during which time he totally transformed it.

Trees had become Robert Holford's passion early in life. When he was only twenty-one, before he succeeded, he was already planting them, and much thought and consideration went into the setting of each. In her scholarly notes on Westonbirt, Margaret Freeman MA, a former Vice-Principal of Westonbirt school, records:

The beauty of the Westonbirt Arboretum and of the garden depends not only on the number of species and the size and symmetry of the carefully tended trees but on the superb arrangement and skilful grouping, the result not only of a knowledge of horticulture, but of the unfailing artistic sense of Mr Holford, and of his son, Sir George Holford, after him. It is said that he would often consider the possible position of a tree that he wished to plant for as long as two or three weeks before finally deciding where it would appear to best advantage.

And Mr Robert Benson, in his book on the Holford picture collection – pictures were Robert Holford's other passion – writes that one of Robert Holford's favourite lines in literature were contained in Bacon's famous essay on gardening: the much quoted 'God Almighty first planted a garden . . . I do hold there ought to be gardens for all months of the year, in which, severally,

Picea breweriana, one of the most beautiful of trees, is rare even in its native California

opposite A group of the exquisite columnar incense cedar, *Libocedrus decurrens*, which is one of the splendours of the arboretum at Westonbirt

Framed in trees, the south façade of the house built by
Robert Holford in 1863 is in Victorian-Jacobean style

things of beauty may be then in season . . . that you may have
Ver Perpetuum'. And Mr Benson goes on to say,

Bacon knew the infinite variety of greens, but he does not mention
the gorgeous livery of autumn, indeed he could not have known the
flaming acers from Japan, the golden maples from Norway, the berberis from North America and China – the glory of Westonbirt in its
Autumn colour.

Westonbirt is on the Wiltshire border of Gloucestershire, about
four miles south-west of Tetbury. The countryside around is
typically Cotswold, undulating, with no high hills. The arboretum lies near enough to the Severn to benefit to some extent from
the proximity of the sea, frosts are not usually severe, and the
soil is particularly suitable for a diverse collection of trees, as it
varies remarkably in range from a heavy limestone on an under-
lying formation of Jurassic limestone, to a lighter and comparatively lime-free soil in its western parts.

When Robert Holford – whose family fortune derived from
shares in the highly successful New River company – decided to
form a collection of trees chosen for their botanical interest as well
as for their beauty, the idea was a new one. In fact, one may say
that Westonbirt arboretum is one of the oldest in the world.

As we have seen, Mr Holford not only planned his arboretum
as an exercise in arboriculture, but he also sought to make it an
attractive feature of his estate. It was not meant to be something
apart – a place for study, and serious observation and experiment
only – but to be an area of beauty at all times of the year as well.

Looking from the house, now a school, towards an
enfilade of splendid trees

The bare branches of deciduous trees and the dark mass
of conifers make a handsome setting for the house

It was to be, in short, an integral part of the pleasure grounds of the Westonbirt estate.

Mr Holford's new trees were not, as can be seen from contemporary survey maps, planted in the shelter of existing woodland, but on open pasture and ploughland: and the avenue and rides were planned with care to align with Westonbirt House itself. The creator of the arboretum used great foresight, knowledge of his plant material and sense of scale, and the avenues he planted, now grown to dignified maturity, are still in ideal proportion to one another.

The early nineteenth century was the heyday for enthusiasts for the many new conifers being imported at that time from North America, and some of the finest trees at Westonbirt are in this category. It would be difficult to find finer specimens anywhere in England of Douglas fir (*Pseudotsuga taxifolia*), California Redwood (*Sequoia sempervirens*) or wellingtonia (*Sequoiadendron gigantea*), all part of Mr Holford's original planting. One wellingtonia is said to be the first ever planted in England. Wellingtonia (known in America as washingtonia) originates in California, where there are specimens known to be over a thousand years old; some authorities even claim that a wellingtonia could live for 4,000 years or more. In their short 120 years in England, wellingtonias have certainly become absolutely acclimatized and one, at Leaton Knolls in Shropshire, was recorded for the Conifer Conference in 1931 as being 143 feet high. There is one at Westonbirt which is 142 feet.

The Westonbirt arboretum is planned in a complex of *allées* of varying widths, each designed to offer distant views and interesting perspectives. For backdrops they have Robert Holford's towering trees, now in their one hundred and thirty-seventh year of life. The later additions, mostly planted by Mr Holford's son Sir George, border the avenues with flower or leaf colour in spring and autumn. Many gardens, for Westonbirt is a garden – a garden of trees – are at their best in spring, but comparatively few have an equally beautiful period in autumn. The author considers that Westonbirt's full splendour comes when the leaves turn, and the maples blaze. Of these the collection at Westonbirt is said to be the best in Europe, with the Japanese varieties in particular offering an eye-catching display of scarlet, crimson and gold in October. These splendid acers were added to the collection by Robert Holford and Sir George Holford, who succeeded to the estate and vast Holford fortune in 1892. He was a very rich man indeed (the Holford town house was Dorchester House, in Park Lane, upon the site of which the present Dorchester Hotel is built) and he spent many thousands of pounds adding to his father's already well-known collections. As well as planting maples, Sir George also planted many other varieties of autumn colouring trees, a form of planting in which he was a pioneer. During his reign at Westonbirt the arboretum was embellished with bold plantings of *Cercidiphyllum japonicum*, an unrivalled tree for autumn colour, though a poor spring flowerer, and of *Parrotia persica*, popularly called the Parrot Tree, though it actually takes

'The creator of the arboretum used great foresight, knowledge of his plant material and sense of scale . . . and the avenues he planted are still in ideal proportion'

its name from Professor Parrot, who the well-informed Canon Ellacombe tells us 'made the first ascent of Mount Ararat in 1829'. Noah presumably descended.

Parrotias have an unusual quality when they colour in autumn. The leaves turn crimson, but not all over, the bases remaining a bright green. Green and red, so perhaps they are not badly named Parrot Tree, after all. Sir George also planted many trees whose beauty is their autumn fruit, like the decorative spindles, gaudy rowans and brightly coloured barberries.

It would be impossible, in print, to visit the Westonbirt arboretum shrub by shrub and tree by tree. Some of the trees and shrubs which particularly interested the author of this book have been noted. He would like to make special mention of two more only.

The first tree at Westonbirt which particularly took the author's fancy, when he visited the arboretum one bleak winter's day – a time of year when Sir George's thoughtful choice of trees for the colour of their barks, like cornus, or majestic winter outline, can be appreciated – was the weeping spruce, *Picea breweriana*. This elegant conifer is a favourite of that well-known connoisseur of plants and gardens, Mr Miles Hadfield. Like the wellingtonia it, too, comes from California, and is uncommon even in its own country, growing only in a few localities. 'To describe it,' says Mr Hadfield, 'is difficult; let us say that one takes a beautifully formed pointed conifer with drooping branches and then drapes them with lace. First seeing it, one stands agape and having seen it again and again, one is confirmed in the opinion that here at last is the perfect tree.'

But for most people the most wonderful of all trees will always be the cedar – of which there are at Westonbirt, besides the exquisite columnar Incense Cedar, *Libocedrus decurrens*, several magnificent specimens of *Cedrus libani atlantica*, the Cedar of Lebanon. These are the trees which so impressed the traveller William Lithgow when he saw them growing in their native land and described them thus:

Their circle spread toppes do kiss or enhance the lower cloudes: making their grandeur over-looke the biggest bodies of all other aspiring trees, and like Monarchick Lions to wild beasts, they are chief champions of forests and woods.

With the death of Sir George Holford in 1926, his nephew the fourth Earl of Morley inherited Westonbirt. The house was sold and became a distinguished girls' school in 1927. But Lord Morley went on with the great work of adding to and perfecting the arboretum. In this, it should be said, he was greatly assisted by his curator, Mr J. Mitchell. Lord Morley died in 1951. Since 1956 the arboretum has been administered by the Forestry Commission. It is the finest garden of trees in England, owing its present dignity and beauty to the vision and devotion of three generations of tree-lovers, Mr Robert Holford, his son Sir George, and great-nephew Lord Morley. Three great arboriculturists. Three good men, for it is said that good men plant trees, and bad men cut them down.

In early spring, even when some trees are still leafless, the lake at Westonbirt is hung around with woodland tapestry

157

Abbotswood

A garden planted by a great gardener

The background trees of the garden at Abbotswood were chosen 'for contrast and foil'. Between them and the hedged rose-garden, with its attractive sundial, lies the heath garden

opposite The elaborate complex of the garden lies to the south. Beyond is the park, with the new circular lake and young plantings of maples

The garden at Abbotswood – now so well maintained by Mrs M. A. Ferguson, owes much of its fame, the present owner would be the first to insist, to the fact that it was originally laid out and planted by a great gardener of seventy years ago, Mr Mark Fenwick, one of the most important plantsmen of his day and one of the most charming men, it is still remembered, in horticultural circles. Gardening was his life-study. Up to shortly before he died in 1945, aged 84 and severely handicapped by arthritis, he would regularly inspect the garden which he had created at Abbotswood, in his electrically-driven wheel chair with, as his daughter Mrs Holland-Hibbert recalls, 'his books, labels and a few tools in a box behind'. And at the fortnightly shows of the Royal Horticultural Society at Vincent Square in Westminster, he made a distinguished, if egregious figure, examining the exhibits with a critical eye, dressed, even during the darkest days of the war, in a frockcoat and top hat.

Mark Fenwick was an immensely knowledgeable gardener, but a very modest one. Though his collection of shrubs and trees in the garden at Abbotswood was impressive, he always maintained that there were no great rarities in his garden, although this was partly owing to the soil – which he would describe deprecatingly as 'an inferior oolite – part clay and part oolite brash', difficult, of course, for rhododendrons, azaleas and all the calcifuges, though good for many other kinds of plants. Berberis were special favourites, and Mr Fenwick grew many unusual varieties, which made a fine show in the garden at Abbotswood in late summer and in autumn – berberis such as the elegant pale yellow-flowered *B. dictophylla yunnanense*, discovered in 1886 by the French missionary Delavay, to whom we owe so many good plants from China. Another favourite berberis Mark Fenwick would indicate with pride was the Himalayan Francisci-Ferdinandi, the last named, one supposes, for the Austrian archduke who was shot at Sarajevo, and whose death started the First World War.

But it was some time before 1914 that the garden at

ABBOTSWOOD

Abbotswood was first laid out, work having started there in the early 1890s. Mark Fenwick knew all that there was to know about the arrangement and planting of gardens, but he also realized, which many good gardeners do not, how important plan and architectural detail are to a garden's success. To help him in this he called in no less an architect than Sir Edwin Lutyens, not as famous then, certainly, as he was later to become, but already a name to conjure with. And quite a lot of conjuring he did at Abbotswood, where between them, in happy partnership, the two men created in a few years a garden of great charm, full of delightful surprises and effective changes in levels.

The house, built a hundred years ago, but not in Cotswold style, stands on the slope rising from the east bank of the rapid Dickler river. Mr Fenwick, rightly thinking that the house did not suit the countryside, and still less the garden he planned to set it in, asked Sir Edwin Lutyens to re-design it. What was worthy in the original house was retained, the rest drastically altered, in Sir Edwin's most high-handed and dictatorial manner. And with considerable success, as can be seen in the picture of the pleasing west façade, with its panelled ashlar blocks and finely pedimented central window overlooking a lily pond, which offers as pleasing a garden frontage as one could imagine. The vast gable which rises above the front door is said to have been inspired by a sixteenth-century outhouse in the neighbourhood of Abbotswood.

It is this lily pond garden, with its wall clad with *Clematis rehderiana* and its pool planted with beautiful Japanese iris, which lingers in the memory of the writer when he recalls his first sunlit hours at Abbotswood. He had just come from Hidcote – surely one of the loveliest of all Gloucestershire gardens – if not of all English gardens, the creation of Lawrence Johnston, the great American gardener who was a friend of Mark Fenwick and a friendly rival. But the scale at Hidcote and the scale at Abbotswood are so different that one after the other comes almost as a relief. At Hidcote all is so contained, intimate, constrained – out-door rooms, certainly, but small ones; which is their charm. At Abbotswood all is so much larger, so much more spacious. It is, in fact, one of the largest and certainly one of the best maintained gardens in England.

Mr and Mrs Ferguson bought Abbotswood in 1946, just after the Second World War, and they were lucky in retaining the services of Mr Fenwick's gardener – one of the great head gardeners of his day, Mr Fred Tustin, who had been at Abbotswood, working as a loyal *employé* and good friend of Mr Fenwick for thirty-eight years.

The Fergusons did not at once make any great changes to the gardens that lay near the house, being wisely content to keep their plan as Lutyens had left it. But the planting was simplified and, of course, many of Mrs Ferguson's favourite flowers added to the gardens.

Further from the house, however, there were great developments. Vistas were cut, and a circular lake was dug in the park

Luxuriant planting in the water garden, with *Lysichitum americanum*, the skunk cabbage, in the foreground. Against the sky is the outline of the house as designed by Sir Edwin Lutyens. The low sweeping gable is a typical Lutyens fancy

on the far side of the lawn to the south, and new trees, mostly maples, were planted nearby. Elsewhere large trees such as limes, Douglas fir, beech, and some Lawson varieties of conifer were cleared to give more space. The general canvas was enlarged, more ground taken in, but at the same time the quality of the upkeep was not allowed to deteriorate, as too often happens when a garden is enlarged. As Mr Lanning Roper has remarked about Abbotswood, 'There is such a high standard of maintenance that the most frequent criticism, and this is one almost never heard in this day of shortage of labour, is that Abbotswood is "too tidy".'

The gardens almost entirely surround the house, with the main flower garden to the south – a paved and box-hedged rose garden to the west, and what was the rose garden in Mark Fenwick's day, set out as a most effective blue and grey parterre. On the hillside to the east of the house there is a heath garden, which was Mark Fenwick's special pride. It was one of the earliest to be planted in England, and unexpectedly successful on such limey soil. Mr and Mrs Ferguson removed a pergola which partially hid this part of the garden from the gazebo in the lower garden.

Beyond the heath garden are the plantings of trees which were Mark Fenwick's delight, and which illustrate two of his favourite gardening precepts – which were 'contrast and foil'. At almost any time of year the different foliage and form of the trees in the arboretum at Abbotswood make a most impressive display – a tapestry of different greens and gold and winy reds, which is totally pleasing to the eye. But their colouring in autumn is especially striking, when the amelanchiers, nyssas and maples fairly burn, and that loveliest of autumn colourers, *Cercidiphyllum japonicum*, puts up its annual firework display of gold and scarlet.

The flower garden on the upper terrace is laid out with boldly designed geometric beds and has for centre-piece a graceful sundial supported by stone cherubs. The planting here is in the modern taste, with herbaceous plants – peonies, delphiniums, evening primroses – interspersed with many plants of grey foliage – *senecio*, *Artemisia canescens* and generous helpings of *Stachys lanata* to edge the beds with its leaves of silver velvet. The general height of the planting is low, though here and there some taller growing plants make a pleasant undulation, and formal yew trees provide exclamation points.

From the upper terrace, garden steps lead down to a lower

overleaf left
'Mulleins also proliferate, seeding themselves everywhere in the Cotswold stonework, and raising their yellow heads of flowers skywards'

overleaf right
The heath garden at Abbotswood was planned and planted in 1905, when a garden of ericas alone was a most novel idea

The lily pond, designed by Sir Edwin Lutyens, is fed by a jet of water from a mask on the house wall. The sides are planted with *Iris japonica*

terrace, which is of simple lawn, with a pool and two fountains in the middle. Here are many roses, both old and new, with several musk roses, like Felicia and Penelope, laying their sweetness on the air in June, when Madame Isaac Pereire, too, is in full flower. This is the rose of which Mark Fenwick once said, 'I believe it is the loveliest and the latest, the largest and the sweetest rose in the garden, but which has been banished from most gardens, because, forsooth, it has not the purity of form of, say, Ophelia.' Mark Fenwick said that many years ago, and the writer was pleased on his last visit to see the old rose he so loved still growing at Abbotswood.

Besides roses, which thrive in such profusion in this part of the garden at Abbotswood, mulleins also proliferate, seeding themselves everywhere in the Cotswold stonework, and raising their yellow heads of flower skywards. Surely one of the most charming of flower families, the verbascums at Abbotswood, belie any possible criticism that the garden looks too manicured, for their almost cottagey character tempers any suggestion of formality.

The rose garden itself is planted with floribundas and hybrid teas, while the grey and blue garden with its beds cut in a charming design of interwoven hearts balances it on the other side of the main terrace. In spring, this garden is neatly bedded out with tulips, but it is in summer that it takes on its most striking colour scheme of blue and silver, the dazzling blue shade being supplied by *Salvia horminum* Blue Beard, and the silver by the argent leaves of *Centaurea sphaerocephalum*. This planting and colour scheme has become a tradition at Abbotswood, and has delighted the eyes of visitors to the garden ever since it was instigated forty years ago.

Forty years ago, too, a shrub which drew the admiration of all who saw it was the *Carpentaria californica* growing in a sheltered place below one of the terrace walks. It was already a good specimen then, and is still growing – a tribute to the care with which it was originally placed, for carpentaria is by no means bone hardy. Near it is a fine shrub of *Garrya elliptica*, a shrub which Lutyens must, in common with the Adam brothers, have much admired, for it is said that the two Scottish architects were inspired by garrya's pendant catkins for the swags which they so often introduced into their architectural designs. Two more shrubs that have added distinction to the garden at Abbotswood for half a century, being mentioned in some notes on the garden which appeared in the 1920s, are *Schizophragma hydrangeoides* and its close relation *Hydrangea petiolaris*; Mr Blakeley, the present young and enterprising gardener at Abbotswood, the redoubtable Mr Tustin's worthy successor, describes them as 'very fine specimens still . . . and two of the main features of the garden.'

Two parts of the garden at Abbotswood remain to be visited – the water garden and the heath garden. The water garden was laid in the early years of this century by the well-known firm of

Pulham & Son, completely to the satisfaction of Mr Fenwick, who wrote, 'water has an annoying habit of finding its way around and under rocks, but there has never been any trouble here'. Already over half a century old, the water garden now looks as if it has been there for ever, and it is a lovely sight in spring, and indeed at almost every time of year, with its massive rock-work quite overgrown with mimulus, primulas, star-studded bushes of yellow potentilla, and the most enormous clumps of *Lysichitum americanum*, or skunk cabbage, the writer has ever seen.

The heath garden at Abbotswood was planned and planted in 1905, when the idea of a garden only of ericaceous plants was something of a novelty, though as we tell elsewhere in this book, Colonel Messel planted a heath garden at Nymans at almost the same date. But at Nymans the acid soil was perfect for heaths, while at Abbotswood the soil is strongly alkali. Of this Mr Blakeley told the writer, 'Mr Tustin always told me that large quantities of peat and lime-free loam were added to the water garden area but not to the heath garden. The heath garden was rough dug in the autumn, prior to a very severe winter which broke up the existing heavy clay. The following spring some leaf soil only was added before planting up with heather. It was a major surprise that the heather flourished in such adverse conditions.'

For flourish it did, with some of the groups of heaths more than ten yards across. From January till April *Erica carnea* Springwood Pink and King George give colour, followed by the silver pink *E. darleyensis*, white *lusitanica* and the tall rose-pink *mediterranea*. In May the crossleaf heath *E. coccinea* takes on, flowering through the summer till the end of September. In July the shrubby ericaceous *menziesias* start blooming, and loyally flower right through till November, when the *carneas* are ready to start once more. No flower could do more, and Mark Fenwick was specially proud of a corner of his garden which showed such cheer and colour all year round. He would often advise his friends to plant heath gardens too, offering cuttings and young plants to start them off – for as a friend of his told the writer, he was the most generous of gardeners, and few visitors to Abbotswood went away empty-handed. Mr Tustin, the head gardener, however, was less so, and would look on with disapproval when plants and cuttings were being given away, and when instructed to send so and so a plant would sometimes, conveniently, forget. But between the two men there was a strong bond of sympathy and understanding, and between them they created a garden which is certainly one of the great gardens of England.

No question of the generosity of that legacy. How fortunate it is that the Abbotswood garden should have fallen into the appreciative hands of Mrs Ferguson and her late husband, who have maintained it so well, and have substantially added to its reputation.

This fine specimen of *Schizophragma hydrangeoides* was mentioned in notes on the garden at Abbotswood in the 1920s

Hinton Ampner

A garden designed by a connoisseur

The Hampshire Hunt meets at Hinton Ampner on a December morning in 1810. The house has subsequently been much enlarged

opposite Through the grove of trees to be seen in the old print above, there is now an informal grass walk, with an obelisk and temple for eye-catchers at either end

There can be comparatively few gardens in Great Britain, though there are several shown in this book, of which the owner is equally knowledgeable about plants as about pictures and furniture. Green fingers do not always go with good taste, and keen gardeners all too often live in houses considerably less well arranged, to put it kindly, than their gardens. And vice versa. The author occasionally stays in a *château* near Paris which belongs to a man whose taste in furniture, pictures and decoration is famous. It has left its imprint on his generation. Every house he arranges is acclaimed and eagerly emulated. His utterances on how to arrange pictures, hang curtains, upholster furniture are treated as gospel by those who care deeply for such things, all over Europe. And his taste is, admittedly, perfect. Imaginative, practical, artistic, original – but only in interior decoration. Only indoors. The gardens that adjoin his *châteaux*, villas, *palazzi*, are very poor relations – neglected, abandoned to gardeners who are never directed, whose achievements are unappreciated. And it is a great pity, for it would be fascinating indeed to see what kind of garden M. de —, the brilliant amateur interior decorator, would conjure.

All of which has little to do with the garden at Hinton Ampner, it might be thought. But wrongly. For Hinton Ampner is the exception – the perfect example of a garden planned, laid out and planted with as much care as a house. In fact, the way in which it is arranged resembles, in some respects, the way a house is furnished. Mr Ralph Dutton, the owner, is a master of both arts. His house is celebrated for the perfection of its appointments. And so is his garden, as befits one laid out and planted by such a recognized authority on garden design. But before passing through the high french windows onto the sunlit terrace, below which the gardens of Hinton Ampner lie, let us for a moment trace the history of the house. It is a tale culminating in recent calamity, and complete renaissance.

Hinton Ampner is in Hampshire, some miles south of Alresford. In the Middle Ages it was the property of the Almoner

'One is not surprised to see in the garden of anyone so architecturally aware . . . acanthus, the favourite plant of all classical architects'

opposite Mr Ralph Dutton's garden is laid out in terraces on the slope where hops were once grown for brewing. One formal parterre, with conical yews, is planted out in summer with bright dahlias 'Park Princess'

of St Swithin's Priory in Winchester – hence Ampner. Records of the house in the mid-seventeenth century (when it was still part of the appurtenance of the Chapter of Winchester) show that it was a sizeable house, with its own brew house and malting sheds. There was in those days an extensive hop-garden where Mr Dutton's present pleasure grounds are now laid out, on a gentle south-facing slope, an ideal situation for growing flowers, shrubs – and hops.

The house Mr Dutton inherited was a Georgian one, originally quite modest but much enlarged and Victorianized in the last century. Mr Dutton, lover of the Georgian and Regency periods, and an expert on the furniture and pictures of those times, transformed it. He encased the old house in weathered brick, added bosomy bow windows to catch the sun, and in the garden only retained the fretted stone balustrade with which his father had trimmed the terrace.

But, even then, the story of the house at Hinton Ampner was not quite finished. In April 1960, one Sunday afternoon, while Mr Dutton was walking in the woods and the staff was out, the new house burned down, with all its treasures – pictures, furniture and its well-known collection of antique and Regency porphyry. Little was saved, only the outer walls survived, and it is a great tribute to Mr Dutton that he had the courage, and the heart, to rebuild his house exactly as it was, though without replacing the attic storey, and refurnish it with more fine furniture and objects of his favourite periods.

The gardens were unaffected by the fire, and looking back at the house from below the terraces, gives the visitor to Hinton Ampner as good an opportunity as any to acclaim Mr Dutton's grasp of architectural detail and his taste in planting.

Above, the house, pink-faced and urbane, with its elegantly spaced windows and restrained stonework. Beneath it, the terraces, with their Victorian balustrading tactfully smothered with roses and clematis and their borders brimful of all the best loved plants of the English border, with colour a-plenty and just those touches here and there of the grey-leaved shrubby plants which the taste of today decrees.

The garden of Hinton Ampner lies to the south of the house, on a falling slope which was once used to grow the hops for the Almoner's brewing. Here, Mr Dutton has laid out his garden on formal lines with many of the component parts that one expects to find in a well-designed English garden.

There are yew hedges, rose borders, a lily pond, borders of old roses, and borders filled chiefly with shrubs. But there is a difference. No one knows a good plant better than the present owner of Hinton Ampner and yet the visitor to his garden quickly notices that it is by lavish use of comparatively simple plants that Mr Dutton achieves his effects. In some chosen corners of the garden there are to be found certain plants that are rare and delicate, but in the main, there are wide areas boldly and generously planted with shrubs which are known to like the local soil, and which can be relied on to grow well. For instance, a

planting which always impressed the writer on his visits to Hinton Ampner, is one which Mr Dutton has used to cover a steep bank facing due south. This is planted with a plant which many gardeners might scorn – *Hypericum calycinum*, the humble St John's Wort. At Hinton Ampner it looks absolutely right, and admirably fulfils its function, which is completely to clothe a bank which would be difficult to mow, and to suppress weeds.

The red brick walls of the house itself are dressed, but not smothered, with magnolias, clematis, and wistarias as fine as those at Pyrford. At the base of the walls is a 'permanent planting' in the popular and practical style of today, of low-growing shrubby material, plants with the silver felted leaves of *Senecio greyii*, lavenders, *Phlomis fruticosa*, all plants which like a warm, sheltered position. A planting rather like the one we see at Haseley Court, which needs little upkeep, looks well all year, and gives a comfortably dressed look to the narrow, usually hot and dry area between the walls of a house and a terrace. Brick steps lead down to the second terrace, laid out as lawn, and more steps descend to a formal parterre, set with conical yews, which of all evergreens, though they do not, in the words of Sir George Sitwell, 'share in the hopes of spring or the regrets of autumn', are surely the perfect accompaniment and foil for the transient brilliance of summer flowers.

In this garden the beds are bedded out in the style of eighty years ago (after all, the terraces and their balustrades are survivals of the Victorian house, so such a planting is perfectly in keeping), with tulips succeeding wallflowers, which in turn are followed by geraniums or dahlias. Looking back from this parterre, up at the house, the eye is delighted with the picture presented, with the terrace walls, atangle with roses and clematis and vines, providing a mass of colour all summer through.

To the east of the house there are more gardens. A small sunk garden laid out with octagonal paving and turf, and again bedded out in an almost Victorian way, with pink geraniums and sweet scented heliotrope. This area is contained in a perfectly tailored yew hedge, backed with high trees, making a delightful entity on its own. The writer especially recalls, in the sunk garden at Hinton Ampner, some fine specimens of that excellent shrub, *Choisya ternata* – the Mexican Orange Bush which we admire in several other gardens in this book, and gardeners in the home counties should be grateful to Monsieur M. D. Choisy, the Swiss botanist, for having introduced his name plant to Europe in 1825, for it is one of the few Mexican shrubs which are hardy near London.

Running the whole length of his garden from east to west, Mr Dutton has laid out a long walk, and on either side of it, he has set 'in even lines the ductile yew', in this case Irish yews which, of all trees, have the great advantage, when quite young, of looking mature, and so give an established look to any garden, even when planted quite small. In the long walk at Hinton Ampner they line the central path of mown grass, and are backed with high borders of flowering trees and roses. It is in these

Beyond the folly's classical façade, 'with its four pillars and pediment bearing the Dutton crest', lie the formal garden and a long *allée* of Irish yews

opposite The folly at Hinton Ampner is set amid brimming beds of shrubs and herbaceous plants. In the foreground grows *Dicentra spectabile*

borders that *weigela* grows in company with pink may, the large-leaved *Aesculus parviflora*, which shows its welcome flowers in August, and those two worthy Viburnums, *opulus* and *tomentosum*. Here too are many of the shrub roses: the golden Frühlingsgold, the purple moss rose William Lobb, and those ever popular musks, Penelope and Felicia. The north side, which is steeply banked and faces south, makes a sunlit curtain of blossom for many months in the summer.

At one end of this delectable *allée* is a statue of Artemis, which is particularly well placed, as is the Folly which faces on to the long walk, on the northern side. This is a four-pillared, classical building, with elegantly swagged frieze and a pediment displaying the Dutton crest. The view this little temple commands is delightful, for it looks due south, between brimming shrub borders towards an old lime avenue, with, as an eye catcher at the further end, an obelisk. Such buildings, as we know, were, and still are, called Follies, and one sometimes wonders why? A pagoda, a pyramid, the late Lord Berners' tower at Faringdon, an artificial ruin, as at Rousham, might all be dismissed as follies, frivolous, and of doubtful decorative value. But a temple such as the one at Hinton Ampner is both elegant and practical – eminently sensible, in fact.

Another part of Mr Dutton's garden remains to be visited: a hollow, once an old chalk pit, which has been planted, one feels, with some of the plants of architectural form and elegance of leaf which are particular favourites of the owner of Hinton Ampner. Here certainly the plant material seems to have been chosen more for its varying texture than for any lavish display of flower. The hollow's plant-clad banks present a picture like John Evelyn's collection of 'curious greenes' at Albury, and seem to be hung with a rich tapestry of different verdure. Here, Mr Dutton has set plants of bold foliage like tree peonies, which delight in the chalk and the giant hemlock, *Heracleum mantegazzianum*, with its jungly leaves, spiraeas of various sorts, the blue-berried *Viburnum davidii* from China, as well as *V. mariesii*. Near by, one is not surprised to see, in the garden of anyone so architecturally aware, several different kinds of acanthus, the favourite plant of all classical architects.

Mr Ralph Dutton is, as we have seen, a connoisseur of plants, but he does not prize a plant because it is difficult to grow. He admits he prefers shrubs to flowers, especially those which put up with his own limey soil, like philadelphus, deutzias, rhus and potentillas. He values any plant for its architectural form, its hardiness, its ability to fulfil a certain function, to create a certain effect. His garden is arranged, as we have suggested, rather like his house – in galleries of green and *enfilades* of outdoor rooms. Each has character, sometimes its own colour scheme. He thinks that the essential of any garden is that it should have good bones – i.e. a well planned layout, 'and that this should be filled in with such luxuriance as one can achieve' . . . He thinks, too, that a garden should 'flow' so that one is carried on to find out what is round the next corner. This succession of garden pictures

The south façade has 'bosomy bow windows to catch the sun'. Below the walls runs a border permanently planted in the popular and practical style of today

Mr Dutton has certainly achieved at Hinton Ampner. It is rare in England to find a garden at once so sophisticated and so simple. Its plan is uncomplicated and yet, at every turn, the visitor is beguiled by planting juxtapositions which he hurries home to emulate, usually with indifferent success. For much scholarly taste has gone into Mr Dutton's thoughtful arrangement.

right The terrace of Hinton Ampner, with a border of shrubby ground-covering plants below. The house walls are carefully dressed with *Vitis coignetiae*

below The trim north façade. To the left *Schizophragma hydrangeoides* has been allowed full rein. In the right foreground *Potentilla arbusculus*, which shows yellow flowers all summer long

Kelvedon Hall

A garden planted in the modern manner

Until 1920 Kelvedon Hall was the home of the Wright family, a branch of which emigrated to America and sired the famous aeronauts Orville and Wilbur

opposite The north façade of the house mirrored in the waters of the lake. In the foreground, azaleas

The bland red brick of Kelvedon Hall looks south towards the sun by day, and at night towards the glowing sky above London. But though only twenty miles from Piccadilly Circus, the early Georgian house lies in perfect country which is unexpectedly undulating for Essex. Its name, Kelvedon, Kelveduna in Domesday Book – for there has been a house on the site for a thousand years – means Battle of the Danes and the wide vista the Hall commands was once the scene of a spirited encounter between the Anglo-Saxons and Scandinavian invaders. Much later, from 1557 until 1920, Kelvedon was the home of the Wrights, a branch of which emigrated to America and there sired two of the earliest and most adventurous of aeronauts, Orville and Wilbur, who were born at Millville, Indiana, and were the first men to fly in a heavier-than-air machine. Occasionally, when the gardens of Kelvedon Hall are open to the public under the National Gardens Scheme, a large Cadillac or Buick noses its way up the drive, dwarfing the Minis and station wagons of the local garden enthusiasts. Out of it will step a prosperous American family – Wright relations – on a pilgrimage to see their ancestral home, and the quite remarkable gardens which lie around it.

For the garden of Kelvedon Hall is remarkable for being one of the earliest in England to be planted in a series of outdoor rooms, each garden enclosed in a hedge or wall, and each planted in its own subtly devised colour scheme. The gardens lie to the south-west of the house on a gentle slope, and are approached through a white painted door, set to the left of the north façade. This first garden, still known as the herb garden, though herbs are no longer grown there, is walled in brick and has for nub a sundial set in what Lewis Carroll would have called a 'wabe' of more brick planted with thyme, a gentle horticultural pun. The colours all round are white and pink. Rose Caroline Testout clothes the wall, with *Buddleia fallowiana alba* planted below it, its honey scent a great attraction for white and, it must be admitted, other coloured butterflies. A border of Mrs Sinkins pinks fills the air with their incense for several weeks in July, and

From the rose garden, steps lead up to a gate painted turquoise blue. To right and left grow shrub roses, pink Grootendorst, and on the wall's edge glaucous-leaved *Othonnopsis cheirifolia*

The orangery with its long Georgian windows gives shelter to tender plants in winter. White geraniums fill the tubs on either side of the door

Choisya ternata, the Mexican orange, thrives in a sheltered corner. The tops of the walls are starry with *Clematis montana* in spring. Through another door a wide vista of park and farmland welcomes the visitor, who finds that the way to the main gardens lies to the left.

On the way there is a long border which, as it is a part of the garden which is constantly and at all seasons in view, has carefully been set, for long lasting effect, with plants more remarkable for their foliage than for a short-lived display of flowers. Here are veronicas – now known as hebes – silver-leaved eleagnus and santolina, with a bold use of an unusual but most effective plant – *Ajuga reptans bicolor* – a ground-covering, weed-suppressing bugle with flowers that are blue in spring, and purple leaves splashed with gold and ginger, which go a brilliant red in autumn.

Next comes the swimming pool garden, with its Baroque pavilion designed by an Austrian architect, Kellner, in 1938. On either side, atop the balustrade, are light-hearted French statues of an eighteenth-century garden-boy and his girl friend, in terracotta. Steps lead down to the pool itself, one of the first ever to be installed in England. Brick walls surround this garden to the north, east and west, giving shelter to flowers chosen for colour and scent at the season when the pool is most in use, such as the cream-coloured rose Gloire de Dijon, white tobacco flowers, wreathing mauve clematis and blue agapanthus in tubs. To the south a wall has recently been lowered to afford a view down a broad expanse of yew-hedged lawn, a most pleasing vista, and an improvement devised by the present owners.

Through another gate, this time of wrought iron, and one of a set brought from Austria, and the visitor reaches the rose garden, sheltered to the north by a further brick wall which is semi-circular in shape. A novel planting here, and a perfect foil to the brilliant pinks and crimsons of hybrid tea roses, are bold groups of *Ruta graveolens* Jackmans Blue – one of the best of our newly introduced plants, with its pungent greenish-blue foliage and debonair habit.

From the rose garden one passes through a holly hedge, down shallow stone steps, and across a long grass path which runs along the main herbaceous border. This not only includes well-grown examples of purely herbaceous material such as delphiniums, lupins, verbascums and so on, but floribunda roses, cushions of lavender and groups of the silver-leaved crimson-barked cornus and other shrubs to give body and interest and some, if muted, colour in winter.

The path now takes on a sharper slope and a broad grass path leads downhill, between tall pointed conifers, which, with the Baroque pavilion and sophisticated iron work, contrive to give this very English garden an almost continental air.

It takes the visitor through three circular gardens, which Victoria Sackville-West would have called rondels, one planted with different white flowers such as white roses, peonies, spiraeas and more pinks; the second in tones of gold, differently textured, both in flower and leaf – a golden catalpa, golden yews, the

above left Pots of plants of differing foliage are grouped around a marble sculpture of *putti* with a goat Above A terra-cotta shepherdess on a carved balustrade in one of the several walled enclosures at Kelvedon

unusual orange *Aquilegia hookeri*, geums, yellow tulips, golden thyme and *Alchemilla mollis*. The last of these three rondels is perhaps the most striking, for it is unusually hedged in closely cut *Prunus pissardii*, which makes a deep claret wall, and it is planted only with red and purple flowers – rose Cardinal Richelieu, scarlet dahlias, purple buddleias and, for punctuation marks and contrast, four symmetrically-placed standard *Pyrus salicifolia*, the silver-leaved Willow Pear. Central feature of this 'red' garden is a giant bear of stone, brought, when such removals were easier, from a deserted garden in the Sudetenland.

From the red garden the path leads on through a little wood of high *Cedrus atlantica glauca* whose blue tones set the colour scheme for the planting beneath, which in spring consists of blue Blackmore and Langdon polyanthus, blue scillas, mertensias and a carpeting of blue flowered pulmonaria. In summer, rose Veilchenblau wreathes skywards, and in autumn the glaucous leaves of *Hosta sieboldii* maintain the note of blue.

Thus the planting of the garden at Kelvedon Hall goes on. Past a sunk garden where there are few flowers and the effect is made by the use of groups of different foliage plants – bamboos, bergenias, giant petasites. This part is rather what John Evelyn might have called a 'Collection of curious greens', all set in paving. It is shaded by an immense weeping willow, and makes a delightfully cool décor. The path then turns back towards the house, past a bank of shrubs which includes a magnificent photinia, a bold group of *Phormium tenax* and a Judas tree grown from a seed of the one that springs from Shelley's grave near the pyramid of Cestius in Rome.

The writer has always been fascinated by the names of plants. Why Judas? Why such a direful name for such a charming tree? It is widely thought that it was from the Judas tree that Judas Iscariot hanged himself after his betrayal of Christ. The legend is, of course, quite without foundation. In Spain the tree is called

Water lilies by the border of the lake, with a fine weeping willow (*Salix babylonica*)

The Baroque bathing pavilion seen through a gate in mellowed brick work. *Stachys lanata* lays a silver carpet by the paving; the terra-cotta urn is planted with sempervivum and the mauve-flowered clematis Belle of Woking grows behind

opposite The pavilion with its attendant terra-cotta statues of a shepherd and shepherdess overlook the pool. The architect was the Austrian Kellner (1938)

Arbol Del Amor, in France Gainier, and sometimes L'Arbre de la Judée. That is probably how the story started, and how a completely innocent tree achieved such an evil appellation.

Cercis siliquastrum, alias Judas tree, never grows very tall in England – a most useful quality in a tree which has to find a place in the smaller gardens of today. But though low in stature it has a curiously mature look from an early age, and a tree only ten years old has a gnarled quality which greatly enhances its pictorial value.

But to return to the garden at Kelvedon Hall. What strikes the perceptive visitor is the care that has been given to choose plants for their leaf rather than for their rarity or brilliance of flower. It is this bold use of hardy plants which gives the gardens their character and extraordinary richness of texture.

Kelvedon Hall is the home of Mr Paul Channon and Mrs Channon. It owes its original plan to Mr Channon's mother, now Lady Honor Svejdar, who devised the elegant lay-out and the pre-war planting. Since the war the present owner's father, the late Sir Henry Channon, replaced much of the bedded-out areas with perennials and shrubs and generally simplified the lay-out, while preserving the garden's original thoughtful plan.

Hush Heath Manor

A very English garden with Italian overtones

The weald of Kent is richer than most English counties in half-timbered manor houses which were the homes of rich sheep farmers and wool-merchants four centuries ago. Of these manors, Hush Heath is one of the oldest. It was built by a master weaver, in 1534 – during the reign of Henry VIII – and ever since, its time-silvered gables have looked over the gentle Kentish landscape dotted with grazing sheep, between Goudhurst and Marden.

The garden at Hush Heath is fascinating in that it is such a happy blending of the Italian and English styles. English with its traditional borders, its roses, and its topiary; Italian with its statues and terraces and general architectural feel. In some notes he made several years ago, the author wrote these words about the owner of Hush Heath who laid out the garden in such an individual way: 'Mr Bower spent his winters in Italy, where he obviously drank deep of the Chianti of Italian culture: for he planted an avenue of slender yews which recall Frascati, built statued terraces which might overlook Fiesole, and designed and planted a circular hedge of castellated and pinnacled cypress which surely must be unusual anywhere . . .'

The gabled and timbered west façade of Hush Heath Manor overlooks a wide lawn, studded with topiary – with a bank to the south which in spring is bright with daffodils and scillas. Stone steps, flanked with ferns and carpeted with moss, mount this bank and lead to the circular enclosure formed by the castellated hedge already mentioned. Here the thought has been to plant few flowers, so that the classic simplicity of the topiary with its differing greens may make its full effect.

From here, an avenue of yews stretches for a hundred yards or more to a statue in marble of a mysteriously veiled woman. But though, again, this vista is of different greens alone, one turn to left or right brings the visitor upon colour a-plenty: broad beds of brilliantly coloured azaleas in spring, parterres of old roses in June and a bold planting of lilies in July and August. More roses – like the snowy Wedding Day, blushing Emily Grey,

Massed geraniums on the terrace at Hush Heath. Beyond, and catching the evening sunlight, a weeping willow

opposite In the shadow of a tubby peacock in topiary, a closely planted bed of bright azaleas fills the eye with colour and the air with scent

above right White roses and pungent-leaved rosemary on either side of an old seat of carved stone

above At the end of a long vista framed in Irish yews stands a figure of a mysteriously veiled woman. Such statues were popular in Italy in the 1860s

opposite The ever fascinating pattern of contrasting leaf and stone. The frosty purple foliage of *Sedum spathulifolium purpureum*, fern fronds and a stone vase of *sempervivums*, said to bring good luck, overgrow a stone bench at Hush Heath Manor

and robust François Juranville – are trained, in the modern way, to grow up and through the many old apple trees which grow around, and are another attractive feature of the garden in summer. Two other interesting parts of the garden lie ahead. A dell, with a central pool which is grown around with a particularly rich collection of moisture-loving plants. Pink and crimson astilbes, broad-leaved rodgersias, huge gunneras, Japanese iris, and as a foil for these, generous groups of hostas whose glaucous blue foliage contrasts for months on end every year with the flower colour and different leaf-forms around them.

Nearby lies the croquet lawn bordered on two sides by hanging banks. These have been planted by the present owner of Hush Heath, Mr Otto Lucas, in a most original and striking way, with shrubs selected carefully for their foliage – evergreens, silver or russet, to make a permanent tapestry of muted colour which persists, in slightly changing beauty, almost all year round. The plants used in this most unusual, yet practical, planting, for all

the shrubs chosen are excellent weed suppressors, include the purple-leaved sage, grey-leaved *Senecio greyii*, *Skimmia japonica* with its scarlet berries and glossy foliage, red berberis, golden-leaved eleagnus and blue-green *Ruta graveolens*.

Thus the garden door of the manor is gained and the visit to the gardens of Hush Heath completed. Nearby an inscription on a sundial reads, '*Horas non numero sed serenas*' – 'I only tell of sunny hours'. But even when the sun is low in the west, too low for its rays to reach the sundial's face, the roses still lay their sweetness on the evening air, and the gardens enjoy the quiet serenity that their very name, Hush Heath, suggests.

opposite The gabled west façade of Hush Heath Manor, built in 1534, one of the finest surviving Tudor houses in Kent

Vines, climbing hydrangeas and roses drape the half-timbered walls of a Tudor gazebo

Pattern in paving. Random paving, uncluttered by planting, but well set off by pots of fuchsias and geraniums

Oxfordshire
Rousham

The only surviving landscape garden designed by Kent

One of Kent's drawings of his alterations to the garden at Rousham: Venus' Vale with its fountains and cascades.

opposite The arcade, named Praeneste for a likeness to the terrace of the Temple of Fortune at Palestrina (anc. Praeneste), Italy. It commands a view of the Oxfordshire water meadows towards the river Cherwell

How lucky for the garden historian that Horace Walpole was so interested in gardens, that he wrote about them so vividly, and that his writings have been preserved. To be able to quote his succinct opinions on so many of the great pleasure grounds of the eighteenth century – complimentary or otherwise – is to be able to illumine any garden's story with flashes of spirited comment. We know that we admire Rousham today, but how fortunate we are to be able to know exactly how it impressed someone of taste soon after it was conceived, when it was quite new, and almost revolutionary. '. . . The most engaging of Kent's works . . . Kentissimo' was Horace Walpole's comment, and he went on to say that it was 'as elegant and antique as if the Emperor Julian had selected the most pleasing solitude about Daphne to enjoy philosophic retirement'.

Before tracing the story of the gardens and park at Rousham let us glance first at the character and career of their creator, William Kent. He was born at Bridlington in Yorkshire about 1685 and early in life was apprenticed to a coach painter in Hull. His talents must somehow have attracted the attention of the local gentry, for in 1709 a group of Yorkshire squires contributed to the cost of sending him to Italy, where he in due course went, with John Talman, the great collector and connoisseur, as travelling companion. In Rome he made many influential friends, including Thomas Coke, the future Earl of Leicester, for whom he was later to build Holkham. While in Italy, Kent also met the Earl of Burlington, with whom he travelled home to England in 1719, and who was to influence him strongly. From then on Kent's career as an architect was established, and he was to originate many famous buildings, including the Horse Guards in London, Holkham and Claremont. He was a man of singular charm and easy-going temperament. After his prolonged sojourn in Rome, the veneer of Italian culture he had gained while abroad, and his taste for the classic won him the nickname of the Signor. Under the influence of Burlington, he became a devotee of Palladianism, and there was always to be a flavour

186

A contemporary plan of Kent's design for the garden at Rousham

opposite Lead statues, which may have decorated the earlier formal garden transformed by Kent, now stand in a setting of sylvan greenery

of that august style in all he designed. His activities were many and varied. Not only drawings and plans for palaces and parks flowed from his busy work board, but illustrations for books, sketches for garden furniture and *cache-pots*, and fancy dress costumes, including 'tragedy-Buskins' and even, his detractors whispered, a design for a woman's ball gown embroidered with columns of the Five Orders, so that its wearer had the look 'of a walking Palladio in petticoats'.

But it is the part William Kent played in the history of English garden design that, in this book, we must acclaim. He was the first of the landscape architects. With his head full of memories of the classical paintings of Claude or Salvator Rosa, he sought to recreate, on his return to England, their sunlit landscapes in his native land. Kent was in the forefront of the revolt against the artificiality of seventeenth-century gardening. Henceforth, he held, there should be no apparent barrier between the immediate pleasure grounds of a gentleman's house and the park. To quote Horace Walpole once more, 'he leaped the fence and saw that all nature was a garden'. Marrying the splendid, ordered formality of the architecture of Palladio to the informality, albeit contrived of the English park he sought to conjure, by thoughtful planting and the well-placed *fabrique*, the dreamy romantic landscapes of the Italian masters. He became 'the creator of the tradition of landscape gardening which has been one of England's most important contributions to the visual arts'. Of all Kent's garden creations, Stowe, Claremont, Gunnersbury, Carlton House, many have either disappeared altogether, or are altered beyond recognition – except Rousham, one of the earliest, and certainly the most characteristic of his essays.

Rousham is in Oxfordshire, equidistant from Oxford and Banbury. From the Bicester–Chipping Norton road, the visitor catches his first glimpse of the house, lying across a smiling valley to the south, with bouquets of high trees on either side, and before its many windowed façade an apron of green grass which falls to the river Cherwell. The house, which was also to be tactfully redesigned by Kent, dates from 1635. It was built by Sir Robert Dormer, whose family, three hundred and fifty years later, still live there. There is no space to examine the architectural changes that Kent made for his patron, Sir Robert's grandson, General James Dormer, an old soldier who had seen service with the Duke of Marlborough and been our Minister in Lisbon. He was a bachelor and, it seems, a delightful man and a dilettante. When he embarked on the alterations at Rousham he was already old and in fading health, but the fame of Kent had reached him, and it was the busy, popular Kent he wanted for Rousham. 'If Kent can be persuaded to come I shall take it very kindly.' Come he did, and having reorganized and redecorated the house in the very individual style that the many visitors to Rousham can still admire, he set about transforming the layout of the garden which is today his monument.

It has been suggested that Alexander Pope had already cast his eye on General Dormer's grounds – he was a friend of the family –

Venus' Vale and the upper cascade, with its basin decorated with lead cupids on swan-back

before Kent set to work. Horace Walpole is not sure: 'I do not know whether the disposition of the garden at Rousham was not planned on the model of Mr Pope's . . . at least in the opening and retiring shades of Venus' Vale.'

Whether Kent followed an early project of Pope's, or not, he certainly put into practice Pope's dictum, to

> Consult the Genius of the Place in all –
> That tells the Waters or to rise or fall . . .
> Or scoops the circling Theatres of the Vale,
> Joins willing Woods and varies Shades from Shades.

His object was to create a dreamlike parkland scene– utilizing existing plantation where possible, planting anew where necessary. The whole verdant scene to be 'traversed' by a series of linking walks and 'vistos', each of which was to axe on 'eye-catchers' in the form of statues, garden seats and temples. The visitor, following the route laid down, for there was a right and a wrong way to visit the glades of any Kent garden, was to be treated to a series of enchanting transformation scenes. Surprise

opposite By the old bowling green there is a sculpture by Peter Scheemakers of a horse being attacked by a lion. Beyond stands one of Kent's elegantly designed 'green seats'

A satyr under a canopy of overhanging yew looks over the green waters of the great pond

and delight were the emotions prescribed, as through the 'opening and retiring shades' he passed, out into the sunlight gilding the grass and silvering the statues.

Let us visit the park at Rousham, grove by grove – as Kent would have had us do – noting as we go on our way what he found, and how he left it. To the north of the house, where once were formal gardens in the old style, he decreed a bowling green, which was enclosed with sloping banks of turf, clipped hedges set with sculptured terms and what in the surviving accounts are described as 'green seats', which probably means bowling green seats, for they are not green, but of white painted wood, elegantly trellised and as pretty garden benches from which to watch a game of bowls as can be imagined. Miraculously, they are still there. Worthily dominating this wide green space is a noble piece of sculpture in stone, by Peter Scheemakers (born 1691), of a lion attacking a horse, of which the original is in the Capitoline Museum in Rome. This part of the garden at Rousham was being worked on in 1738, when the old terraces were being re-sculpted. Contemporary records tell of the enthusiasm for the improvements to the gardens of the clerk of the works, Mr White: '. . . upward of seventy hands have been employed. The slope will this evening be turfed . . . the banks everywhere pared. All things thereabouts appear Magnifique.'

From the bowling green the visitor bears left and comes to what Christopher Hussey in his scholarly note on the garden has described as one of Kent's 'most dramatic garden structures: the massive Arcade'. Garden historians have, and will have in future, as much cause for gratitude to Mr Hussey as that they bear to Horace Walpole, for his vivid, lively descriptions of English gardens. Of Rousham Mr Hussey goes on to say: 'One of Kent's problems was to deal with this important hinge in the lay-out in such a way that it came as a surprise on the outward tour and provided another impressive incident on the return . . .' But the arcade 'must not be discovered at once. The visitor was therefore conducted along the top of it by a balustraded terrace . . .' This arcade was nicknamed Praeneste from a likeness it bore to the terraces over an arcade at the Temple of Fortune at Palestrina near Rome, which Kent may have taken as his model.

On the outward journey, did we not note that there was a right and wrong way to tour the garden at Rousham? the visitor sees first a balustraded terrace, with a fine statue, also by Scheemakers, in stone of the Dying Gladiator, commanding a wide view to the north towards the Cherwell and its watermeadows beyond. The important architectural complex of the arcade – below his feet – remains for the moment unsuspected. The tour goes on, and soon the visitor gains Venus' Vale. This, when Kent found it, was a series of ponds, shaded by thick trees and probably unpromising and dank enough. Hey presto, and suddenly the attractive upper and lower cascades were conjured, with the arch of the upper one surmounted by a statue of Venus and the basin decorated with groups of cupids riding swans in lead. The lower cascade is simpler and without statuary. Between the two cascades lies the great pond, and around stand statues, also of lead, which came from the same workshop as those we admire at Powis: Jan Van Nost's, who had a workshop at Hyde Park Corner in the reign of William III. These lead statues are dated 1701, so may well have been originally placed in the earlier, more formal garden at Rousham.

From the lower cascade, along an avenue of limes, there is a distant view of a statue of Apollo, named in the Rousham records as Colossus, and as we approach between the tree-canopied glades which lie to left and right of the lime walk, we pass, on the left, the Cold Bath, with its eight-sided pool of inky water. On Apollo's left hand, beneath a towering cedar and in a plantation of conifers – were they supposed to re-create the cypresses of Tivoli? – stands another in the series of enchanting buildings which decorate the grounds of Rousham: a temple, called rather unromantically Townsend's building. This elegant little Doric structure, with its classic columns and portico, is said to have been the work of William Townsend, the Oxford architect, and though he may have had a hand in the mechanics of its actual building, the design and siting is typically Kent's.

Before returning to the house, two more *fabriques* must be noticed. First, the Temple of the Mill. A distant view of this is obtained from the portico of Townsend's building, beyond the Cherwell river, and closer inspection reveals it as originally a simple mill, promoted and romanticized complete with flying buttresses, ogee window and pinnacles of rusticated stone. As if this was not enough, another 'eye-catcher', this time an entirely artificial ruin, was built under Kent's direction, on a further slope, to close the vista in the fashionable way.

From Townsend's building, we retrace our way by the lime walk and as we near the house the full ingenuity of the placing of Praeneste is made clear. Passing the lower cascade on our right, we mount the slope, and come obliquely upon the arcade. Within, alcoved seats invite one to relax and enjoy the view across the Oxfordshire fields that is framed in its massive arches. It is the moment to brood on the genius of Kent, and record one's gratitude that this extraordinary garden survives, painstakingly maintained for our delectation by the present owner, Mr Thomas Cottrell-Dormer.

Christopher Hussey has written:

Kent made his reputation by managing to transform the theoretical 'garden of idea' into pictorial landscape. He was painter enough to see that garden and park design, however linked with a theoretical ideal, was essentially a visual business: there must be principles of composition, light and shade, colour, to give shape to the philosopher's dream.

The philosopher's dream – whatever feelings Horace Walpole had had before about Kent's work, Rousham 're-instated' him with him, and he wrote to George Montagu in 1760: 'The garden is Daphne in little; the sweetest little groves, streams, glades, porticos, cascades, and river imaginable. All the scenes are perfectly classic', in short, 'Kentissimo'.

A gate of airy ironwork invites the visitor to Rousham to leave Kent's Arcady for the comparative formality of a straight garden path between herbaceous borders

Exbury

The parent-garden of a famous azalea

Exbury, framed in the red leafy sprays of a Japanese maple, with a soaring cedar to the right

opposite Rhododendron yakusimanum—described as 'the most beautiful rhododendron species of them all'— was recently found growing wild on an island in Japan. Its pink flowers open to white and the plant, with its compact habit, is one of rare distinction

Exbury is the most famous rhododendron garden in England. The Exbury strain of azalea has spread the fame of the garden of its origin far and wide, as *Eucryphia nymansay* has done for the Sussex garden of Nymans, and a spectacular hypericum hybrid has done for Rowallane in Ulster, two other great gardens shown in this book.

And yet, for all its pre-eminence, Exbury is a very much younger garden than either of the other two. It was only in 1922 that the late Mr Lionel de Rothschild began planting rhododendrons there in earnest.

The estate prior to its purchase by Mr de Rothschild had belonged to Lord Forster. There was a garden of two or three acres near the house (which was soon to be largely rebuilt) but it was overgrown and neglected, and contained little planting of any interest, save for a few magnificent cedars, as fine and as old as any in England. The area now covered with the famous rhododendron plantations was, in those days, nothing but rough coppice and woodland and its soil was poor, though of a gravelly acid loam which is just the right soil for rhododendrons. And, of course, Exbury had the perfect climate for the plants for which it was soon to become so well known. It has much the same almost frost-free climate as nearby Pylewell, elsewhere described in this book – soft and temperate, with a general temperature several degrees higher than that found in Hampshire only a few miles inland. All rhododendrons, save a few from the tropics, will grow happily at Exbury. Before many years had passed, the collection that Lionel de Rothschild assembled there was taking on impressive proportions, so that today every informed gardener knows that the collection of rhododendrons and azaleas at Exbury is as comprehensive as any in the country. Under the green canopy of its cedars or in the dappled sunshine of its glades, are to be found rhododendrons of every description, rhododendrons like the great sino-grande; falconeri, with leaves that are underfelted with golden fur; campylocarpum, with yellow flowers; the blue flowered augustinii; the red, pink and white

Ferns and the feathery wine-red foliage of *Acer japonica* complement each other along a rocky path

flowered arboreum; orbiculare, which has leaves that are round; or the most rare and delicate concatenans, which has leaves that smell of incense.

The first rhododendron which is recognizable as such to be imported into England and to become an established, too well established, plant of English gardens and woods, was the *Rhododendron ponticum*. This was discovered growing in the wild in southern Spain near Gibraltar by the Swedish botanist Baron Clas Alstroemer, and reached the British colony of Gibraltar about 1763. Alstroemer was a friend and gardening colleague of the celebrated Linnaeus, who gave his name to the alstroemeria. *Rhododendron ponticum* is too well known to need any description; in some parts of England and Scotland it has almost become a weed, and of course to the connoisseur it is a plant to be treated with mild disdain. But it has its qualities – it is useful as a stock on which to graft more delicate varieties, and it transmits its astonishing vitality to all its scions.

It was in the early nineteenth century that the flow of rhododendrons into England really started. They came from all over the world, because, except for Africa and South America, rhododendrons are native to every continent. Most experts agree that two of the most important plants to be introduced into England after *R. ponticum* were the tall *Rhododendron arboreum*, the first of the great Himalayan rhododendrons to reach England, and *Rhododendron caucasicum* from Azerbaijan on the shores of the Caspian.

From *R. arboreum* most of our red and pink hybrids are descended, and *R. caucasium* has bequeathed its hardy Russian blood to many of the lower growing, neater plants which are so popular in the smaller gardens of today.

Another important arrival at about this time came from across the Atlantic where the well-known Chelsea nurseryman and botanist John Fraser (1750–1811) had been sent on a plant-collecting expedition by the 'Mad' Emperor Paul of Russia. This was *Rhododendron catawbiense*, which Fraser found growing in the south-eastern United States, where it made such dense thickets that the traveller could 'only make his way by following old bear tracks'. *R. catawbiense* was not a particularly beautiful plant, and its flowers were not unlike those of the despised ponticum, but it had great qualities as a sire which it was able to pass on to all its descendants, a comfortable rotund habit of growth and, above all, complete hardiness.

These, then, were three of the earliest rhododendrons to be imported into England, and, as we have seen, they came from Spain, the Caucasus and America. Many of the splendid hybrids that grow in the garden at Exbury, and in gardens all over the world, one hundred and fifty years later, are descendants of these early rhododendrons.

With the succession of great expeditions following that of Sir Joseph Hooker in 1849 – those led by Wilson, Ludlow, and Sherriff – hundreds more rhododendrons were discovered growing in the wild. Seeds and plants were sent home, to be used by eager and painstaking hybridists to produce more and more beautiful plants. But two strains in particular were to find their way to Exbury, soon to be so celebrated in the world of rhododendron growers, to be crossed there and to produce a strain of rhododendron which was to make the fame of the garden on the Solent. These were *Rhododendron campylocarpum*, parent of most of the yellow-flowered hybrids, and the more generously flowered, taller *Rhododendron discolor* of the grey-green leaves. The result of this cross was a rhododendron which Lionel de Rothschild called after a friend of his, Lady Bessborough. Lady Bessborough, child of the garden at Exbury, first flowered in 1933 and was in due course crossed with another rhododendron of clear yellow, *Rhododendron wardii* (called after one of the last and greatest plant collectors, Kingdon-Ward), to become the parents of the impressive Hawk hybrids, which rank amongst some of the best yellow rhododendrons in cultivation.

Another product of the Exbury garden, and result of the important work of hybridization that went on there thirty-five years ago under Lionel de Rothschild's direction, was the beautiful and still rare Lady Chamberlain. This too was called after a personal friend of Mr de Rothschild, the wife of Sir Austen Chamberlain. It is a lovely, most graceful plant, and a child of the glaucous leaved *R. cinnebarinum*, collected by Sir Joseph Hooker in Sikkim, and the hybrid Royal Flush, from which it inherits its tubular flowers of an uncommon apricot colour. Lady Chamberlain, to be seen at its best, must be planted in thin woodland, where the sunlight can catch and hold its curious, most attractive flowers. It is one of the writer's favourites of all varieties of rhododendrons.

Another strain of plants raised by Mr Lionel de Rothschild, which has made the name of Exbury resound in the world of horticulture, is the Exbury strain of azaleas. The breeding of these was first started forty years ago by the well-known hybridist and nurseryman Anthony Waterer at his nursery at Knaphill. The parent plants were the ordinary *Azalea mollis* and the orange *Azalea calendulaceum* – the burning 'Sky Paint Flower' of the Cherokee Indians, and the grandparents *Azalea occidentale*, which contributed its strong scent, and *Azalea arborescens*. The Exbury azaleas flower in May and June, and with their delicious scent, spreading habit of growth and large well-shaped flowers are among the loveliest of the shrubs of early summer.

But to return to Exbury. Lionel de Rothschild died in 1942, in the middle of the war, difficult days for gardening. Exbury house was occupied by the Admiralty, and its great plantation had, therefore, to undergo neglect. Many of the finest specimens there were choked and died; and yet today, twenty-five years later, so well do rhododendrons grow in the gentle climate of the shores of the Solent that the gaps have been more than made up and yearly thinning is necessary. From April onwards the garden presents scenes of the greatest beauty. It is difficult to choose one particular moment when they are at their peak. One of the loveliest moments is perhaps when the magnificent Red Admiral

The garden at Exbury is in woodland watered by streams. *above* A bridge of wood, canopied with chestnut leaves; *Osmunda regalis*, the royal fern, grows in the foreground

below A bridge of rustic stone, with white azaleas

The gnarled and twisted trees of the woods of Exbury provide shade and shelter for younger, rarer plants

One of the many exotic rhododendrons in the garden is the yellow-flowered Rhododendron Fortune, a cross between falconeri and sino-grande

flowers in March, one of the earliest, and lights up the shade of the home wood, not far from the golden brightness of *Rhododendron lutescens* – or perhaps it is the following month, when the glade planted with the blue *Rhododendron augustinii* and the yellow *Rhododendron campylocarpum* are in flower, growing in wide drifts under the high canopy of the Scots pines, with daffodils everywhere echoing the yellow tints of the *campylocarpum*. In May, Exbury's own azaleas come into bloom, and edge one side of the lake with colour, planted in company with the shining leaved *Griselinia littoralis*. In the centre of the lake is an 'island' upon which grows *Taxodium distichum*, the Swamp Cypress of the southern United States, a tree which revels in just that situation.

In 1950 it was decided by Mr Edmund de Rothschild, who had inherited Exbury eight years before, to run the estate commercially, and the talented and enterprising Mr Peter Barber was put in charge of the venture. The project prospered. Exbury's reputation as a garden grew. It was already well known for the quality of the plants, and could boast more awards for rhododendrons and azaleas than any other garden in England. Soon the estate was exporting hundreds of rhododendrons a week. The magnificent hybrids raised there found their way all over the world. Exbury became a name to conjure with.

The author asked Mr Barber, and he knows his plants like he knows his children, which, in his own opinion, was the best group of plants to be seen at Exbury. After a pause for consideration, for there was so much to choose from, the answer was the planting of the rose pink flowered hardy rhododendron Naomi near the bridge, which has won an Award of Merit for its profuse flowering and was, in Mr Barber's opinion, 'perhaps the best all-round hybrid for the general garden produced at Exbury'. Naomi's clones include the excellent award-winning Stella Maris, FCC and Nautilus, AM. Next Mr Barber named a hybrid of *Rhododendron falconeri* and sino-grande, rhododendron Fortune FCC which is hardier than both its parents, with larger flowers and a better-formed truss, and an example, which occurs often with rhododendrons and azaleas, though rarely with other plants, of a hybrid being better in every characteristic than either of its parents. Another plant which was singled out for special praise was rhododendron Crest FCC (Hawk), which grows near what has been described as the most beautiful rhododendron species of them all, *Rhododendron yakusimanum*, shown opposite page 194.

Some rhododendrons have been singled out for special mention in these notes on Exbury, because Exbury, of all gardens, is famous for its rhododendrons. But, of course, there are many other fine plants there, not in such quantity perhaps, but which more than deserve special mention. A magnificent *Picea breweriana*, for instance, noted elsewhere in this book, and considered by some to be the most beautiful of all conifers; there are tall specimens of the rare *Magnolia campbellii*, groves of Japanese maples with their leaves of winy purple which make such a perfect foil for other flowers, and the splendid cedars near the house, which have stood at Exbury since the reign of James I.

opposite The brilliant colour of the Exbury strain of evergreen azalea Bengal Fire, set off by the paler cream of Rhododendron A. Gilbert beyond

Mount Stewart

A garden which benefits from the Gulf Stream

Mount Stewart has a very wonderful garden, beautifully and interestingly planted. It is laid out not only with wisdom and knowledge but with wit as well, an unusual quality in gardening. The fame of the garden stems from its ownership for two hundred years by the celebrated Londonderry family of which Mairi, Lady Bury is a daughter.

The first of her family to live on the estate, as noted by that dedicated diarist and writer of unreadably dull travel books, Bishop Richard Pococke (1704–65) was, in 1752, 'one Mr Stewart', a descendant of John Stewart who had emigrated to Ulster from Scotland – had been 'planted' in fact, about 1630. Records tell that he lived at Ballylawn, Co. Donegal. And it was a most successful plantation. The Stewart family prospered. By a series of successful marriages they quickly gained riches and influence, and by the last half of the eighteenth century they were building their fine house at Mount Stewart. 'Athenian' Stuart (1713–88) has been suggested as the architect.

The house is built of the local brown stone with dressings of lighter stone, and its long, rather low, façade on the north side centres on an imposing four-pillared portico built by the third Marquis of Londonderry about 1825. 'One, Mr Stewart's' family had certainly gone up in the world; his son, Robert, Tory MP for Co. Down, having quickly become Baron Londonderry in 1795, Viscount Castlereagh (the name derived from the ancient Castle Royal of the O'Neill family), then Earl and finally Marquis of Londonderry in 1816. His eldest son was the famous Lord Castlereagh of the Congress of Vienna, and one of Europe's most distinguished statesmen. It is from his second son, Charles, that the seventh Marquis descended, whose wife Edith, also known as Circe, and with good reason as we shall see, created the present gardens of Mount Stewart.

Edith, Marchioness of Londonderry, mother of the present owner of Mount Stewart – Mairi, Lady Bury – was a charmer, a political seductress who turned Socialists into Conservatives, and at the same time a green-fingered Circe who conjured one of the

The garden at Mount Stewart 'is decorated with figures and fantasies in stone'

opposite Primulas, azaleas and banked rhododendrons fill the eye with colour in early spring

Topiary at its most intricate: one of the galloping figures which surmount a clipped hedge at Mount Stewart

Clianthus puniceus, the curious Lobster Claw plant, bright red, with feathery foliage, only grows in a few very sheltered gardens

most fascinating and beautiful gardens in Britain.

When Lady Londonderry first came as a bride to Mount Stewart there was little garden round the eighteenth-century house – like many places of that period there was only a large walled garden nearly a mile away. Lawns surrounded the house, running right up to the large Georgian windows, and these were darkened by a too-close grove of immense ilexes. Some of these, with regret, Lady Londonderry cut down.

After the 1914–18 war there was unemployment in Ulster, and landowners were encouraged to take on demobilized soldiers as extra labour. Twenty came to Mount Stewart, and with their aid, Lady Londonderry set about creating the gardens as they exist today. To the south a formal garden of terraces and fountains was laid out, to the west a sunk garden, and all round, in the surrounding woodland, paths were cut, steps were laid and the ground was prepared for the rhododendrons, eucryphias and embothriums for which the garden at Mount Stewart was soon to become well known.

The south garden was, and still is, decorated with figures and fantasies in stone – carved by an *employé* of the Mount Stewart estate, who if not an actual rival of Ferdinand Dietz, sculptor of the inimitably humorous garden statues at Veitshöcheim in Germany, displayed a jovial turn of invention which invites comparison. The figures at Mount Stewart are a series of portraits of Lady Londonderry's friends – all members of the 'Ark Association' over which Lady Londonderry used to preside. But as she was not nicknamed Circe for nothing, they are all portrayed as animals. Of the Ark Association, which was formed in the dark days of the first world war, Lady Londonderry once wrote:

We used to meet every Wednesday at Londonderry House, for relaxation and refreshment. Members comprised Cabinet Ministers, King's Messengers, ladies of low and high degree, soldiers, sailors, tinkers and tailors. All were given the names of birds and beasts, and were always referred to by these names at 'Ark' meetings. For instance Lord Halifax (Edward Wood) was known as Edward the Woodpecker; Lord Templewood, a great skater, was Sam the Skate; and Lady Astor, Nancy the Gnat. As hostess to all these 'creatures', I was given the name of Circe the Sorceress.

The Ark Association comprised many of the most influential figures in political life till the early 1920s, and in its time wielded considerable power. Their 'portraits', in stone, still stand in the garden at Mount Stewart, reminders of a more privileged, aristocratic age.

Circe could not only transform politicians into penguins and generals into water-rats, but also the wild wooded surroundings of her house into the most civilized of pleasure grounds. It is in the sunk gardens to the west of the house that the visitor to Mount Stewart first comes on some of the rare plants which Lady Londonderry collected, and which in the last forty years have all grown into magnificent specimens. The garden lies on two levels and on the stone pillars which support the pergola surrounding

opposite An Irish Harp in close-cut yew in the Shamrock Garden, enclosed in high hedges of *Cupressus macrocarpa*. Set in the paving is the Bloody Hand of Ulster planted with low-growing *Iresine herbstii*, of which the foliage is red throughout the summer

Palms of every kind revel in the favourable climate of Mount Stewart. Here they grow by a sunlit path leading to high arches of clipped *Cupressus macrocarpa*

One of the most spectacular plants growing by the waterside is the giant-leaved *Gunnera manicata* from Brazil

the garden grow the white-starred *Clematis indivisa*, above the tender tree poppy, *Dendromecon rigidum*.

Below, in a flowery hedge of low-growing shrubby planting, are the purple spotted *Calceolaria violacea* from Chile, spicy-leaved shrubby salvias such as the red-flowered *S. greigii*, as well as the sky-blue *pitcheri*, together with fuchsias, the scarlet Mitre Flower, *Mitraria coccinea* and the brilliant blue-flowered Corsican rosemary.

Nearby is another garden, enclosed in a high hedge. This shows, as do the stone figures in the Italian garden, further evidence of the wit which animates some parts of the garden at Mount Stewart. For it is shaped like a giant shamrock, and has for centrepiece a towering yew tree carefully cut into the shape of an Irish harp. Round the top of the surrounding hedge of *Cupressus macrocarpa* is clipped a fox hunt in full cry. It is topiary in the tradition of Levens or the chessmen at Haseley Court. Cut into the paving is a 'Bloody hand' of Ulster, which is always suitably planted with red flowers.

What is most impressive about the garden at Mount Stewart is the speed with which everything has grown. The gardens were first planted in 1920, but many of the trees and shrubs, thanks to the gentle maritime climate, already look a hundred years old or more. And thanks to this, the woodland around Mount Stewart offered the perfect terrain for wild gardening, on the scale of Exbury and Logan. Lady Londonderry has described how she was first introduced to this most specialized but rewarding form of horticulture:

When I began gardening here, my two mentors were the late Sir John Ross of Bladenburg, and Sir Herbert Maxwell of Monreith, in Wigtownshire. These two opened my eyes to the possibilities of gardening in what is called a 'favourable' climate. Never shall I forget my first visit to Sir John Ross's famous garden at Rostrevor. He called it Fairyland, and he was perfectly justified; on all sides grew rare and most exquisite plants. In my ignorance, I exclaimed: 'This is like Kew Gardens.' Sir John stopped dead in his tracks and said, 'Dear Lady, never mention Kew to me again, I grow things here that Kew has probably never heard of!' This was how my initiation began into a form of gardening which I had never dreamed existed.

A few more of the rarities which grow at Mount Stewart are worth special mention – the Chilean tree *Guevina avellana*, for instance, certainly not hardy at Kew; many embothriums, also from Chile; a twenty-foot high *Ceanothus arboreus* which scents the air all round in spring when its pale blue flowers are out; Banksian roses – both yellow and white – grow on the house walls up to the eaves. and fill the rooms indoors with scent; the Senna tree, *Cassia corymbosa*, all too rare in British gardens, with its yellow flowers; the sweet scented white *Mandevilla suaveolens* (or *laxa*) which flowers roof-high and weaves itself in and out of the odd-looking Lobster Claw plant *Clianthus puniceus* which only grows in a few very sheltered gardens.

At Mount Stewart, the winters are so mild that geraniums from the Cape can be wintered out of doors, and echiums, of

which seed was obtained from Tresco, a famous garden in the Scilly Isles, hundreds of miles to the south. There are cestrums and eucalyptus and a pair of *Erica arborea* said to be the largest in Great Britain. These are two of the few rare plants growing at Mount Stewart before Lady Londonderry developed the garden, and must be a century old. They are still in full vigour and on warm spring days fill the air all around with their honey-laden breath. Some weeks before she died Lady Londonderry repeated to the author of this book a remark made to her by her old gardener, as they walked together under arching rhododendrons, many of which they had grown from seed collected by Forrest and Kingdon-Ward. 'We must give up going round the rhododendrons, my lady, they date us too much.'

The gardens of Mount Stewart, under the able direction of Mairi, Lady Bury, are open to the public for many days every summer. The shilling or two they pay purchases endless treats. Snow seldom falls at Mount Stewart and hard frosts are virtually unknown, so even in March, when English gardens are still asleep, there are flowers on every hand, and delicious scents, stirred by the breezes from the nearby Strangford Lough.

Below the southern façade of the house lies a formal paved garden with a pool and lofty hedges

overleaf Two very different styles of garden architecture at Mount Stewart *left* The humorous sculpture by Thomas Beattie of Newtownards, with the Ark of the Ark Association, which was set up forty years ago *right* The cold classicism of James 'Athenian' Stuart's Temple of the Winds, built at the end of the eighteenth century

Wigtownshire

Lochinch

A garden on the grandest scale

John Dalrymple, Earl of Stair – a diplomatist, field-marshal and great gardener – is said to have been one of the first landowners to advocate the growing of turnips as a crop

opposite The garden at Lochinch, like the garden at nearby Logan, benefits from the Gulf Stream, which washes the shores of Wigtownshire. Palms thrive in its gentle climate

Lochinch, in Wigtownshire, like nearby Logan, enjoys the Gulf Stream's beneficient influence. Lochinch is situated on the narrow neck of the land which separates Lochryan and the Bay of Luce. The story of the garden of Lochinch really starts with the accession to the title of John Dalrymple, second Earl of Stair (1679–1747). This delightfully clever and civilized Scotsman, after a meteoric career – an officer's commission when he was thirteen, and active service in the field at Steenkerk the same year – became aide-de-camp to the Duke of Marlborough when he was twenty-six. By the time he was thirty he was Ambassador in Paris, and was only recalled from there in 1720 owing to his inability to see eye to eye with a fellow-Scot, the Regent Orleans' Finance Minister, John Law.

In this, Lord Stair was proved right, for Law was disgraced for sharp practice in 1720 and exiled from France. When Lord Stair returned to his native Scotland, he interested himself in agriculture, and it is said he was the first landowner to advocate the growing of turnips as a crop. These, however popular they became in Scotland as a food, never found favour in the south. Was it not Johnson who said, 'In Scotland men eat turnips, in England they are only food for horses'? Whereupon the answer came, 'And where else do you see such horses, . . . and where else do you see such men?'

Lord Stair's turnip-growing period was short-lived – he was a favourite of the Hanoverians who did not leave him long in retirement. He was soon offered the post of Lord High Admiral of Scotland, and he shortly after received a Field-Marshal's baton, and a series of other important appointments. But by 1733 he was out of public life once more, and quite happy, it seems, to settle down on his estates in Wigtownshire and take to landscape gardening and 'place-making' on the largest scale.

It was the second Earl who planted many of the magnificent stands of trees which now dress the landscape round Lochinch. Accounts for consignments of beech trees survive to this day, and though he planted trees for beauty, certainly he also planted

Much of the garden at Lochinch lies round the ruins of the ancient Castle Kennedy, the medieval residence of the Earls of Cassilis

A feature of the gardens in late summer are the many flowers of an avenue of eucryphias

them for protection, knowing that though the Gulf Stream warms the sea round the west coast of Scotland, and lessens to a great degree the onslaught of frost, it is powerless to stay the wind which blows over the Black and White Lochs as keenly as anywhere. It is these plantations – now two hundred years old – which so well protect the rare and tender trees and shrubs which make the beauty and interest of Lochinch garden today.

But Lord Stair did not only plant trees. He used the soldiers and horses of the Royal Scots Greys and the Inniskilling Fusiliers, then stationed under his command nearby, to sculot – no other word is adequate – the impressive series of turf terraces which today are such a feature of the policies of Lochinch. The soldiery were in Wigtownshire to hunt down Jacobites, but Lord Stair, who had seen and admired the great gardens at Versailles, considered that they would be far better employed making him a new garden in the French style. And it was his fancy to devise garden features for it which recalled his distinguished military career – such as Mount Marlborough, and Dettingen avenue.

After the death of the second Earl of Stair, Castle Kennedy and its domains passed through changing times. The lame seventh Earl, who was known as Hobbling Jack, let his great estate fall into decay, felling many of the trees and allowing the famous terraces to become overgrown with whins and gorse. It was not until the succession of the tenth Earl, the present Lord Stair's great-grandfather, that the place was taken in hand. The old castle having fallen into almost complete decay, a new house, in the Scottish baronial style, was built a mile away on rising land, with its own flower garden and elaborate parterre. But it was the ruin of the old castle which was made the centre point of a complex of newly-planted avenues and vistas, each planted with a different species of conifer imported from North America. Two of these deserve special mention – one, which was called 'the blue avenue' by the great arboriculturist Sir Joseph Hooker, is planted with the frosty-leaved *Abies nobilis*. Another is planted on either side with Monkey Puzzles, *Araucaria imbricata*, a tree so often seen languishing in suburban gardens. When planted in company with British natives such as beech or birch, Monkey Puzzles look egregious and out of place. But it can, as visitors to the great Irish garden of Powerscourt will confirm, make a splendid avenue.

It succeeds nowhere better than at Lochinch, and being a tree of the mountains (its native habitat is the foothills of Chile) asks only for sharp drainage and a cool root-run to thrive. Recently the araucaria avenue at Lochinch has been trimmed and tailored and now presents a very magnificent appearance indeed. There are other impressive tree-plantings at Lochinch, especially of Norway spruce, and the Dettingen avenue, which runs from the old castle gardens to the White Loch, is especially fine, with its impressive ilexes, and inner avenue of alternate embothrium and *Eucryphia glutinosa*.

But to the gardener the greatest interest of the gardens at Lochinch is the lavish plantings of rhododendrons, including

A circular lily pond, planted all round with rhododendrons, azaleas and rare trees

several hybrids first raised at Lochinch, and many fine specimens of *Rhododendron arboreum* over a hundred years old, grown from seed brought back by Hooker from Himalayan expeditions. These rhododendrons, with azaleas, embothriums and magnolias, present a magnificent spectacle in early summer, and seldom can such well-grown, well-chosen plants have been grown in such a splendid setting.

Of the garden at Lochinch Sir Herbert Maxwell wrote nearly seventy years ago,

The dominant idea, the sense which pervades the whole, is that of size and atmosphere. There are broad stretches of the wood-girdled and reed-bordered lochs : there are fine hill prospects. . . Nothing small, nothing petty or miniature, could be introduced into a natural scene of which spaciousness was the governing factor and chiefest charm.

One of the loveliest rhododendrons in the garden of Lochinch in spring is Loder's White

Middlesex
Hampton Court
The garden for a royal palace

The warmest admirer of the English garden must admit one thing. There are few formal gardens in England which can be compared with the great formal gardens of France. There is no real rival to Versailles or Vaux le Vicomte. In fact, unlike Germany and Spain, there are no gardens that were modelled on the vast creations of Andre Le Nôtre and his school. None, except perhaps Hampton Court.

Conditions in England were so utterly different from those on the continent. There, gardens were the pleasure grounds of kings. When the parterres at Versailles were being planned there was no king in England, and Cromwell did not favour such status symbols of monarchic power. Perhaps he felt that his position was too insecure.

Even after the Restoration, his royal successor, Charles II, the solar Louis' pensioner, must have longed to copy the Great King, his cousin, but he just did not have the money to do so. In 1685, the year the Orangerie at Versailles was completed, James II succeeded to the throne of England, and he was not sure how long he would be king, and was, in fact, deposed three years later.

It was Dutch William and his Mary, securely throned, who created Hampton Court and its garden as we know it today – a royal garden, planned on the grandest lines, which has survived through the years for all to visit and enjoy. But the story of the gardens at Hampton Court, though it reaches its climax in the reign of William and Mary, began 150 years earlier.

It starts, on as good a day as any, Midsummer Day, 1514, when 'Prior Docwra and the Knights Hospitaller of St John of Jerusalem' rented the Manor of Hampton for £50 a year to the 'Moost reverend Fader in God Thomas Wulcy Archbishopp of Yorke and primate of England'. The Manor stood in two thousand acres of land, which the Primate proceeded to enclose in strong brick walls, decorated every fifty yards with a design of crosses. The development of the gardens began at once, for an account exists for 1515 in *The Book of Payments* of Laurence Stubbs, a steward of Archbishop Thomas Wolsey, for various items of

Cardinal Wolsey, who rented the Manor of Hampton in 1514. His 'unbounded stomach' and pride lost him his favour with King Henry VIII

The sunk garden, with its tulips, wallflowers, fountain and conical clipped yews, lies by the junction of Wolsey's old Tudor building and William III's palace

above Hampton Court today: the river façade, showing the Privy Garden and the Knott and sunk gardens *below* Hampton Court in the time of William and Mary, showing the bow-shaped fountain garden and present Privy Garden with elaborate broderies designed in the manner of Daniel Marot (1660–1720)

garden equipment: 12d for two iron rakes, reasonable enough, and 10d for a wheel-barrow. At the same time payments are recorded to four gardeners of two shillings each for a week's work.

Wolsey's extravagance and pride soon made Henry jealous, though the Cardinal's fall was not only brought about by his 'unbounded stomach' and his ambition, but by his opposition to the King's marriage to Anne Boleyn. In an attempt to regain Henry's favour he even presented him with his great domain of Hampton itself, but to no avail. The king would listen to no other voice than Anne's, 'all my glories in that woman I have lost for ever . . .' His garden at Hampton Court among them, so a tenuous thread of history links Hampton Court with Hever Castle, which was the scene of the start of the romance which was so disastrous to the Cardinal.

Henry VIII soon added bowling greens and 'tennis plays', as the earliest tennis courts were called, and archery butts. These covered much of the ground formerly taken up with the Cardinal's gardens, and to replace these he laid out new pleasure grounds. A rose garden was planted, to supply roses for his new queen, his 'Awne Darling', for a while, Anne Boleyn, and an orchard was planted, and a herb garden. By 1533 the King's new garden was complete, and filled the piece of ground now taken up by the present privy garden.

There was a mound, with a summer house on top of some elaboration: it had three storeys with a copper cupola and weather vane. From the glazed windows there were views over the nearby Thames and the gardens, which by this time were embellished not only with flowers, but with those Tudor conceits, the Kinges Beastes. These were a series of heraldic animals such as the Black Bull of Clarence, the Griffon of Edward III, and the curiously horned and toothed Yale of Beaufort, painted in brilliant colours. Perched on green and white poles, they were a favourite decoration for many years, and must have presented a gay, if slightly garish, sight with their shields displaying the arms of the King and Queen – though the colour they supplied was probably a welcome supplement to the generally muted colours of the Tudor garden scene, and their bright tints must have stood out bravely against the sombre shades of yew and holly.

In 1533 Henry and Anne were married. Improvements and additions to the garden at Hampton Court went on. Four hundred more roses were bought at 2d. for fifty, but the new Queen, triumphant during her short reign, never saw them grow to maturity. In 1536 she was imprisoned in the Tower (how far away her carefree days in the garden at Hever must have seemed) and soon after she was executed. Her badge, a falcon, disappeared from Hampton Court. The falcon had soared too high.

Henry, fat, diseased and prematurely old, died in 1547, and the second chapter of Hampton Court's history came to an end.

All the Tudors loved their palace on the river. The boy Edward VI preferred it to Windsor, Mary passed some time there quietly with her Spanish husband Philip, and died there in 1558. Elizabeth gave audiences in its trellised arbours and, in the intervals of ruling the country better than it had been ruled for centuries, interested herself in the garden. During her reign many new additions in the way of plants made their appearance in the garden, sent home by the Queen's ambassadors, or brought from the four quarters of the globe by her far-adventuring sea captains. These included 'Blew Pipe, the later physicians do name Lilach'.

The Stuarts, too, spent much time at Hampton Court. James I enjoyed the hunting, until it was spoiled for him by the intrusion of what he called 'vulgar people'. James never had Elizabeth's magic touch with his subjects. But during his reign the gardens were well cared for, and in her excellent book *The Gardens of Hampton Court*, which the author has found a mine of information, Miss Mollie Sands has quoted an account submitted by George Hopton, Esq., for extensive work done in the garden in the year 1614. The account shows that the Knotts were still being maintained, peaches and apricots were being planted and earth was being renewed and manured to as great an extent as ever.

Charles I succeeded his unloved father in 1625, and soon, for he was artistic and more interested in improving his palace and garden, than in governing the country, set about embellishing the garden at Hampton Court. In his plans, water for the first time in English garden planning played an important part.

A path near the Privy Garden lined on both sides by ancient pollarded lime-trees

Two of the 'Kinges Beastes' by the entrance to the Tudor palace. They were a favourite form of decoration in Henry VIII's garden

opposite 'Most dramatic of all the changes brought about by William was the partial demolition of Wolsey's palace and its replacement by a magnificent new building by Sir Christopher Wren'

Fountains had always been popular features in gardens, but Hampton Court was the first garden in England in which there was to be a large decorative *pièce d'eau*; canals in the French manner were to come later, but meanwhile more water was needed at Hampton Court, 'for the better accomadation of the Palace and the recreation and disport of His Majesty'. The waters of the river Colne were brought to Hampton Court by means of a canal eleven miles long – a most unpopular move as it caused flooding, spoiling crops and pasture on its way.

Statues were the new fashion borrowed from Italy for Stuart gardens and sophisticated gods and goddesses were gradually replacing the crude and somewhat childish 'beastes' of the Tudors. The Yale of Beaufort gave way to Diana and the Greyhound of Richmond to Ganymede. The days of Le Nôtre and the great Gardens of the Intellect were not far off.

The gardens must have been an attractive sight in the days of Charles I and Henrietta Maria, with the silken throng of courtiers and their women folk walking in the alleys, dipping their long Vandyke fingers into the fountains, admiring the new statues, particularly one of Cleopatra; but quite soon their bright day, like hers, was done and they, too, would be 'for the dark'. Between the final tragedy and the end of the first Civil War, there were several incidents in Hampton Court's history, such as when the King was there as a prisoner and was to be seen in conversation with that great gardener John Evelyn, who lived nearby at Sayes Court. A more remarkable conversation also took place at this period when Oliver Cromwell, still friendly and deferential, could be seen pacing the gravel walks in company with the short, stuttering, but immensely dignified figure who was still his King.

Charles' last walk through his gardens took place soon after, on a cold November night when he was on his way to short-lived freedom, before the final scene on the scaffold.

Cromwell passed much time at Hampton Court, but during his tenancy there were few additions to the garden. The right of way across the Harewarren was enclosed, because it interfered with the Lord Protector's hunting, which was an unpopular, undemocratic move, but little else was changed. Cromwell was surely too occupied with the affairs of state to care about flowers, and gone were the days when it was 'his highest plot, to plant the bergamot'.

The Restoration, however, saw great changes to the garden. Charles II in exile had seen and admired some of the great gardens then being laid out in France. He was certainly told much about them by his sister Minette, who was married to Louis XIV's brother. And, though he hardly had the money or power to do so, he soon was trying to copy his brother-in-law, and the work done for him by the great Le Nôtre at Versailles.

In spite of statements to the contrary, Le Nôtre never came to England – though his plans and designs almost certainly did. And these designs had great influence on English garden planning. The enclosed intimate Tudor and Stuart gardens suddenly seemed poor and cramped. For Le Nôtre the horizon was

the only boundary he recognized for a king's garden. Such gardens were unheard of in an England impoverished by the Civil War; furthermore there just was not room, let alone the money, to make them. But the idea was born, and the first garden to reflect it was the garden at Hampton Court.

Charles' gardener was John Rose, a pupil of Le Nôtre. Between them they devised the canal which still runs from the centre of the east façade. This new canal was lined with lime-trees, brought from Holland, and there were more avenues of lime-trees radiating from the palace *en patte d'oie*. The gardens were beginning to take on the general plan as we see it today. That devoted Royalist John Evelyn returned to Hampton Court after a discreet sojourn on the Continent during the Commonwealth, and much admired the changes: 'The Park, formerly a naked piece of ground, now planted with sweet lime-trees'. He was full of praise for the perplexed twining of the pleaching in the privy gardens, which was the framework of what was going to be Queen Mary's bower.

Once more the gardens must have presented a gay appearance, with ladies such as Lely painted and their lovers walking in it, and making the most of what the visiting Duke of Tuscany describes as 'snug places of retirement, in certain towers'.

Charles was not only popular with the ladies, but also with the people round Hampton, for he gave orders that the right of way over the Harewarren should be reopened.

James II played little part in the story of Hampton Court, but his son-in-law William of Orange transformed the palace and made more great changes to the gardens. During his reign the Maze was planted, the long and broad walks were laid out, the great Fountain Garden was designed below the east façade of the palace, to make room for which the end of Charles' canal had to be filled in. The Great Fountain Garden, still one of the most spectacular parts of the pleasure grounds at Hampton Court, owes something to William's native Holland and something to France, with its *broderie* of box trees in an almost Baroque design of flowerbeds set with hyacinths or tulips or relying for colour on a filling of powdered brick – *brique pilée*, such as Le Nôtre used in his great creation at Vaux le Vicomte.

Orange trees, new introductions and suddenly popular because of their name, stood about in the then fashionable blue and white 'vauses', and were stored for the winter in Queen Mary's new Orangery. Mary took a great interest in gardening; and Switzer reports 'the active Princess' as being most knowledgeable, 'especially in exoticks'. She had a passion for 'fforeigne plants'. They were her only extravagance, but Bishop Burnett reports that she was conscience stricken that her hobby 'drew expense after it'.

Most dramatic of all the changes brought by William was the partial demolition of Wolsey's palace and its replacement by a magnificent new building by Sir Christopher Wren. But, sweeping though this transformation was, the exact position of Wren's new façade was dictated by the existing lay-out of the gardens, and he had to align his new building with Charles II's lime trees.

Two famous names, besides that of Wren, now take their place

opposite In April the sunk garden near the riverside banqueting house, relic of the Tudor palace, is bright with beds of tulips in May *above* Lilacs, known as 'Blew Pipe', were first grown at Hampton Court in the reign of Queen Elizabeth I

in the story of Hampton Court: Daniel Marot, who had designed a garden for William in Holland at Het Loo (still the palace of the Queen of Holland), and Jean Tijou. Marot was another versatile pupil of Le Nôtre; he designed not only gardens but furniture, looking glasses and flower vases of blue and white Delft china as well. Among his published designs there is an engraving entitled 'Parterre D'Amton Court Inventé par Daniel Marot' and he certainly had a hand in the design of William's new parterre, which, one can see from engravings of the time, is very much in Marot's individual style.

The other name which we must acclaim at this period is that of Jean Tijou, whose twelve grilles are still one of the great beauties of the garden. These are typical of the period of the introduction to English gardens of the *clairvoyée*, an attractive form of partition, half wall, half screen but combining the qualities and function of both. Two of Tijou's grilles remain in their original position in the Great Fountain Garden – the others were moved to the privy garden at the beginning of this century, and are still there.

The work started by William and Mary went on, after a short break following the Queen's death in 1694, when Switzer records 'gardening and all other pleasures were under an eclipse'. Had war with France not broken out in 1701 the whole of the Tudor palaces might have been lost to us. As it was, the last traces of Henry's garden disappeared, including the tiltyard, with its attractive towers; and his mound, which interrupted the view of the Thames, was swept away. The famous gardeners George London (a pupil of John Rose) and Henry Wise, whom we meet again at Blenheim, were now in complete charge, and were to be, well into the reign of Queen Anne.

Anne came often to Hampton Court, for she loved the hunting there, and we know she would drive round the park in a one-horse chariot, at furious speed. Of her interest in the garden we know only that the smell of box made her sneeze, so much of the low hedging of the parterre, which must just have been becoming established, was rooted up. '*L'odeur pénétrant des buis*' was not, apparently, for her. But Anne's association with Hampton Court has been caught for us in an amber moment by Alexander Pope in an exquisite vignette – the opening lines of the *Rape of the Lock*:

> Close by those Meads for ever crown'd with Flow'rs
> Where Thames with Pride surveys his rising Tow'rs
> There stands a Structure of Majestic Fame,
> Which from the neighb'ring Hampton takes its name.
> Here Britain's Statesmen oft the Fall foredoom
> Of foreign Tyrants, and of Nymphs at home;
> Here thou, great Anna! whom three realms obey,
> Dost sometimes Counsel take – and sometimes Tea.

George I was the dullest of rulers, and he is commemorated at Hampton Court by a walk – called the Frog Walk, after two very unattractive Fraus, Schulenburg and Kielmansegge, whom he brought from Hanover as his mistresses, and who used to take

One of the twelve elaborate grilles made by the French iron-smith Jean Tijou, who came to England in 1689. The grilles were added to the garden in the reign of William and Mary

the air, arm-in-arm, on the path by the old tiltyard wall. The gardens which had seen so many pretty faces were more attractively peopled when the palace was occupied by the Prince of Wales, Dapper George, and his clever wife Caroline, who brought with them a flock of flower-like Maids of Honour, among them Mary Bellenden and the enchanting Molly Lepell. Their laughter was to give the garden a liveliness it was not to know again.

When George became King he engaged William Kent, whose only surviving garden, Rousham, we show elsewhere in this book, and he carried out various alterations to the garden, bowing to the new taste for natural gardens, and sweeping away the already old-fashioned scroll work in the east garden, replacing it with gravel and turf. Topiary was also out of favour – and Charles Bridgeman, who had succeeded London and Wise, did away with any that was left at Hampton Court.

In 1728 Batty Langley wrote, 'The Parterre garden of His Majesty's Royal Palace of Hampton Court would have a very grand aspect were those trifling plants of Yew, Holly etc. taken away, and made plain with grass.' And away they went. But George II did the one thing which, as we have seen, was guaranteed to make the occupant of Hampton Court unpopular. The Harewarren right of way was closed again, and was only opened again, following public protest, eight years later.

George III never lived at Hampton Court but he put Lancelot Brown, whose career and achievements we examine in several other chapters of this book, in those on Blenheim and Luton Hoo in particular, in charge of the gardens. Lancelot Brown had long lived near by, and knew the gardens well. For once he treated the formal gardens, or what was left of them, with a light hand, and it is probable that he advised the planting of the great vine which is one of the sights of the garden at Hampton Court to this day, and has been ever since 1769.

George III's granddaughter, Queen Victoria, made the last great change to the gardens at Hampton Court, which had been royal and private, except to the privileged, for nearly three hundred years. She opened them to the public. It was a sensational thing to do at the time, and in the first year 120,000 people flocked to see them. Since then, of course, the character of the gardens was bound to change. They were no longer royal, except in name, and yet there is still an air of grandeur, a flavour of history about them which is at once apparent.

In the last century there have been many innovations. The herbaceous borders are particularly fine and the new Knott garden would surely have gladdened the eye of the great Lord Cardinal . . . who once upon a time, one midsummer day, nearly five hundred years ago, first rented the Manor of Hampton, and so began the story of the gardens of Hampton Court.

A sundial, bearing the entwined initials of William and Mary and possibly designed by Thomas Tompion, has 'only told of sunny hours' for over three centuries. Tompion made many of the clocks for Hampton Court

Gloucestershire
Lyegrove

A garden laid out like a Persian carpet

A 'scented path leads to a wide gateway flanked on either side by tall piers of stone'

overleaf The sunken lily pond at Lyegrove: plants grown in the warm grey stone of the Cotswolds—iris, valerian pinks and Sun Roses—are an attractive feature of the garden

'A pleasant seat in the midst of a large park', is how Sir Robert Atkyns in *The Ancient and Present State of Gloucestershire* described Lyegrove three hundred years ago in his massive history of Gloucestershire. How much pleasanter it is today, with the house enlarged and embellished, and surrounded by one of the most beautiful gardens in the country.

Lyegrove, which belongs to Diana, Countess of Westmorland, is situated in the south Cotswolds, about two miles west of Badminton. The house is seventeenth-century, but was substantially altered and enlarged in about 1820 when the south façade, which overlooks the forecourt, was given its present slightly continental look.

The gardens lie to the east of the house and are entirely the creation of Lady Westmorland, who employed the distinguished architect G. H. Kitchen. Their co-operation was extraordinarily successful and Mr Kitchen's graceful, but highly architectural lay-out of paths, steps, and gateways, all in the attractive grey, but golden-lichened, stone of the Cotswolds, has now mellowed after forty years into the happiest possible garden pattern.

The visitor to Lyegrove enters the garden by way of a broad stone path unusually planted on either side with rose bushes set in the actual paving—shrub roses such as Fantin Latour, Celestial and Duc de Guiche. This scented flowery path leads to a wide gateway flanked on either side by tall piers of stone, ball capped, which came from the now vanished Little Sodbury Manor. From this entrance most of the garden, for it is on a lower level, can be surveyed, and the author of this book can well remember the feeling of delight he experienced when first seeing the garden, fifteen years ago. Afterwards, in his enthusiasm, he described them 'like a spreading carpet with its design woven not in silk or wool, but in walls and paving, leaf and petal. As in a Shiraz or an Isphahan, its background colours are the soft rose of brickwork, and the silver grey of stone and the muted greens of turf and yew. And brighter colours, as in a carpet, are given by scattered bouquets and borders of flowers.'

above A loggia and path of orange lichened stone which seem reminiscent of
an Italian garden

opposite Old roses and tall fox-gloves (the splendid new Excelsior strain) give a
typically English look to this corner of the garden at Lyegrove

There is a strong architectural feeling about the garden, with stone and leaf in constant contrast

By a border planted with blue and white flowers is this graceful entrance, with stone pineapples amongst the delphiniums and roses

Lady Westmorland is an experienced and knowledgeable gardener and has had forty years at Lyegrove to perfect her plans and devise her colour schemes. For colour, in the setting of stone, plays an important part at Lyegrove – whether it is colour offered by flowers planted actually in the paving, a favourite form of planting of Lady Westmorland's, or in wide borders devised in subtle and individual tones. The pavement planting round the lily-pond is particularly effective, as can be seen in our pictures. Iris star the terraces in June with lilac and mauve, while their tufts of grey-green leaves are striking for most of the year. *Stachys lanata* – the homely Lamb's Ear of cottage gardens, lays its mats of silvery velvet here and there, while valerian, a plant that actually looks out of place not growing in stone-work, shows its feathery crimson or white flowers all summer through, and seeds itself freely. Blue campanulas, too, run about everywhere, and self-set foxgloves – the creamy Excelsior strains, in particular – raise their heads around.

Lady Westmorland's borders too, have great distinction. One, backed by a wall curtained in Shot Silk roses, is planted in shades of mauve, blue and white, colours which are supplied by bold clumps of anchusa, the Californian strains of delphinium and the airy flowers of the cultivated Meadow Rue *Thalictrum acquilegifolium*, with a broad swathe of aubretia followed by nepeta at their feet. Here and there in this blue border are plantings of the brilliant *Salvia patens* which, though now too seldom grown (it is an annual and demands special treatment) in the opinion of the author, offers the brightest blue of any flower. But brilliant colours at Lyegrove are always linked by a leitmotif of grey and silver foliage, a way of planting, which has long ceased to be a fashionable gimmick, and has become a sound tenet of taste in English gardening décor. Everywhere at Lyegrove are to be seen the cool frosty foliage of close cropped santolina, the grey-green of senecio, and as already noted, the silvery velvet of *Stachys lanata*, with for contrast here and there the purple-shaded grey of the shrubby *Salvia atropurpurea*.

Like all good gardeners Lady Westmorland prizes plants for their foliage as much as their flowers, and some of these leaf contrasts which struck the author as particularly effective were tree lupins, with their many-fingered leaves, growing hard by *Viburnum rhytidophyllum*, a noble member of a noble family which that great plantsman Reginald Farrer dubbed the Pew Opener for its dignified and austere look. Its leaves are like old book leather, and their undersides are thickly felted. Nearby the trefoil leaves of *Tropaeolum speciosum*, each like a tiny emerald ace of clubs, contrasts with the handsome tomentose foliage of *Hydrangea sargenti*. And so it goes on. Though in the limey soil of Gloucestershire the visitor, fresh from Pyrford or Exbury, will look in vain for rhododendrons, there is at Lyegrove an abundance of foliage and flowers to delight him. The lavish use of annuals – blue salvias, antirrhinums, and heady-scented heliotropes – give the borders in high summer an exuberance and lavishness seldom met these days.

opposite Old roses Fantin Latour, Celestial and Duc de Guiche grow alongside the path leading to Lady Westmorland's garden

Hampshire
Pylewell Park

A garden on the shores of the Solent

With the New Forest for shelter to the north and the Isle of Wight to the south, Pylewell Park, near Lymington, enjoys a climate which is as frost-free as any one could find in England. There is a tenderness in the air which encourages an exuberance of vegetables seldom found elsewhere. But before enumerating, in admiration and envy, the botanical rarities which thrive in the gentle climate of Pylewell, let us for a moment trace the history of the estate, which has been one of the most important in Hampshire for hundreds of years.

In the early eighteenth century the house belonged to the Worsleys – a branch of the Yarborough family – and it was during their occupation of Pylewell that the grounds achieved an odd notoriety. In 1750 the Prince of Wales – 'Poor Fred' – father of George III, was staying with the Worsleys for the good of his health, as his grand-daughter Princess Amelia was to do forty years later. It is said that some of his more light-hearted attendants played a joke on the village folk by pretending to have heard groans issuing from an ancient elm on the estate. Whether it was a hoax, and whether there was something about the tree which creaked in a specially eery way, has never been established, but in his *Old Times Revisited* Edward King records that for some time the Groaning Tree was a source of wonder, alarm, curiosity and amusement to all the neighbourhood, and that the park at Pylewell, in which it stood, was 'thronged like a fair, with rustics and residents of all ranks'; so much so, that the offending tree was eventually cut down, though the legend of it lingers to this day.

In due course, the Worsleys sold Pylewell to Ascanius William Senior, who must have been one of the earliest pioneers of aeronautics, for there exists in the Huntington Museum in California a Rowlandson drawing of a balloon ascent from the Park at Pylewell during his ownership.

Later the house passed into the hands of the Welds, relations of Mrs Fitzherbert, the love of the future George IV, who, in spite of her equivocal position as unacknowledged wife of the heir to

An engraving of a portrait by Sir William Beechey of Princess Amelia, delicate daughter of George III

opposite An oak bridge spans the stream which feeds the lake. Beyond, a bank of azaleas, and in the foreground the bold leaves of *Gunnera manicata*

229

right The garden, with the Solent beyond, in the Worsleys' time
below The south parterre today

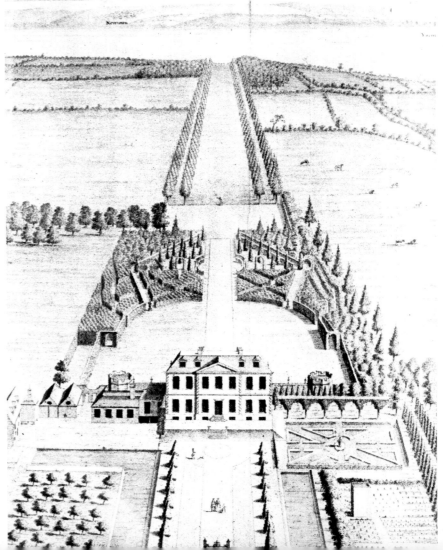

above A drawing by Thomas Rowlandson (1756–1827) of an early balloon
ascent in the grounds of Pylewell

the throne, appears always to have been on good terms with his
royal sisters. It may have been she who recommended the climate
of Pylewell to the Prince's delicate sister Amelia, who rented the
place for a time.

In Princess Amelia's day the garden looked very different from
the way it does today. In an old print, a wide double avenue of
trees runs down to the Solent and the house, much smaller, is set
as the central point of an elaborate complex of pleached walks,
parterres and symmetrical *bosquets*. Nothing remains of all this,
so one does not know for certain whether the lay-out ever existed.
It may have been never more than an ambitious project.

The projects of the present owner, Mr William Whitaker's
father, however, were indeed realized, for Mr Ingham Whitaker
was one of the leading gardeners of his day, and he enthusiastically set about developing the garden at Pylewell soon after he
inherited the property in 1892.

The vegetable garden, at least, seems to have been in perfect
order, for a local guide book of some years before describes it as
being 'on a large scale, kept in fine condition' and goes on to say
that it produced 'every delicacy of the vegetable world which the

Framed in trees, the south front of the house looks over a
formal layout studded with standard rhododendrons

One of the finest of all rhododendron hybrids is *Rhododendron loderi*, a cross between *R. griffithianum* and *R. fortunei*. This is the white-flowered variety King George

Growing through the mauve racemes and light foliage of wistaria, the white-flowered clematis Duchess of Edinburgh

most fastidious taste can desire'. But the pleasure grounds were uninteresting, and consisted only of the formal lay-out to the south of the house, which still exists today, though very differently planted, as we shall see.

But east of the house, a quarter of a mile away, there lay a romantic lake surrounded with oak-woods, the trees of which had enriched the soil beneath with the humus from their fallen leaves. Mr Ingham Whitaker was quick to realize that here was the ideal place to grow rhododendrons, and of the collection he made, more than seventy years ago, many were grown from seed sent home from early Himalayan expeditions, and can now be seen in the woodland of Pylewell, grown to splendid maturity. Pylewell is near Exbury; both are on the Solent and so enjoy the same gardening climate. Though Exbury is the larger in extent of the two, many rhododendrons at Pylewell are older, and the gardens are equally beautiful when the shrubs for which they are celebrated are at their best, in May and June.

Among Mr Whitaker's many rhododendrons, some are of especial interest to the connoisseur. Among these is an early hybrid raised at Pylewell by a former head gardener there, Mr Hamilton, and now named for him W.F.H. This is a particularly fine plant, with orange scarlet flowers and dark glossy leaves. It is the result of a cross between *R. haematodes* and the well-known Tally-Ho.

Another very beautiful plant at Pylewell is an eighteen-foot-high bush of the cream-coloured form of Penjerrick, while on the other side of the lake is a pale pink *griffithianum* hybrid, Isabella Mangles, which especially aroused the enthusiasm of Mr Patrick Synge, a connoisseur of rhododendrons, who described it in the *Rhododendron and Camellia Year Book* with the words: 'To say that it is a much improved Pink Pearl is faint praise, yet gives some idea of its character'. After mentioning other good specimens, such as *R. arizelum*, and *R. fictolacteum*, a tree fifteen feet high and twenty feet across, Mr Synge goes on to say: 'Perhaps the finest plants were the forms of *R. cinnebarinum* and *R. roylei*. We measured one across, and it was 20 feet and must have been nearly as high, the branches heavily weighed down with the dark plum red flowers glowing where the sun shone through them like a glass of wine held up to the light'.

The beauty of the rhododendrons at Pylewell is much enhanced by the proximity of the lake, glimpses of which are continually to be had while walking round the garden, which is fed by a stream bordered by *Osmunda regalis*, the Royal Fern, with groves of azaleas behind. Mr Ingham Whitaker did not, like many rhododendron addicts, care as much for azaleas, and the plants, which are now seven and eight feet high and scent the air around in May, started life in pots as ballroom decoration sixty years ago and were planted out, without too much care, afterwards. Such is the climate at Pylewell, they have thrived ever since. It is a garden anecdote that is, somehow, typical. Throughout the garden's history, providing flowers for the house has been one of its most important functions and there still lingers about the

above By the lake and growing among moisture-loving astilbes, the striking leaves of *Hosta marginata alba*

left A Japanese garden lantern in green patinated lead and a twisted pine create an oriental effect at Pylewell

below Daffodils flower by the lakeside. Beyond the thatch-roofed boat house are the woods which shelter Mr Whitaker's collection of rhododendrons

gardens at Pylewell an unusual air of almost Edwardian ease.

As the visitor to Pylewell retraces his steps back to the house he passes through groves of well-grown shrubs and trees which he must pause to admire. Among these are *Eucryphia nymansay*, *Embothrium coccineum*, the Chilean Bottlebush Tree, a splendid *Photinia serrulata* and several parrotias. A wall gives added shelter to callistemons, *Actinidia kolomikta* and the tender *Trachelospermum jasminoides*.

But a too long list of Latin names can be wearisome. Under the south façade of the house itself lies the former Victorian parterre. This is no longer extravagantly and laboriously bedded out twice a year, but thoughtfully planted with many of the silver- and grey-leaved shrubs so rightly popular, for their long lasting effect, in English gardening today. Here are many of the shrubs with good old English names that once figured in Perdita's catalogue, and among them 'lavender and rosemary and rue', that 'keep seeming and savour all the winter long'.

Julians

Exuberant plantings in a neat architectural frame

Against a background of yew a stone statue of a monkey keeps look-out on the very English scene

opposite An informally planted path runs to the garden door of Julians

In January 1941, in the darkest days of the war, a very beautiful woman bought a very beautiful house. It was an act of faith, a gesture of confidence, when the future seemed so obscure, for Mrs Pleydell-Bouverie to embark on the acquisition of an estate, with all its attendant obligations, at a time when there was no possibility and indeed little heart for the embellishment of new country houses and for the planning of gardens.

It was in 1947 that the writer visited Julians after five years' war service overseas, and he well remembers his excited pleasure.

In India, in the plains, he had seen roses, petunias, tobacco flowers. On leave in the Himalayas, there had been dahlias and zinnias and, of course, rhododendrons. But in Mrs Pleydell-Bouverie's garden there were many very English flowers of which one does not necessarily think when indulging in 'home thoughts from abroad'.

Mulleins (verbascums), which Christopher Hussey describes as 'accommodating and glorious plants', galtonia or *Hyacinthus candicans,* heavy with their white bells, and *Salvia turkestanica,* an improved form of the old-fashioned Clary with furry grey-green leaves and spires of mauve flowers – these were the flowers, though all the other flowers of the English border were there too, that, for one visitor at least, first made the delight of the Julians borders. Verbascums particularly in several varieties – the soft amber, purple-centred Cotswold Queen, the pristine pale yellow Vernale and the perennial Pink Domino. It was at Julians too that the writer first met another quite outstanding mullein – *V. broussa,* called, as we have noted elsewhere, after the ancient Seljuk capital of Turkey, and now re-named by the Linnaei of today, more ponderously, *bombyciferum.* By any name it would be a remarkable and lovely plant, with its leaves, stems and flower warmly dressed in the purest white wool, or tomentum, and brilliant yellow flowers, which it bears, if only a few at a time, through June till autumn. *V. broussa* is, unfortunately, a biennial, which means that one must sow it every season in July to flower the following year. But it is well worth the effort.

A circular pond, planted with tufts of sagittaria, has as *genius loci* a fine bronze specimen of *Phoca vitulina*

Two other impressive biennials much in evidence in the garden at Julians are foxgloves (digitalis) and onopordon. Not only the much loved mauve and white varieties of foxglove, but the Excelsior hybrids as well. This is a truly magnificent flower, which makes a plant six feet tall and carries its freckled spotted flowers all round, instead of only on one side of its towering stem.

Onopordon acanthium, the other biennial which is such a feature of the Julians borders, is another superb plant which the writer met for the first time in Mrs Bouverie's garden. Onopordon is the Scotch thistle, and a most impressive plant which rears its silver white heraldic, heavily-spined leaves on a five-foot stem. It is the most fiercely armed of any garden thistle (though the rose Mermaid runs its close), and strikes a fine architectural attitude in any border in which it is planted, its cool silver colouring a good foil for other flowers.

A quality Mrs Bouverie values in a garden is the ability to provide continued interest and surprise. She likes gardens like Sissinghurst and Hidcote, gardens which are divided up into outdoor rooms. She dislikes plantings which make a spotty effect, and prefers, like all good gardeners, to plant boldly in large groups, as has been done at St Pauls Walden Bury – shown elsewhere in this book, another Hertfordshire garden, and one Mrs Bouverie particularly admires. Tall plants are her favourites; she admires delphiniums and eremurus, and of lower growing

flowers she is particularly fond of the blue cynoglossum.

The gardens at Julians lie on three sides of the house. The garden door, in the south façade, is approached by a neatly paved path, its stone symmetry only discreetly broken by a planting here and there of clumps of dianthus, thrift and thymes, and other plants which grow in stonework. More grow in the paved 'wabe', which surrounds the sundial which came from an old house in Northamptonshire and is a recent addition.

The main part of the garden lies to the north of the house and is gained by passing through the house and onto a terrace, which, as it lies on the shady side of the house, provides a cool retreat in summer, and is set with inviting white-painted table and chairs. This terrace looks onto a lilly pond with, as its centrepiece, the piece of sculpture which is such a feature of the gardens at Julians, and was an addition of Mrs Bouverie. This is of a seal in bronze, balanced on an imposing ball. It is the work of Wheeler Williams and makes a bold yet unexpected *genius loci*.

Beyond the lily pond, with its many varieties of nymphaea and fine presiding specimen of *Phoca vitulina*, lies the rose terrace, walled and completely clothed with climbing roses. Here are all the old favourites which cannot be bettered to curtain a terrace wall – the scarlet Etoile de Holland, the thorny Mermaid with its late and long-blooming flowers of sulphur yellow, coral-budded Albertine and pink New Dawn. To the east of this terrace lie the

A flower-strewn path runs at right angles to a Claire-voie, a low wall surmounted by a graceful iron-work railing. Beyond lies the broad grassland of Hertfordshire

A new addition to the garden is a formal parterre of box-edged beds of different coloured thymes, with an obelisk as centrepiece

herbaceous borders which are such a feature of Mrs Bouverie's garden, with bosomy parterres of delphiniums, tree peonies, which are special favourites, lavender, and several groups of grey-leaved aromatic shrubs like *Phlomis fruticosa* such as we admired at Pusey, and the verbascums and *Salvia turkestanica* already noticed.

In one corner, heavily shaded with trees and in a thicket of foxgloves, there lurks a statue of a monkey, eyeing the very English scene which confronts him with a somewhat sardonic eye. In its humour it recalls the monkey statues in the great Italian garden at Collodi, or the ones in the garden of the palace of Queluz in Portugal.

Near the monkey are more well-planted borders, and the writer, out of the profusion of flowers they contain, remembers with particular affection some magnificent poppies – the annual 'horned' variety, called horned on account of the conformation of their seeds, in every shade of pink and crimson and mauve, with flowers the size of peonies, some with picotee petals, two or three to a stem, lolling over their glaucous leaves; and valerian, with their beautiful flowers of pink, crimson and white, tumbling about among the other flowers.

The borders at Julians have some of the quality of cottage flower beds. Their pattern is haphazard, though unusually successful. One feels perhaps they lack the drawing board perfection of the parterres of the Courts of Hampton and Hascombe; they more resemble those at Haseley. There is nothing polite about their plan – here and there their colours clash, and here and there a tall plant has pushed itself to the front and been allowed to stay. And yet with the grey leaves of lavender and the silver velvet of stachys to act as catalyst, and a lavish interplanting of white flowers, so important to any border – *Lilium candidum*, papery romneya, Mrs Sinkins pinks, white achilleas – a good-humoured harmony is achieved. And the general plan of the garden at Julians is contained in a rigid frame, with the width of the paths measured to a fraction and the proportions of the main axial paths in perfect proportion to the lesser cross-axial ones.

Recently Mrs Bouverie planned and planted a new section of her garden in a most original way, as a small formal garden, with the beds surrounded by clipped box and filled with various varieties of thyme. Some of the beds contain dwarf umbrella-shaped apple trees, and two sides of this new garden are planted with espaliered pear trees – a most effective little parterre, which in its symmetry is in great contrast to the remainder of the garden and recalls a French *potager*.

At Julians the garden and house are closely interlocked. If the garden's influence is felt indoors, the house's influence is strong outside. The house can be seen from every part of the garden, and its Georgian façade coolly returns the garden's gaze, exercising, as it were, a gentle restraint on the exuberance of the coloured borders. And the brick walls and classical gate piers, too, reaffirm the pattern, even though it is a design which is blurred here and there by climbing roses or by a purple cloak of clematis.

Sun roses, *helianthemum*, grow in coloured cushions in the interstices of a paved path at Julians

An astrolabe on a carved stone base, in a setting, or 'wabe' of flower-grown pavement

Easton Neston

A setting for Hawksmoor's masterpiece

There are some, but not many beautiful gardens in Northamptonshire, a county where gardening zeal in the past has seemed to lag behind the enthusiasm for building large houses. Easton Neston is an exception. A house of great beauty, of unique architectural importance, married to a garden which exactly suits it in temperament. It is an alliance, it must be admitted, of fairly recent date. The smiling parterre of gardens, terraces and *pièce d'eau* which lie today to the east of the house, did not exist fifty years ago. But so thoughtfully have they been devised, and they are carried out with such taste and sense of period, that they might have been planned as a setting for the house at the time that this was originally built. Originally built – but by whom? Sir Christopher Wren or Nicholas Hawksmoor? The name of our greatest architect is often mentioned in connection with Easton Neston. But before considering this question let us turn back the pages of the history of Easton Neston till they fall open at the date 1535, the year the present family came into possession.

In 1535, Richard Fermor acquired Easton Neston following the death of Richard Empson, whose family had owned the property since the time of Henry VI, and whose father, once a simple sieve-maker's son, had acquired a fortune under Henry VII, was arrested for peculation by Henry VIII, and died on Tower Hill. Richard Fermor, who had made a fortune as a London merchant, lived in his new house in the greatest luxury, employing a vast number of servants, grooms and foresters, and even including on his pay-roll a jester, Will Somers, who plays an important part in the story. In 1540, at the height of the unrest of the Reformation, Richard Fermor, who was a Roman Catholic, visited his confessor, who had been arrested, and was in gaol. When he left he gave him two shirts and eight pence. As a result of this bounty – which today sounds so meagre – he too was arrested and imprisoned, like Mr Micawber, in the Marshalsea, and his estates were forfeited. When the Fermor household collapsed, Will Somers, who had a high reputation as a joker, was taken on by no less a personage than King Henry VIII himself, but

A lichen-grown stone lion finds a bed of roses under the east façade of Easton Neston, Nicholas Hawksmoor's architectural masterpiece. The date 1702 appears above the central window

opposite Flowers curtain a wall in a sheltered corner of the garden

loyally never lost an opportunity, in his privileged new employment, to put in a word for his imprisoned employer. His efforts were rewarded, and it is said that the King gave orders on his deathbed for Richard Fermor's release. Be that as it may, Richard Fermor certainly regained his house and lands, and the family returned to Easton Neston. It was his great-great-grandson who had the present house built as we see it today. The family had been well-off for generations, had achieved a knighthood under King James I, but only reached the higher rungs of the social ladder when the twice-widowed Sir William Fermor made a third marriage in 1692. His bride was a daughter of the first Duke of Leeds, Lady Sophia Osborne. To match this ducal connection it was felt that he should have a grander house, which brings us to the troubled question of who was the architect of Easton Neston.

In 1682 Sir William Fermor had, there is no doubt, been in touch with Sir Christopher Wren, a personal friend and a remote relation of the Fermor family, about his new house; and it is possible that he showed the great architect his projected plans, asking for his comments. No documentary evidence exists that Wren did more than correct or perhaps merely approve the plans, which had probably been prepared by a local architect. Hawksmoor was only twenty-one in 1682, by which year two wings of the new house were already built, one of which still exists, following the plans which Wren must certainly have approved, if he did not actually re-draw them. Between these two wings, a space was left for the main house, a space which was to remain empty for several years. How much did Wren have to do with the wings of Easton Neston? His connection was a shadowy one – made more obscure by a letter which exists, that he wrote to Sir William Fermor, in which he gives some general advice about the building of greenhouses, but does not mention the house at all, and even seems imperfectly acquainted with the site generally.

But John Bridges, who was an authority on Northamptonshire and its houses, definitely credits Wren for the wings of Easton Neston, and Hawksmoor for the central block. In about 1724

below 'There is something of the palace about Easton Neston . . .' Bold piers of rusticated stone frame the view of its classical façade *right* The formal east parterre with its bow-shaped pièce d'eau and hedges set with terms. The curling hedges are of golden yew in the form of an Archimedean spiral

he wrote, 'The only house at Efton is the magnificent seat of the Earl of Pomfret . . . the wings are of brick and were built by Sir Christopher Wren. Finished 1702 about 20 years after Erection of Wings. It was built by Hawksmoor who hath very much departed from the first design.'

Whoever built the wings, whoever planned the foundations of the house we see today, there is no doubt whatsoever as to who was the architect for the central block. It was Nicholas Hawksmoor, and it is his masterpiece.

Nicholas Hawksmoor was born in Nottinghamshire in 1661, and was to be the architect of several great London churches, St Mary Woolnoth and St Georges, Bloomsbury, among them. He is well known for his work on the library of Queen's College and at All Souls, Oxford. When still a youth he entered Sir Christopher Wren's entourage as a junior member of the Office of Works. In the course of time he rose to be King William III's Clerk of Works at Kensington Palace, then being rebuilt. By the time of the completion of Easton Neston he was already an acclaimed architect, and Wren himself may have recommended Sir William Fermor, soon to be Lord Lempster and Earl of Pomfret, to employ him in the creation of the exquisite house which Hawksmoor himself, with understandable pride, was to refer to as his 'owne child'. The new central block was largely completed in 1702, and built of a luminous local stone of great beauty.

John Morton, author of *A Natural History of Northamptonshire*, extolled especially the material of which the house was built. 'Easton, my Lorde Lempster's house is built of a fair white and durable stone from Helmdon, which is freer of an intermixture of yellowish spots than in that of Ketton, and is indeed the finest building stone I have seen in England.' As one looks at the façade of Easton Neston, carved with lapidary detail and reflected, on the eastern side, in the waters of the great ornamental pool, one must recognize the fact that it owes much of its beauty to being built of Helmdon stone.

Perhaps, for a book about gardens, too much space has been devoted to a history of Easton Neston and to the question of its architect. But there are few houses in England which have even the most tenuous claim to have been designed by Wren. And the architecture, whoever its author, of Easton Neston plays a more than usually important part in the garden picture, so subtly has the garden been designed to act as a framework and setting for the house.

First sight of the garden is obtained when leaving the house by the high arched garden door in the centre of the east façade. Steps, balustraded in neat ironwork, descend to a paved parterre of rectangular box-edged flower beds and clipped conifers. Beyond is a bow shaped pool set in a yew hedge, which gives a dark background to stone terms which were brought, when the garden was reconstructed in 1921, from Stowe. This pool was part of the great alteration made to the garden by the present owner's grandfather, the first Lord Hesketh, a collateral descendent of the Pomfrets, assisted by his head gardener, Mr Swainson.

Set between bushes of clipped box, a statue of a Roman matron raises her marble hand in greeting

When it was dug land pipes are said to have been discovered which proved that an ornamental stretch of water may have been part of Hawksmoor's original formal plan.

Though the stone terms are importations, they make dignified punctuation marks to the elliptical hedge, while the lead figure in the centre of the pool is the embodiment of light-hearted gaiety. It is of a spouting dolphin, jockeyed by a child. The other lead statues, though from time to time they may have been moved, have always been in the garden at Easton Neston.

There are two openings in the yew hedges – and the view they frame makes a cross axis of the garden, and centres on the lead dolphin and its rider. To the north the vista is closed by a high pedimented garden pavilion backed with the trees of the arboretum, planted eighty years ago and containing several remarkable specimens, among them some fine *Sequoia sempervivum* – redwoods – from California. The little garden house dates from the seventeenth century – back to an earlier Easton, demolished when the present house was built. It contains the tomb of Pug, a dog thought by some to be Lady Bertram's dog immortalized in Jane Austen's *Mansfield Park*, of which Easton Neston is said to have been the inspiration.

Lady Hesketh, mother of the present owner who is fifteen years old, has planted her gardens with imagination and fancy. Though she is modest about her contribution to the garden at Easton Neston, she has strong ideas about the sort of garden she admires:

I like a combination of French classicism and English imagination, though on the reverse side it has to be said that sometimes the French dislike of colour leads to monotony, and that English gardens can be too untidy . . . My favourite English garden is Sissinghurst because it is so poetic and full of surprises. In Scotland I have never seen prettier gardens than Kinross and Logan. I cannot say what I consider to be an ideal garden. There are so many beautiful gardens, all different, but if one must generalize I think the best gardens are either within sight of the sea or have water very close.

Lady Hesketh's favourite flowers seem those that are strongly scented – she loves pinks, lily of the valley and moss roses. There is something of a Victorian Valentine, or perhaps rather of a Meissen bouquet, in her choice. Certainly her gardens, though reconstructed, breathe the very air of the eighteenth century. They have been planted accordingly, with many of the flowers which might have scented the pleasure grounds surrounding the Petit Trianon at Versailles, a building which Easton Neston architecturally resembles to a degree which is startling, when we consider that it was built fifty years before Gabriel's gemlike palace. And there is something of a palace about Easton Neston, too, especially late on a summer evening, when the roses are reflected among the lilies in the pool and the first lights are lit behind the high arched windows. One listens expectantly for the music of the flute.

above A spouting dolphin jockeyed by a *putto*. *below* 'The little garden house dates from the seventeenth century —back to an earlier Easton, demolished when the present house was built.' Behind it grow some fine specimens of sequoia, or Californian redwood

Surrey

Hascombe Court

A garden with some of the best herbaceous borders in England

The period between 1918 and 1939, those short twenty-one years of peace, were great years for gardening. Labour was still available, people had time to make plans, to look ahead. The war to end wars was won, there was time for Candide to cultivate his garden. It was during this comparatively halcyon period that the great pleasure grounds at Hascombe Court were laid out.

The corner of Surrey in which Hascombe Court is situated is a part of England famous for its gardens. It is, as is the garden at Pyrford Court, in the Gertrude Jekyll country. Hascombe Court lies between the village of Hascombe and Godalming, standing on high ground, with its grounds and gardens covering a gentle slope to the south-east. In their acreage they combine several outstanding examples of gardening as practised by connoisseurs of gardening in the twenties and thirties. There is an area devoted to daffodils naturalized in grass in a planting of silver birches and flowering cherries, a handsome rock garden, and perhaps the best herbaceous borders in England. It is proposed to visit each of these different parts of the garden in turn, starting with the herbaceous borders, which lie near to the house, and are such an outstanding feature of the garden.

The herbaceous border, like the landscape garden, is a peculiarly English invention. It would be interesting to know who first used the phrase which is now so well known. William Robinson, who is credited with the invention of the herbaceous border, does not refer to it, in those words, in his classic, *The English Flower Garden*, first published in 1883. This is how he opens his fourth chapter:

We now come to the flowers that are worthy of a place in gardens and to consider ways of arranging them. Their number and variety being almost without limit, the question is, how the garden lover is to enjoy as many of these treasures as his conditions allow of. As during all time a simple border has been the first expression of flower gardening, and as there is no arrangement of flowers more graceful, varied, or capable of giving more delight, and none so easily adapted to almost every kind of garden, some ideas of the various kinds of borders of hardy flowers mainly deserve our first consideration.

The white-flowered *Viburnum plicatum*, one of the best of a noble family of shrubs, flowers well in the garden of Hascombe Court

opposite The twin herbaceous borders run alongside a broad grass path towards the house, which was built by Sir Edwin Lutyens (1869–1944)

From the shelter of a summer house, a long view of the herbaceous borders to the west of the house

The lavender-topped terrace wall and set-in lily pond are typical of Lutyens' garden architecture

And he goes on to describe various types of borders, several only of herbaceous plants, but the words 'herbaceous border', specifically, do not occur.

By the time Gertrude Jekyll, whose famous garden at Munstead Wood is only a few miles away from Hascombe Court, was writing her classic book, twenty-five years later, the words 'herbaceous border' were accepted and she has, as always, words of wisdom to say on the subject. In the introduction to her *Colour Schemes for the Flower Garden* she writes:

To plant and maintain a flower border with a good scheme for colour is by no means the easy thing that is commonly supposed . . . I believe that the only way it can be made successful is to devote certain borders to certain times of year: each border or garden region to be bright from one to three months.

What, in fact, is a herbaceous border – the kind of border that Miss Jekyll advocated planting? That august publication, the Royal Horticultural Society's *Dictionary of Gardening*, defines a herbaceous border as:

A characteristic feature of the English garden which in its true sense is a border consisting solely of hardy herbaceous perennials which can be cut down to the ground in winter and will come up again the following year . . .

'Consisting solely of herbaceous plants' – and the earliest herbaceous borders were doubtless planted with herbaceous material only. Lately, for a variety of reasons, the rule has been relaxed.

But let us first examine the kind of herbaceous borders that were being planted at the beginning of this century, in the heyday of Edwardian affluence and luxury, when quite small gardens had two or three gardeners to look after them. They were borders, usually fifteen or twenty feet wide, preferably sited to face south. If they ran on either side of a path, the path had to run north and south. North is a bad aspect for herbaceous plants. The aim was to maintain, by the thoughtful choice of plants, a show of colour over a period of several months, beginning in May and only ending with the first frosts. Colours were carefully blended. The oblong clumps of plants were bold, seven feet or eight feet long or more, and five feet through. Heights were exactly graded, with low plants in the front and loftier plants, like delphiniums, macleayas and hollyhocks at the back. Lucky were the gardeners who could plant their herbaceous borders in front of a high brick or stone wall, for walls not only give shelter but provide an opportunity for vertical planting of climbing roses, clematis, vines and tender wall shrubs.

The actual disposition of the plants and their placing, with regard to their colour and flowering period, was a matter for deep thought. The plan for the border was set out on paper and hours were spent in its preparation. Areas were shaded in different colours, to indicate peak flowering periods. In fact, planning a herbaceous border was a very serious business indeed. And, of course, when it was successful the result could be superb. But such a border demanded a lot of upkeep. Soil preparation,

opposite From a lily pond, with its attendant lead crane, a shrub-grown bank rises towards the gabled house

Laburnums in May with their showers of golden flower were first introduced to English gardens in the reign of Queen Elizabeth I

planting, staking, weeding, dead-heading were all tasks which had, inexorably, to be done, one after the other. With an army of gardeners there was no problem – but with two wars and drastic labour shortage the grandiose borders of Edwardian England became impossible, save in very few gardens, to maintain. Moreover, their high peak of popularity, through necessity, was past. Discriminating gardeners recognized the value of a less brilliant show of colour, of subtler shading. Evergreens and even more, 'evergreys' were introduced into herbaceous borders to give body and form and at least a little colour in the winter.

The old herbaceous border had presented a picture of brown earth merely from November to April, Now plants were chosen for their long flowering periods, and low shrubs and even roses, which would seldom have found a place in an Edwardian border, were included. The border was simplified, made more practical, but in the change lost little of its beauty. To have a good herbaceous border is still the aim of many gardeners, for it is still the only way of attractively assembling a large number of different plants. And as much thought as ever must go into its planning. A collection of plants, however different, if not carefully juxtaposed, is a collection of plants and nothing more, but if arranged with skill, a herbaceous border can be a work of art whether it is a mixed border or a classical herbaceous border as at Hascombe Court, with its bold groups of all the favourite plants of English gardens – misty nepeta, golden heleniums, starry Shasta daisies and the rich purple *Salvia superba*. Particularly impressive in July are romneyas as fine as those at Mereworth and campanulas, those useful bell-flowers which ring the changes between mauve, blue and creamy white, and fill so satisfactorily the gap between the flowers of June and those of later summer.

If the great William Robinson was the prophet of the herbaceous borders there is, at Hascombe Court, another example of a type of gardening of which he was a pioneer: a rock garden. Robinson visited Switzerland for the first time in the late sixties in the last century, following a visit to Paris. After the formality and grandeur of French gardens, and especially Versailles, which he detested, the simplicity of the flora of Switzerland delighted him, and soon he was advocating the planting of specially constructed gardens for alpine plants in England.

The rock garden at Hascombe Court lies to the south of the house and is approached from the balustraded terrace down a flight of steps. The lie of the land was one which lent itself readily to the creation of a rock garden. And siting a rock garden is all important. It should be on a slope – for drainage is all important for all rock plants. It should lie – like the foothills of the Alps – open to the sky. There should be no spreading trees to deprive the garden's denizens of a moment's sunlight. All these requisites were, at Hascombe Court, to hand, and the few shrubs and low trees there are in the rock garden were carefully chosen to accentuate a knoll, or to clothe a fall of stone with a cascade of green.

The author of this book, as a small boy, was already fascinated by plants and gardens. One of the first books on the subject which he read was Reginald Farrer's *My Rock Garden*, published in 1907, a book which every rock gardener of today still reads with respectful attention. For it is full of wisdom and sound sense, though perhaps today Farrer's English seems a trifle turgid. Clarence Elliot, the well-known writer on gardens, has described Farrer's classic as invaluable, though he was put off by 'his un-bridled purple passages and frequent slabs of sheer clotted verbiage'. But to one young garden enthusiast, curled up on a sofa in a chilly billiard room of a large Victorian house in Scotland, his descriptions of plants were enthralling, and it is to that early introduction to Alpine plants that the author of this book largely owes the dawn of his interest in gardening – a great debt.

One other section of the garden at Hascombe Court has been overlooked – a part of the garden which is particularly beautiful in spring. As the visitor leaves the walk between the herbaceous borders at the far end of the house, and turns south, he comes to an area devoted to natural gardening at its very best. A region of turf, planted with silver stemmed birches and flowering cherries which rise from drifts of daffodils naturalized in grass. They flower from March – 'before the swallow dares' – till the middle of May. The daffodils and narcissi in this part of the garden at Hascombe Court are planted in very large groups, as such plants always should be, of one kind, and they flower in succession for several weeks, old, favourite varieties, as well as new ones. One of the oldest of yellow trumpeted daffodils is Winter Gold, and though it has been grown in English gardens for many years, it is still one of the best of all. Other reliable flowerers, which pay their way with gold year after year, at Hascombe Court and in many other good gardens, are King Alfred, Hunter's Moon, King's Court and Magnificence. John Evelyn is another good daffodil, called after the great gardener of the seventeenth century whom we meet in our chapter on Hampton Court, in converse with the doomed King Charles in his garden there. Evelyn's own daffodil is a bicolour – white and yellow – a quick spreader and lavish flowerer.

This part of the garden at Hascombe Court presents a scene of enchantment every spring, and shows what delightful pictures can be created by the gardener with an artist's eye, who has noticed and can copy how daffodils grow in the wild, and repro-duce in some small way, on his private canvas, a scene that Nature herself composes so successfully.

The gardens of Hascombe Court were laid out in the 1920s by Sir John Jarvis. The architect of the house and the attractive terraces which surround it was Sir Edwin Lutyens. The paving, with its telling contrast of patterns in brick and stone, is typical of Sir Edwin's work. The gardens are a perfect example of the period, a pleasure-ground in which a series of picturesque scenes have been created and a collection of good plants assembled in a setting which blends perfectly with its surroundings.

The present owners, Mr and Mrs Claude Jacobs, maintain the gardens meticulously, and generously open them to the public several days every summer, in aid of the National Gardens Scheme.

above Reflections in a formal pool. Geraniums with decoratively marbled leaves fill the stone vases

below An informal treatment of water bordered with a luxuriant planting of shrubs and ferns

Pyrford Court

A garden in Kipling's Merrow Down County

Gertrude Jekyll (1843–1932) had a garden at
Munstead Wood, not far from Pyrford Court, and
had a great influence on the planting of this great
Surrey garden

opposite 'Gardening by colour demands . . . an artist's
eye for the refinements of colour of flower and form
in foliage': the Silver Garden

Pyrford Court, in Surrey, has a garden which is justly celebrated
for its rhododendrons and azaleas, but almost more spectacular
in early summer are the wistarias which clothe its welcoming
façade. Mr A. J. Huxley, that well-known connoisseur of gardens,
has recorded that 'In early summer the eye rests in amazement
on the house . . ., for it is draped on every side with wistarias of
varying shades . . . further wistarias climb into trees near the
house, and are equally the eye-catchers in the gardens to the
north of the house'. The Pyrford wistarias are extraordinary in
that their racemes of flowers, whether mauve or white, are even
longer than those of the often grown *Wistaria multijuga*. Mr Huxley
measured one 4 feet 7 inches long.

Pyrford Court is not an old house. The owners, the Earl and
Countess of Iveagh, started building it before 1914, when their
project was interrupted by the war, and the house was not
finished until 1927. Lord Iveagh found time, in spite of his duties
as an M P and a director of the Guinness Brewery, to be his own
architect, and the resulting house, large and comfortable, owes
something to the style of Queen Anne but even more to Lord
Iveagh's own very personal tastes. From its many windows there
are magnificent views to the south over the countryside watered
by the River Wey, with Hindhead to the west. It lies in Kipling's
Taffy Country, near Merrow Down.

'An hour out of Guildford town – above the River Wey it is.'

It is also in the Gertrude Jekyll country, and Miss Jekyll's
famous garden at Munstead Wood lay not far distant, enjoying
very much the same porous acid soil, rich in peat, as the garden
at Pyrford. Lady Iveagh was a friend of Miss Jekyll and was a
student of her books. Inspired perhaps by the classic *Wood and
Garden*, she aimed to make as much of the woodland at Pyrford
as of the garden itself. Many planters of new gardens in rhododendron country fall into a kind of euphoria, so over-excited are
they at being able to draw on such a rich family of plants. These
are the gardeners, and how many of them there are, who plant

rhododendrons without any regard to colour or form. Not so Lady Iveagh, who was a serious and thoughtful gardener, and who, from the outset, closely studied the precepts firmly laid down by her illustrious neighbour.

In her book *Wood and Garden* Miss Jekyll describes how she herself planned her own rhododendron garden at Munstead.

The plantation was made about nine years ago, in one of the regions where lawn and garden were to join the wood. During the previous blooming season the best nurseries were visited and careful observations made of colouring, habit, and time of blooming. The space they were to fill demanded about seventy bushes, allowing an average of eight feet from plant to plant – not seventy different kinds, but, perhaps, ten of one kind, and two or three fives, and some threes, and a few single plants, always bearing in mind the ultimate intention of pictorial aspect as a whole.

She goes on to suggest another useful rule for 'wild' gardeners.

Azaleas should never be planted among or even within sight of rhododendrons. Though both enjoy a moist peat soil and have a near botanical relationship, they are incongruous in appearance and impossible to group together for colour.

Though closely allied by family, the French maxim *Cousinage meilleur voisinage* does not apply to rhododendrons and azaleas.

The visitor to Pyrford, as he steps on to the terrace, sees in the foreground a belt of dry wall cushioned with rock plants, and beyond, a grand panoramic view towards the distant Downs. In spring the woodlands to left and right of the great central glade are bright with rhododendrons, and as he approaches, he finds paths literally carpeted with primroses, bluebells, gaultherias and the bronze rosettes and azure flower heads of *Ajuga reptans*. In this 'wild' part of the garden at Pyrford there is a kind of controlled abandon, for many plants have been allowed to run wild, to spread beyond their allotted boundaries, in fact, to take over. The result is a tapestry of colour, with the pattern blurred a little here and there perhaps, but with the general effect all the more telling for just that.

Elsewhere in the garden a stricter discipline is maintained, and nowhere more than in the Gold and Silver Gardens, where more of Miss Jekyll's rules – this time for 'gardening by colour' – are closely observed. These gardens are enclosed in hedges of evergreens and the colour of their different schemes is established, today at least, more by the foliage of the plants with which they are planted, than by their flowers. Entering the Gold Garden, even on a dull day, is like suddenly coming upon sunshine, for the glowing leaves of golden hollies, of *Eleagnus aureus*, *Veronica cupressoides*, and golden yew, supply such different tones of bright yellow as to create a glittering effect. Even the workaday golden privet has been effectively used, and visitors to Pyrford will agree with Miss Jekyll's words of praise, when she wrote of this underrated shrub: 'Its clear, cheerful bright yellow gives just the right colour all through the summer.' On the author's first visit to Pyrford he remembers noticing that there was no goldfish pool

An Italian stone seat in the garden at Pyrford Court is sheltered by a curved yew hedge

opposite The Gold Garden, 'even on a dull day, is like coming upon sunshine', with its golden hollies, *Eleagnus aureus* and bright-leaved golden yews in the Gold Garden and at the time wondered why. The answer probably is to be found on page 108 of the useful book, *Colour Schemes for the Flower Garden*: 'In the Gold garden . . . if there is a tank, do not have goldfish, their colour is quite wrong . . .' Miss Jekyll was a perfectionist.

The Silver Garden, equally satisfying, lies next door and is gained by means of a gateway in the dividing yew hedge. Here, by contrast, the colours are all cool and glaucous. *Senecio greyii* – that favourite and well-named silver-leaved shrub – is much in evidence, with species of the frosty-leaved *Chamaecyparis lawsoniana allumii* above; these contrast well with the feathery leaves of *Pyrus salicifolia*, the weeping pear. Other plants to add their tones of silver are the Jersualem Sage, the pungent Cotton Lavender, spicy-leaved *Helichrysum angustifolium*, velvety *Stachys lanata, Verbascum bombyciferum*. Near these grows the giant almost white-leaved thistle of Scotland, *Onopordon acanthium,* so well supplied with spines as to confirm the ancient Scottish motto *Nemo me impune lacessit.*

These two coloured gardens are fascinating features of the gardens at Pyrford. Given the right soil, rhododendrons are not difficult to grow, though, as we have seen, it takes thought in planting them, to grow them effectively. Herbaceous borders and rock gardens can be found in many gardens of England and Scotland, but gardening by colour demands more. It needs not only a knowledge of plants and a knowledge of soil but an artist's eye for the refinements of colour of flower and form in foliage.

The gardens at Pyrford are large, and in these short notes several interesting features have been omitted – the pergolas, for instance, which, like the house face, are completely draped with wistaria in early summer. And the wall nearby, which gives shelter to many delicate plants, such as the golden buttercup-like *Fremontia californica*, as well as fine specimens of the more frequently planted carpenteria, climbing hydrangea, and the *Garrya elliptica.*

Which is the best season to visit an English garden? For the more sophisticated gardener late summer is perhaps the right moment. It is then certainly that rarer plants are at their best, when leaf form is fully developed and when carefully devised planting schemes make their richest effect. But, surely, at Pyrford it must be May, 'As the faithful years return', and the woods are scented with lily of the valley, and we think of books we read long ago, and 'Taffy dancing through the fern – to lead the Surrey spring again'.

Wistaria, for which the gardens at Pyrford are well known, was named for Caspar Wistar (1761–1818), an American of German descent. Wistaria originated not in the Orient, as is generally supposed, but in America

In a framework of *Vitis coignetiae* an Italian fountain with dripping dolphins stands in the garden at Pyrford

A pergola hung with the long mauve racemes of wistaria shades a wide paved path

Wigtownshire

Logan

A spectacular garden of exotic plants

In the shelter of a high wall at the base of a palm grows *Euphorbia wulfenii*, a decorative spurge which shows acid-green flower heads early in the year

opposite Revelling in the blessings of the Gulf Stream a line of noble cordyline palms, which stand more than forty feet high

'Nobody,' once wrote the late Sir Herbert Maxwell in a book on Scottish gardens, 'wants to speak disrespectfully about the Gulf Stream', which recalls Sydney Smith's friend Jeffery, who was once bold enough to denigrate the Equator. And Sir Herbert goes on, 'But hydrographers have differed amongst themselves in estimating the extent of its effect upon the land temperature of Western Europe, and perhaps the popular tendency has been to exaggerate it.'

Opinions vary as to its effect. One expert holds that it still accounts for one-fifth of the total heat of the North Atlantic, which without it, in his opinion, would freeze. Another affirms that though the Gulf Stream certainly raises the temperature of the sea off our west coasts in winter, it can also lower it in summer. Summing up, Sir Herbert generously concedes it to have 'a genial influence', and no one who knows the gardens of the west coast of Scotland will disagree with him. And especially no one who knows the almost sub-tropical garden of Logan in Wigtownshire. But before describing this beautiful garden in detail, and the rarities that grow there, a few words about the difference in the gardening climates of Scotland and England. It is all-important to remember that the two countries are divided, climatically, not into north and south, but into east and west. And that, whatever anyone may say, is the direct result of the Gulf Stream.

Logan House is sited to the north of its celebrated garden. For centuries the place belonged to the MacDouall family, who, according to Sir Herbert, were originally of Pictish origin and descended from a Lord Fergus, who, writes the seventeenth-century historian McKenzie, held sway over Galloway 'many years before Christ'.

The last MacDouall lairds were two brothers – both bachelors – and it was they who first planted the garden. In 1949 the late Mr Olaf Hambro bought the property, attracted by the possibilities of gardening in such a gentle climate, where he was confident that many of the delicate and exotic plants which he had seen and envied at Tresco in the Scilly Isles would thrive. He was

above Logan House from the south. The Georgian house was revealed when the much larger Victorian baronial mansion was demolished. The walls are painted a warm pink. Under the cherry is a fine group of *Phormium tenax*. *left* The formal lines of the garden are broken by luxuriant planting. *below* Not only rarities are grown at Logan, but daffodils as well

One of the loveliest of sweet-scented rhododendrons is *R. edgeworthii*, with waxy white flowers tinged with pink. In the background is a group of the Australian tree ferns (*Dicksonia antarctica*) for which the garden at Logan is noted. Tree ferns grow only in the mildest of climates

opposite Palms (cordylines, chamaerops and dracaenas) are set out in avenues at Logan and look far more impressive than the single specimens which are usually planted

right, and now a visit to the garden at Logan affords the plant connoisseur endless treats.

On entering the garden, an avenue of Chusan palms (*Trachocarpus fortunei*) promises more interesting plants to come. These palms, which originate in China, were named for Robert Fortune, the Scottish plant-hunter who introduced the much-loved Japanese anemone to English gardens. Further on, the lobster-claw flowers and ferny foliage of *Clianthus puniceus* greet the eye. This spectacular plant grows in very few British gardens out of doors. Nearby runs another avenue of palms, this time of the tall *Cordyline australis*, the Cabbage Palm which was so dubbed by Captain Cook when he saw it in New Zealand in 1771. Captain Cook was a better navigator than botanist, for *Cordyline australis* is one of the lilaceae, a particularly striking variety of which grows at Logan, with nobly sculpted leaves, *C. indivisa*.

The path leads on – on either side are plants, some of more rarity than beauty, but all of the greatest interest to the connoisseur. The climbing white-flowered *Decumaria barbara*, from California; the odd Asiatic fern, *Drymoglossum heterophyllum*; and the uncommon white-flowered form of *Lapageria rosea*, named for the Empress Josephine, born Mlle de la Pagerie of Martinique, who was a passionate lover of flowers and a great patron of horticulture. If her errant shade could visit Logan today, leaning perhaps on the ghostly arm of her Scottish gardener, Monsieur Hewitson, as she used to do at Malmaison, the Empress would find much to take her eye. Plants quite unknown in her day, like *Euphorbia mellifera*, *Mitraria coccinea*, the scarlet Mitre flower, and *Meterosideros lucida*, which is seldom grown in Britain outside a greenhouse. But a catalogue of Latin names can soon pall, so the author proposes to list only a few more of Logan's rarities. Many come from Chile, far though the distance seems from the Sierras to the Rhinns of Galloway. *Crinodendron hookerianum* – the Lantern Tree – whose branches are alight with little red globe-shaped flowers in June, and a twenty-foot high Winter's Bark – *Drimys winteri* – which shows white, strongly-scented flowers in May.

Other interesting Chileans at Logan are the beautiful Myrtle – *Myrtus luma* – with its ginger-coloured bark, snowy flowers and black fruit, and on a sheltered wall the very rare *Lardizabala biternata*, which is odd in that it bears two different kinds of flower, pendant racemes of purple male flowers and simpler female ones. Other rare and tender plants on this wall are the lovely blue-flowered *Clematis macropetala*, the sea-green leaved *Lonicera splendida*, Banksian roses, the sweet-scented *Jasminum polyanthum* and the Japanese *Stauntonia hexaphylla*, a relation of *lardizabala*, and the white form of *Clianthus puniceus*.

Another plant the author would like to salute, for to him it seems almost to be the most fascinating plant at Logan, and one that he found growing there as in no other garden he knows in Britain – *Myosotidium nobile*, the Chatham Island forget-me-not, with leaves as large and glossy as those of *Bergenia crassifolia*, and heads of blue flowers. All gardeners have some plants which have

a special magic for them. Myosotidium has just that for the author of this book. Excessively difficult to grow – it likes sea-air, sandy soil and a diet of dead fish – it is not particularly beautiful. But it has a *mystique* of its own, and many is the gardener who has tried to grow it and failed. At Logan it proliferates.

But the garden at Logan is not only one of rarities. For many months of the year there are rhododendrons in flower: the writer especially remembers the exquisite scented edgeworthii and some magnificent twenty-foot-high red arboreums, over a hundred years old. And it is not only while they are flowering that the rhododendrons at Logan are beautiful. Some of the rarer kinds have foliage which is very attractive too. '. . . There is a tremendous diversity in size, shape, texture and colour,' the guide book proudly claims,

from leaves a quarter-of-an-inch long and even less in breadth, to leaves 3 ft long and 1 ft broad; from round, to oval, from oblong to egg-shaped; from thin to thick and leathery, from light to lettuce-green through blue-green to deep bottle-green on the upper surface from green through shades of fawn, yellow, orange, orange-red, cream and silver. In many the young foliage is even more lovely than the adult – bold cockades of kid-white, ice-blue, sea-green, amber, golden-fawn, or burnt-orange, often brushed over with a frosty iridescence and ribboned with crimson or yellow bud scales . . .

So the leaves at Logan offer sharp competition to the flowers, though these are everywhere, and there are drifts of pink and yellow Himalayan primulas which grow four feet high and seed themselves everywhere; there are drifts of blue poppies, there are lilies growing, as the late Captain Kingdon-Ward wrote, 'waist deep in a sea of dwarf rhododendrons'. There are camellias and tree peonies. There are great tufts everywhere, in beds, in borders, sometimes in the paths themselves, of a very seldom grown plant, *Fascicularia bicolor*, which shows violet heads of flowers and scarlet leaves in late summer.

Such is the delicacy of the climate which is almost, but not entirely, frost free, that wild scillas, as blue as the nearby sea, and pink carnations grow wild by the shore.

Almost, but not entirely, frost free. And the disastrous winter of 1962–3 caused many casualties, while recent gales have wrought havoc with the MacDoualls' carefully-placed shelter belts. These now have been replanted with Monterey and Corsican pines and Sitka spruce, while in the beech and ash woods around, Western Hemlock, which enjoy light shade, have been generously set.

A garden is never static. It is for ever developing or being developed. A bad winter takes its toll. A hot summer ripens the seed, and there are a number of connoisseurs' plants which seed themselves most generously at Logan – primulas, as we have seen, and the very rare Chinese *Rhododendron rubiginosum*, seedlings of which come up 'like mustard and cress'.

Sir Herbert Maxwell was right to treat the Gulf Stream with respect. No garden is more blessed by it than Logan.

Pensive *putti* rest their elbows on the rim of a stone vase in the lily pond. Behind grow tree ferns and tall cordylines, or cabbage palms, so named by Captain Cook, who first saw them in New Zealand

opposite Himalayan poppies delight in the gentle climate of this great Scottish garden. A favourite is *Meconopsis betonicifolia*, first introduced into western gardens in 1924

Great Dixter

A garden for a house by Sir Edwin Lutyens

The garden at Great Dixter seems to be the most English of all the gardens in this book. It was designed by Sir Edwin Lutyens in 1910–12, so it is not, in fact, a very old garden. Yet, so happily is it married to the ancient house it surrounds, that it seems far older than it is. It is, first and foremost, a plantsman's garden, for there is not a plant in the garden at Great Dixter which is not an interesting plant, a good plant, and not only that, but, having been planted by Mr Christopher Lloyd, probably the best plant of its kind available. So the garden might legitimately be described as approaching the ideal – an architect-designed garden planted by a connoisseur among gardeners, which is a very rare combination indeed.

It was in the nineties of the last century that Sir Edwin Lutyens met the celebrated Miss Gertrude Jekyll, the foremost amateur gardener of her day, and probably of her century. Mr Robert Lutyens, Sir Edwin's son, assesses the importance to gardening of their friendship, when he wrote of his father:

His contribution to the assured and lovely development of modern English gardening is incalculable. But here he was aided by the only fruitful and abiding collaboration of his career, with Gertrude Jekyll, for whom – alone among contemporaries – he retained an admiration only equalled by his affection for her. The influence of this wise, eccentric and cultivated woman on her generation, in general, and on my father, in particular, has been on the whole insufficiently acknowledged. Much has he owed to her companionship and encouragement; much to her great knowledge of rural tradition. She fostered his love of ingenious contrivance, so patent in all his assembly of finished detail, and shared his pleasure in the wit and economy of old-fashioned workmanship. How odd must they have looked, this curiously assorted pair, as they drove in her armigerous ponycart along the Surrey lanes in search of rare survivals!, the lank young man and the inordinately stout and bespectacled spinster – the dreaded 'Aunt Bumps' to us children on our rare visits, later on, to Munstead Wood.

Mr Lutyens goes on to say that whilst Miss Jekyll elaborated, with an infallibility of taste and sensitive craftsmanship, the growing feeling for natural and picturesque planting . . . she

Sir Edwin Lutyens (1869–1944) was the architect, or rather re-creator, of Great Dixter for Mr and Mrs Nathaniel Lloyd. Lutyens' influence on the garden is still apparent

opposite Luxuriant planting laps the edges of a neatly paved path leading to the brick and beamed façade of the house

Boisterous groups of eryngium, scabious and Japanese anemones threaten to take over the pathway to a formally castellated yew hedge

Carefully designed steps, their formality tempered by discreet overgrowth, lead up to an arched doorway in this great East Sussex garden

found in Sir Edwin Lutyens the ideal interpreter, who eventually exalted her limited conception on to the plane of creative design.

The Lutyens family's Aunt Bumps had no hand in the planting of the garden at Great Dixter, though Mr Christopher Lloyd, as a boy, remembers being taken to see her at her house at Munstead, and being very impressed at being blessed by her. 'She expressed the hope that I should grow up to be a great gardener . . . I was very interested in plants even at that age. I suppose she saw this.'

Mr and Mrs Nathaniel Lloyd, for whom the house of Great Dixter was re-created, were great gardeners, but it is certain that, even now, so many years later, the famous borders show something of the Jekyll touch. And it is sure that Sir Edwin Lutyens was the architect of the garden, and devised its subtle plan of interlocking terraces and steps, which sets the house so happily in its flowery framework.

The house at Great Dixter dates from the mid fifteenth century and it was in a sorry state, with haphazard additions and two floors inserted into the great hall, when Mr and Mrs Nathaniel Lloyd acquired it in the first years of this century. With Sir Edwin Lutyens as their architect, their reconstruction and re-creation of the house was masterly. And it was a bold stroke to weld on to the ancient framework of Great Dixter a whole new, or rather old, house – which was transported beam by beam from nearby Benenden. It is this addition with its many timbered façade, which fills much of the south façade and shows its mellow face above the garden terraces below.

The series of gardens at Great Dixter lie all round the house, and the first on the visitor's itinerary is a sunk garden richly bordered on three sides, with a central lily pond, and a fourth side formed of a low out-building, in summer almost entirely smothered with roses and climbing plants. This sunk garden and the topiary were designed, not by Sir Edwin, but by Mr Nathaniel Lloyd himself.

Few English gardens, in these years of labour shortage, make a feature of growing annual flowers, and yet it is the lavish use of this type of flower that quickly strikes the visitor to Great Dixter. The author of this book first visited the garden in September and, even as late as that in the season, the garden was full of colour – colour provided, in the sunk garden at least, largely by annuals. One combination in particular was memorable, an annual seldom grown in other gardens, *Salvia farinacea*, Blue Bedder, a sage of a most telling blue with flowers a little like those of lavender, except that the very stems of *S. farinacea* are a brilliant blue. Near it were growing a large group of another annual, making a striking contrast, the golden yellow, Black Eyed Susan daisies of *Rudbeckia hirta* Autumn Glow. Mr Christopher Lloyd denies that he has any special preference for annual flowers, though saying:

The only difference, here, between me and many other gardeners is that they cannot be bothered with the recurring business of sowing, pricking and planting out, whereas, to an extent, and in the interests of, say, the smell of mignonette and stocks, or of a good contrast in colour and form, I can. But I like biennials too: Sweet Williams and foxgloves in particular, but as these go over in July, it works well, I find, to sow some annuals like tithonias or cleomes, in early May, and have them coming on in readiness to take the biennials' place. Of course, another nice point about annuals and biennials is that you can come back to or take a rest from them so easily. No major decisions have to be made as to what must be sacrificed or eliminated or worked up again by some long-winded propagation technique.

But Mr Lloyd, being an expert plantsman, has very definite favourites, admitting:

It may sound snobbish, but I do like unusual plants. The storehouse of plant material that we can grow in these favoured islands is prodigiously rich and yet is drawn upon so niggardly that I am continually goaded into championing things that should be seen more, like aciphyllas (the Spear Grasses of New Zealand), the South American *Eryngium pandanifolium*, with its sea-green scimitar leaves, *Zigadenus elegans*, with sprays of starry green flowers, the bold-disced alpine thistle, *Carlina acaulis*, and *Euphorbia wulfenii* with its glaucous foliage and pale green flowering columns in spring. If, as in these cases, the plant has good positive structure yet subtle colouring, so much the better.

Handsome foliage appeals to me very strongly; I would sell my soul for a shrub like Melianthus major, and the fact of its being tender seems quite beside the point to me. Who would shirk the little bit of trouble needed on such a plant's behalf? And I am crazy about variegated foliage: a grass like *Arundo donax variegata* or the sword leaves of a variegated yucca or of the green and yellow phormium; these plants make for big moments.

And yet I like the showy and the obvious as well, as a contrast, if not used indiscriminately and without imagination. I like dahlias and cannas, not in solid beds on their own, but taking their place among border plants and shrubs like buddleias, hypericums, perovskias and caryopteris. In fact, I like mixing all categories of plants. It seems the natural thing to do. Their different habits act as foils one to another.

From the sunk garden, paved paths, with brimming borders on either side, lead southward under the drawing room and study windows of the west front. In late summer these borders are full, not only of dahlias and michaelmas daisies as one would expect, but with many different fuchsias, once treated as only half hardy but now thought of as herbaceous, dying down to the root in the winter, and springing up again in April – fuchsias like the flesh pink Lena, red and mauve Display and strong-growing Madame Cornelissen. Nearby grew some attractive hebes, once known as veronicas, with two of the most impressive, the hardy Autumn Glory and elegant pale lavender Midsummer Beauty. These two plants, in the opinion of the writer, add much to the beauty of the garden at Great Dixter in September.

To the south part of the house, and one feels that this was a Lutyens touch, an old cow-shed has been left, but with its walls removed, to make an airy garden house, and a delicious place to sit out on summer evenings, with the butterflies still busy with the buddleias, and Tobacco Flowers – more annuals – laying their sweetness on the air. This overlooks the rose garden from where a long paved walk runs the length of the south façade,

Rotund clipped evergreen stud the lawn at Great Dixter. Beyond is the roof of the old cow house

Planting for pleasing combinations of colour as well as for contrasting form should be aimed at in any herbaceous border. Two plants which achieve this effect are the flat-pink-faced *Sedum spectabile* and the taller, willowy *Verbena bonariensis*

shaded at one point by a pair of splendid mulberries. The path, which is over a hundred yards in length, runs below the old Benenden house, in front of which Sir Edwin laid another terrace, and at right angles to it. This terrace, which juts out over the falling ground to the south, still studded with its old apple trees, is a typical Lutyens fancy and is designed in a series of circular steps, set with planting.

Beyond these steps, and to the east, the paved path runs on, with the mixed borders for which Great Dixter is celebrated making a high hedge of flower on the left. It terminates in a seat sheltered by a yew hedge. To the left again lie more enclosed gardens, mostly given over to beds for the plants which Mr Lloyd raises, and markets, in his far too tempting nursery.

He is an expert, as we have seen, on many plants, though he admits that his oldest love, in the plant world, was and still is clematis, about which he published a book in 1965. It was a taste he developed early in life, and has lasted until now.

At first I was attracted, as any wide-eyed child would be, to the glamorous, large-flowered satiny-textured hybrids such as W. E. Gladstone and Lasurstern, but now I find I love nearly all of them, even the tiniest and most insignificant, in their different ways, and for their fascinating diversity of habit, colour and flower form.

In the list of the writer's favourite gardens, Great Dixter must take a very high place. For any informed gardener, it has the greatest possible fascination. There are many well designed gardens dully planted, and amorphous gardens, like so many in Ireland, full of botanical treasures. There are very few gardens which were laid out by the foremost architects of the day, and then planted and maintained by a great plant connoisseur. Thus, the garden at Great Dixter can be compared to a beautiful house furnished with museum pieces.

right Disraeli once asked 'What is a nobleman's garden without peacocks? Live peacocks are notoriously bad gardeners, but these are of yew

below A Lutyens touch: 'An old cow house has been left, but with its walls removed, to make an airy garden house . . .' In front is a bed of sweet-smelling annuals

From the checkered shade cast by a mulberry tree a mixed border stretches out into the sunshine

opposite The sunk garden at Great Dixter and lily pond, designed by the late Mr Nathaniel Lloyd. Notable are the richness and variety of the planting

Oxfordshire
Haseley Court

A garden which shows American influence

Contrasts in form, not only in flower, are the aim of every careful gardener. They could not be more effectively exemplified than in these pictures. *above* A spirally clipped yew on a base of golden ivy *opposite* The exotic leaves of *Yucca gloriosa*, or Adam's Needle, with jade rosettes of echeveria and the different shapes of topiary

The owner of Haseley Court is a Virginian and echoes of the South sound round her most English of gardens. There's a whisper of Williamsburg in the many hedges of box and the trelliswork garden pavilion, and of the Apammonax in the stirring of the Confederate flag against the Oxfordshire sky.

Mrs Nancy Lancaster is an intrepid woman and in her gardening her motto might well be *de l'audace, toujours de l'audace*. It certainly took courage to embark on saving Haseley Court (which might otherwise have been demolished) after the rigours of army occupation, dry-rot, and general dilapidation. It took courage, too, to replant the park denuded of its ancient trees. But the visitor to Haseley today – twelve years since the scene was one of towering nettles, broken bricks and mouldering debris – will quickly see how Mrs Lancaster's enterprise has been rewarded, how successful her rescue work has been. In the words of Mr Valentine Lawford, 'Today by some magic touch, rust and rubble have been replaced by a maturely beautiful sequence of interlocking gardens, as surprisingly harmonious as a maze of disparate rooms in an ancient, rambling, time-cemented house.'

Haseley Court is built on a site which has been inhabited for a thousand years. William the Conqueror, after the Battle of Hastings, rewarded a relation with the land around. From then it passed, through the centuries, from family to family – all, as it happens, Roman Catholics. Two or three hundred years ago Catholic families were debarred by law from holding high offices. Their households were generally impoverished but, in spite of that, early in the eighteenth century the occupants of Haseley managed to rebuild it in the fashionable style of the moment. Only a wing remained, and still remains, to hint how the earlier edifice may have looked.

The gardens lie all around, and though each is very different from the others, some old, some quite new, they relate comfortably to one another, their link perhaps being in the planting and the recurring use of certain favourite plants, and certainly in the quality and colour – silver grey with orange lichen

In the topiary garden at Haseley Court there are 'no bright colours, only low beds of lavender and *Stachys lanata*, to make a haze of silver-grey at the bases of the thirty-two chessmen in box-wood and yew. Beyond lie the open fields . . . and the few ballooning elms that escaped the wartime axe. The contrast is a striking one of rural nature and artifice triumphant'

overtones – of the local stone.

The house is approached by way of a broad terrace, for which the architect was Mr Geoffrey Jellicoe, and up stone steps, on either side of which are stone lions bestraddled by paunchy cherubs. The note of restraint, even elimination, is immediately struck. No rock plants disfigure the symmetry of Mr Jellicoe's neat paving and trip the unwary visitor. Bay trees in grey and white painted *caissons de Versailles* and some strutting fantail pigeons are the only embellishments. The planting under the windows, and to either side of the front door with its curved pediment, is well understated too. No garish colours here, no reds or crimsons, but a spreading shrubby herby hedge of plants of good form and foliage – starry, long-flowering golden potentillas, phlomis, the Jerusalem sage, with its felty leaves and flowers like Roman helmets, yellow *Rosa harrisonii*, blue-flowered shrubby rosemaries with their strongly aromatic leaves. All these plants, all favourites of Mrs Lancaster, have as good foliage as flowers, cover the ground, and smother weeds; in short they are plants of high garden value.

Facing the house, the visitor to the garden at Haseley turns right, through a path cut in a yew hedge and into the Box Parlour, under the walls of the old wing – a garden of paving and cobbles and gravel, furnished like a room, not only with table and chairs, but with crisply tailored box and yew trees, standard fuchsias, terra cotta vases of geraniums and heavily scented daturas.

Nearby, to the right again, beyond a balustrade festooned with roses, is the Chess Garden, the most celebrated feature of the garden at Haseley and one which only exists thanks to the devotion of Mr Shepherd, a gardener during the war, who, though the rest of the garden had to be let go to rack and ruin, regularly trimmed what he fondly called his 'Kings and Queens'. Though of no great age compared with the topiary gardens at Levens or the hedges at Powis, the Chess Garden at Haseley is remarkable. Here again, Mrs Lancaster has planned the planting with restraint and an artist's eye. No bright colours, only low beds of lavender and *Stachys lanata*, to make a haze of silver-grey at the bases of the thirty-two chessmen in box-wood and yew. Beyond lie the open fields, with their grazing cattle and the few ballooning elms that escaped the war-time axe. The contrast is a striking one of rural nature and artifice triumphant.

Leaving the chessboard garden on his right, the visitor to Haseley descends a sloping path of pebble and flint, edged with honeysuckle grown as miniature trees. A turn to the left through a narrow Gothic door leads to a turfed courtyard with an Astrolabe for centre-piece. Another doorway leads to a great walled enclosure which has been called the Baroque garden, though except for its flowing basic design of cobbled and gravel paths, now almost submerged in exuberance of flower growth, there is little there to remind one of the arid splendours of the Baroque gardens of Wurzburg or Collodi. It is in this part of the gardens at Haseley that one of Mrs Lancaster's garden precepts is forcefully illustrated. 'A garden should have an architectural

Under the walls of the older wing, a paved and cobbled courtyard gives shelter to pots of delicate plants

The word 'topiary' derives from the Greek *topos*, 'a place', and so *topiarius* came to mean 'the man in charge of the place', hence gardener. Topiary chessmen in shorn box at Haseley Court

'The owner of Haseley Court is a Virginian and echoes of the South sound round her most English of gardens . . . and of the Apammonax in the stirring of the Confederate flag against the Oxfordshire sky'

The elegant design of the trellis-work pavilion which
stands in the centre of Mrs Lancaster's flower garden
was adapted from that of one in a garden in Virginia

opposite A sundial in an enclosed garden of corkscrew
yews and classic busts is framed in a gateway of grey
Cotswold stone. To the left grows a fig, to the right
Schizophragma hydrangeoides

feel and formality – but the formality should be "thrown away", half hidden with roses, vines, anything you like, even ivy . . . a garden, I feel, should have a tight corset, but the plants should be allowed to burst out and overflow. I like flowers that take charge. . . .' Thus, the owner of Haseley, and in her walled garden the planting has literally taken over; both flowers and vegetables, roses and raspberries, lilies and artichokes, the red leaves of beet near the mauve velvet foliage of *Salvia candelabrum*. Roses everywhere, of course, to scent the air, and the honey-laden breath of buddleia – but the riot is controlled, the rumpus of colour and fragrance not quite out of hand, for box-lined paths subdivide the giant rectangle into four lesser enclosures, one paved and pebbled in the 'Baroque' design, one left to lawn and one a fruit garden, and one a *potager* where cabbages are kings. Nub of the whole complex design is a superlatively elegant pavilion of trellis work, based on a design of one that Mrs Lancaster saw in Virginia. So charming is this little building that it is to be hoped that Mrs Lancaster, in her indulgence, will not let its crisp outline be entirely smothered even by her most favourite roses.

There are other parts of the garden at Haseley yet to be visited. There is a wild garden, carpeted in spring with snowdrops and aconites and shaded in high summer by the higher cartwheels of the giant hemlock. There is a canal, formerly a fish pond or possibly a moat, reflecting in its green surface statues and grotesque masks brought from the Brenta. Everywhere there are statues and urns, though these are not dotted at random, but thoughtfully placed 'eye-catchers' to close a vista or give importance to a gateway.

Mrs Lancaster is a true gardener. Everything she says about gardening, in her sweeping, highly characteristic way, makes sense, 'I hate borders, but I like a garden to have a definite layout and a plan on the grandest possible scale', 'I like all plants with green flowers'. Indeed, ordinary herbaceous plants are not particular favourites at Haseley; nearer to Mrs Lancaster's heart, one feels, are species plants, wild plants, plants which are not the product of the careful hybridist. She loves Christmas roses, golden elders, wild geraniums, periwinkles. Like many highly sophisticated gardeners, Mrs Lancaster's tastes are simple.

above Reflections in a moat of an enfilade of tall trees in their green panoply of summer lead the eye to a Baroque fountain, which can be seen more closely in the picture on the right . . . a giant shell and flower-crowned mask of stone set in a Cotswold wall hung with single white roses. The bold-leaved plant to the right is damp-loving *Saxifraga peltata*

opposite Pyramids of white trellis give support to roses and clematis in a corner of the flower garden at Haseley Court. In the foreground, proof that vegetables can be as decorative as flowers, grows sea-kale (*Crambe maritima*) with glaucous blue-green leaves and heads of creamy flowers

Mereworth Castle

A garden of classical perfection

A plasterwork portrait of Colin Campbell (died 1729) at Compton Place in Sussex. Mereworth has been called his masterpiece

opposite 'One path . . . is typical of the restraint and sophistication' with which the garden has been planted. Simple beds of *Yucca gloriosa* are set in turf

In the summer of 1752 Horace Walpole described a visit to Mereworth. He started in the most enthusiastic terms: 'Since dinner, we have been to Lord Westmorland's at Mereworth, which is so perfect in the Palladian taste, that I must own it has recovered me a little from Gothic.' But he went on to say in the carping way he sometimes assumed, 'It is better situated than I had expected from the bad reputation it bears, and has some prospect, though it is in a moat, and mightily besprinkled with small ponds. The design, you know, is taken from the Villa del Capra by Vicenza, but on a larger scale; yet though it has cost a hundred thousand pounds it is still only a fine villa: there are some dismal clipped hedges . . .'

Mereworth's position, though certainly not on the top of a hill, is a good one and the views from its many windows, over the rolling park, through vistas of cedars, are as fine as any in Kent.

It is an exquisite building, as unexpected in Kent as a Cotswold manor would be in the Campagna, or the Brighton Pavilion is at Brighton. It is an exotic, and no one quite knows why it ever happened, or indeed who had it built. It was either the seventh Earl of Westmorland or his brother the sixth. Whoever it was, we should be grateful to him, and to the architect Colin Campbell, who said of the house that 'nothing was wanting for strength, convenience or ornament', and that 'never architect had a more beneficient and liberal patron'. The house was constructed soon after 1723, a Palladian Villa, exact in every detail, set down in all its classical perfection in the weald of Kent. It is Colin Campbell's masterpiece.

Colin Campbell died in 1729, six years after the completion of Mereworth. He owed his early success to the patronage of William Benson, Sir Christopher Wren's successor as surveyor-general, and to that of the Earl of Burlington for whom he re-modelled Burlington House in Piccadilly in his favourite Palladian style. He was the architect of Houghton, Compton Place at Eastbourne, and Stourhead in Wiltshire. His literary fame rests on his publication in 1715, 1717 and 1725 of *Vitruvius Britannicus*

Contrasts in the garden at Mereworth *above* Lady Anne
Tree's bridge in chinoiserie painted in 'brilliant
colours such as folly needs' *right* The ordered formality
of a statue surveying a vista of yew hedges and cedars

in which there is an impressive sectional view of Mereworth.

From the Westmorland family, Mereworth passed first to the
Stapletons and then to the Falmouths. During Victorian times,
the moat, of which Horace Walpole complained, was filled in – a
great pity, as the extra dimensions that water provide would
have added even to Mereworth's perfections. For it is said that
architects of the Renaissance, devising gardens for newly transformed *châteaux* built on a medieval plan, were often careful to
retain their ancient moats, valuing the extra check that water
offers to architectural nicety. And it is true that any building
reflected in water has the truth and purity of its lines accentuated:
the reason an artist will hold a looking glass to his portrait to
check its likeness to the sitter. Mereworth would have stood up
well to the test. It only lost its moat a century ago, and the
seventh Viscount Falmouth, who died in 1918, remembered
fishing from the portico. But though it is sad that the walls of the
house no longer rise from the water which Colin Campbell
designed for them, time has dealt unusually kindly with the
surroundings of Mereworth. The twin pavilions, added by Lord
Westmorland in 1736, are not marred by any Victorian accre-
tions. Nothing spoils the cool and triumphant formality of the

architectural whole. In fact the added pavilions were built sufficiently clear of the moat and far away enough one from another as not to compete in any way with the proportions of the house, or detract from its imposing silhouette.

It was the seventh Lord Falmouth's widow who created the gardens as we see them today. These have been most imaginatively maintained by the present owners, Mr Michael and Lady Anne Tree, and the outlines have been little changed in the last eighty years. The plan of the garden reflects the cool Classicism of the architecture. Grass paths set in turf, restrained planting near the house, clipped hedges with airy windows cut into them to give glimpses of the main building, make a complex which is a suitably severe framework for Mereworth's Palladian perfection. One path looks today exactly as it does in old photographs taken nearly half a century ago, and is typical of the restraint and sophistication with which Lady Falmouth planted her garden to be in keeping with her unique house. It is a long walk which stretches direct from the loggia and is of gravel, bordered on each side by some of the yew hedges which so depressed Horace Walpole, though one wonders why.

So far so good, but how many enthusiastic gardeners fifty years ago would have resisted the temptation to plant a herbaceous border, never so popular as in 1910, or at least indulge in some elaborate bedding out on either side of that path? Lady Falmouth knew better. She edged the path with stretches of turf, setting on either side at regular intervals large beds of *Yucca gloriosa*, of which the exotic leaves recall, as no other plant of an English garden could, the luxuriant foliage of an Italian parterre.

Lady Anne Tree is a gardener full of enterprise and fancy. On the lake she has conjured a bridge in *chinoiserie* painted in the brilliant colours which such a folly needs. This sprightly little building was the work of Mr Tolhurst, the house carpenter at Mereworth, and the design was taken from an old Dutch book on garden ornament – *Magazin Van Tuinsieraden*, published in the eighteenth century, at about the same time as Sir William Chambers published his design for Chinese bridges and buildings in 1757. In another part of the garden, there is an aviary, also in the Chinese taste, which is a masterpiece of airy imagination, and is based on a sketch made by Lord Snowdon. When the writer first visited Mereworth, the romneyas, favourite flowers of Lady Anne, were all out in this garden, and were looking beautiful, for all the Californian tree poppies are at their very best in July and August. They are called romneya and one wonders why; did the Reverend T. Romney Robinson (1792–1882) combine botany with his study of the stars?

Near the aviary garden, with its brimming beds and attractive bird-house, there is a long border of old roses which are other special favourites of Lady Anne, and reflect their flowers in the stream which borders the path on the other side.

Here grow the kind of roses that Lady Anne likes best, 'roses with green centres – moss roses – which retain on their petals drops of water that remind one of Dutch flower paintings – white

The Aviary Garden with its pagoda-roofed bird-house and brimming beds of herbaceous flowers. Beyond is the rolling parkland of Kent

roses that show up at dusk and night'. Roses like the pink shell-like *Rosa alba* Celestial and the green shadowed Paul's Lemon Pillar.

In the garden at Mereworth the observant visitor notices, through the year, many species flowers, for these too are specially favoured. 'Hybridization usually spoils both quality and colour.' Lady Anne likes species crocus and tulips, all poppies, cistus with their flowers that are as fleeting and papery as romneyas, and Madonna lilies. In pots on Mereworth's several terraces she grows citrus trees, and their oranges and lemons look curiously at home in Colin Campbell's architecturally Italianate setting. In the wilder parts of the garden are bold plantings of hostas, for the pictorial value of their foliage, and Lady Anne has here and there succeeded in creating what she refers to as a Douanier Rousseau effect, with giant hemlock (*Heracleum giganteum*) and tall polygonum growing by a wood, and casting their long shadows on the grass beneath.

But it is already evening and the sun is low, though its fading rays still fill the petals of the roses with light; as the air moves gently from the lake, their scent is borne upward and away. Through the windows cut in the hedges – through the Chinese carving – round Campbell's cupolas, past the Palladian dome, permeating everything with magic. For as the Kentish historian Edward Hasted wrote of Mereworth, 'Throughout the whole, art and nature are so happily blended together as to render it a most delightful situation'.

'Nothing spoils the cool and triumphant formality of the architectural whole . . . The added pavilions were built . . . far away enough . . . not to compete . . . with the proportions of the house'

In June roses grown on arches or as standard bushes scent the air in the rose garden at Mereworth

Acknowledgements

The following photographers took the photographs of the gardens mentioned against their names:

ROBERT BELTON: Powis Castle; Great Dixter

PETER COATS: Haddon Hall; Kelvedon Hall; Hascombe Court; Pyrford Court

ANTHONY DENNEY: Nymans; Luton Hoo; Cranborne Manor; Exbury; Hampton Court; Pylewell Park; Easton Neston; Mereworth Castle

BRODRICK HALDANE: Drummond Castle; Kinross; Newby Hall; Tyninghame; Lochinch; Logan

PATRICK ROSSMORE: Rowallane; Abbotswood; Hinton Ampner; Hush Heath Manor; Mount Stewart; Lyegrove

EDDIE RYLE-HODGES: Pusey House; Anglesey Abbey; Westonbirt Arboretum; Hascombe Court; Haseley Court

PENNY TWEEDIE: Blenheim; Stowe; Wakehurst Place; St Paul's Walden Bury; Hever Castle; Sezincote; Rousham; Julians

Additional illustrations were used in each chapter, and we are grateful to the following persons or institutions, mentioned below in italics, for permission to reproduce them. The author would also like to express his appreciation to the head gardeners of each garden, and to thank those persons mentioned below in roman type for their help and co-operation.

INTRODUCTION: *National Portrait Gallery, Edwin Smith, Kerry Dundas, J. E. Downward, Radio Times Hulton Picture Library*

BLENHEIM: *National Portrait Gallery,* David Green

DRUMMOND CASTLE: *J. R. Freeman & Co.*

STOWE: *National Portrait Gallery, Library RIBA,* George Clarke, R. Q. Drayson

WAKEHURST PLACE: *British Museum,* Sir George Taylor, R. L. Shaw

ST PAUL'S WALDEN BURY: *Country Life*

PUSEY HOUSE: *National Portrait Gallery*

ROWALLANE: *The National Trust of Northern Ireland,* The Hon. Mrs Terence O'Neill

TYNINGHAME: *J. R. Freeman & Co.*

HADDON HALL: *National Film Archives, J. R. Freeman & Co.,* Kathleen, Duchess of Rutland, Lord and Lady John Manners

NYMANS: *Edwin Smith,* Oliver Messel

LUTON HOO: *National Portrait Gallery*

SEZINCOTE: *The Architectural Review*

POWIS CASTLE: The Hon. C. V. C. Herbert

CRANBORNE MANOR: *National Portrait Gallery*

WESTONBIRT ARBORETUM: E. Leyshon

ABBOTSWOOD: Mrs Sheldon, Mrs Holland Hibbert, Mrs Fleischmann

ROUSHAM: *Country Life*

EXBURY: *J. E. Downward,* Peter Barbour

LOCHINCH: *Tom Scott, J. E. Downward*

HAMPTON COURT: *Aerofilms Ltd, National Portrait Gallery, A. C. Cooper Ltd,* Miss Mollie Sands

PYLEWELL PARK: Miss Penelope Whitaker

PYRFORD COURT: *National Portrait Gallery,* A. Nicholson

LOGAN: Mr and Mrs Jocelyn Hambro

GREAT DIXTER: *National Portrait Gallery*

HASELEY COURT: Valentine Lawford

MEREWORTH CASTLE: *National Buildings Record*